More Praise for
Use the Power You Have

"*Use the Power You Have* isn't just the story of the remarkable journey of Congresswoman Pramila Jayapal, although her sincere telling is an inspiration in itself. This book is a blueprint for women of color who are ready to seize the moment, build with movement, lead with heart, and create a just country and world."

— Aimee Allison, founder and president, She the People

"This book is a rare treat: a look into the mind and heart of one of the most inspiring political figures in our landscape today."

— Ilyse Hogue, president, NARAL Pro-Choice America

"This hopeful book not only chronicles an immigrant's political successes, but, more significantly, the enduring faith in American democracy that inspired them. A passionately articulate memoir and political manifesto."

— *Kirkus Reviews*

USE THE POWER YOU HAVE

USE THE
POWER
YOU HAVE

A BROWN WOMAN'S GUIDE TO
POLITICS AND POLITICAL CHANGE

PRAMILA JAYAPAL

THE
NEW
PRESS

NEW YORK
LONDON

A portion of Chapter 1 was originally published in "Be Here Now" in *Orion* Magazine.
A portion of Chapter 2 was originally published in "Speaking For Justice" in *YES!* magazine.
A portion of Chapter 8 was originally published in "A New Moral Imagination on Immigration" in the
New York Review of Books.

Published in the United States by The New Press, New York, 2020
Distributed by Two Rivers Distribution

ISBN 978-1-62097-143-7 (hc)
ISBN 978-1-62097-145-1 (ebook)
CIP data is available

The New Press publishes books that promote and enrich public discussion and understanding of
the issues vital to our democracy and to a more equitable world. These books are made possible by
the enthusiasm of our readers; the support of a committed group of donors, large and small; the
collaboration of our many partners in the independent media and the not-for-profit sector; booksellers,
who often hand-sell New Press books; librarians; and above all by our authors.

www.thenewpress.com

Book design and composition by Bookbright Media
This book was set in Adobe Garamond and Questa

Printed in the United States of America
10 9 8 7 6 5 4 3 2 1

For my parents:
Boundless gratitude, across continents
for everything

Contents

USE THE POWER YOU HAVE

Part I

POLITICS

1

My Immigrant Story

A FRIEND OF MINE SAYS THAT WE IMMIGRANTS LIVE IN THE HYPHEN: we live in the space between the places we bring with us and the places we go, in that complex space of change. And if there is one thing that is true about migration, it is that everything and everyone who is touched by it changes. Our collective experiences as immigrants—willing and unwilling, brought over on slave ships to build this country or traveling across deserts to seek refuge—have shaped a nation on territory solely inhabited by indigenous peoples who had the only real claim to the land.

Migration and immigration do not just affect the United States. They are worldwide phenomena, brought about by the increasing ravages of climate change, inequality, poverty, and war. We are a global people of movement. Today, an estimated 258 million people live in a country other than the one where they were born.[1] One in seven people in the world is a migrant and, right here in the United States, we are home to the largest share of immigrants in the world—50 million or 20 percent of the world's migrant population lives within our borders.[2]

Like so many generations of people from all over the world who have come to America, my immigrant experience has shaped me.

I was born in India, and then lived with my family mostly in Indonesia.

I finished my high school education at an international school with a large percentage of American teachers. At the time, my father worked for an American oil company and had caught his own American fever: unlike many of his Indian colleagues who—as products of a colonial empire, loved the United Kingdom—he truly believed that the United States was the place where his daughters would get the best education and have the most opportunity. Using most of his meager savings, he first sent my older sister, Susheela, to the United States. His intent was to send me as well, but in the three years between Susheela's departure for America and mine, he lost his job and whatever he had left in savings became even smaller. Much of my senior year of high school was spent worrying that I would not be able to follow my sister to America. But my parents were determined. They sacrificed everything so that, in 1982, a few months before my seventeenth birthday, I arrived in America with the two suitcases allotted to me by the airline.

I still remember arriving alone at JFK airport and being amazed at the grandiosity of the place and the strangeness of it all: a couple kissing passionately in a public display of affection like I had never seen before; the smell of french fries from McDonald's, which still had not made it to Indonesia; the bustle of a population that looked so different from the people of the countries in which I had lived.

I had applied and been accepted to Georgetown University without the luxury of a visit or even much knowledge other than it was in Washington, DC, and had a good number of international students. That first year was a study in anxieties: what should I wear? Collar inside my sweater or outside? Would people know I was a foreign student? What were the prevalent TV show and pop culture references? I tried to blend in as best I could, but I constantly mixed up common phrases. It wasn't until I got to business school six years later, to the amusement of my friends, that I found out the phrase I thought was "doggy-dog world" was actually "dog-eat-dog world!"

In retrospect, my entry into America was incredibly privileged compared to so many of those I would later work with through the course of my immigrant rights work. I was on a student visa, I spoke fluent English, and I was not completely new to American culture, given my international school education in Indonesia. Still, I was far away from my parents, with money to call home only once a year, and I was homesick.

My first week of college, I decided to combat the homesickness with a reminder of home: I walked into town and bought a beautiful poster of the Taj Mahal to pin on the wall of my dorm room. My next-door neighbor, who came from a very wealthy family, came in and excitedly asked if it was a picture of my house. I honestly thought she was joking, so I decided to joke back. "That's just the servant's quarters," I said. "The house is too big to fit on there." To my complete amazement, she believed me! "Oh my goodness," she said. "Are you a princess?" It was beginning to occur to me that she thought I was serious, but it was too good a prank to let the opportunity go. "Yes," I said modestly. "I am a princess but I don't like people to know that." She left and I laughed myself to sleep. Some days later, I was at a party and as I was introducing myself, the person said in awe, "You're the real live Princess Pramila!"

That was when I realized that many people in the United States really didn't know much about the rest of the world. In Indonesia, my friends were from everywhere: what was then Yugoslavia, Turkey, Japan, Mexico, Kenya, and across Europe and the United States. My parents spoke multiple Indian languages, and my mother was learning German as we were growing up. At school, I took both Bahasa Indonesia (the language of Indonesia) and French as an elective. Most of my friends spoke languages other than English. Places on the big globe that rotated around in our world history class felt near and relevant. It made the whole world seem so small and familiar. America was relevant to everyone else in the world, it seemed, but the rest of the world didn't seem that relevant in Washington, DC.

America!

I found a friend living on the floor below me who was from New Orleans and we made a pinkie pact that when the first snows fell, we would find each other to share our first sighting together. When that moment came, we ran out with no shoes or gloves or hats, caught snowflakes on our tongues and made angels in the snow. We were completely and totally enthralled by the white blanket that covered the Georgetown steeples.

Every Sunday, I sat down to dutifully write to my parents. For school breaks, I would either go to visit one of my aunts who lived in Maryland and Ohio, respectively, or I would go to my best friend's house just half an hour from Georgetown. Her family was a wild and welcoming Irish Catholic family with six girls and a cooking fiend of a mother; they welcomed me in completely, like another daughter. In the midst of the family cacophony around a Washington NFL football game and a heaping table of food, I tried to forget that it still wasn't home.

People often ask me what it was really like to leave home at sixteen and come to America by myself. The truth is, I think I put away all the hardest experiences in the recesses of my mind. It was not until recently that I revisited those memories; I was visiting my parents in India when I came across a treasure trove of my old aerograms and letters my mother had saved. The aerograms—which consisted of a folded sheet of paper that was the cheapest method of airmail—were crammed with tiny writing. The letters were on thin onionskin paper (also cheap to mail), some typewritten on the brand-new IBM Selectric typewriter I had purchased so I could make a little money—a dollar per page—by typing papers for my classmates. I spent hours reading those letters at my parents' house, sometimes with tears pouring down my face. I viscerally reexperienced the pressure to succeed that an immigrant daughter feels.

There were regular reports on my grades, accounts of how hard I was studying, and the apologies and expressions of disappointment I felt if I didn't get a perfect score. I felt, too, the burden of responsibility at a young age. Almost every letter expressed my deep and constant fear about money, given my father's still precarious position: I sent monthly accounts and talked about the joy of receiving my first $100 paycheck for my on-campus library job while also apologizing for having to spend an unexpected amount on a pair of long underwear that would help me weather the cold. I had completely forgotten until I read those letters that I was perpetually ill, dealing with the challenges of adapting to the cold and the new place. Many of the letters were about my frequent visits to the doctor to deal with everything from rashes on my stomach—were they stress induced?—to ear infections and colds. But perhaps hardest of all to read was the deep homesickness, which nibbled at the edges of so many of my letters. It seemed to come in waves: I would start to pour out my sadness and loneliness to my parents and then immediately apologize, feeling badly for dumping these emotions on them when they were so far away and could do little to help. In many ways, my letters sounded like they were written by a forty-year old, not a teenager, gravely and seriously considering how to make ends meet, how to live up to the opportunity I had been given, and how to hide or absorb the sadness and confusion at this brand-new place where I had so much to learn.

Reading my letters from those early years reminded me again about an important truth of the immigrant story: There is so much pain but also so much resilience. We adapt because we have no choice. We learn, change, grow—all the while trying to make sure we contribute and succeed because so much is at stake and we simply cannot afford to fail.

In the words of Lin-Manuel Miranda, from the musical *Hamilton*, "Immigrants, we get the job done."

There's a story that's told that the most successful paths are linear, that you plan your life so that it takes the shortest route to your destination. There's also this idea that successful people knew all along that they would be successful—and that the success they achieve is somehow preordained.

At least in my case, neither is true. Today, as I mentor young people about their hopes, dreams, and futures, I tell them about the slogan that I have emblazoned on one of my t-shirts: "All who wander are not lost." That seems to be a much more apt motto for my life so far—in many ways, my life has been an ongoing exploration with no preordained endpoint. The one thread through it all was that I listened to myself. I gave equal credence to what my heart said, not just what my head said. I pushed away expectations of me—from others and even from myself—to allow a different path to unfold. I took each thing as it came and hoped that when it was time for that next step, it would reveal itself to me. Sometimes it felt like I was lost, but now I have the hindsight to see it as a determined sort of wandering. I knew that I just had to have faith in myself and my future, and then work my ass off to get whatever it was that was right there in front of me.

It's hard to know exactly what it was that set me up to develop my "women can do anything" attitude. Some of it came from my parents. Too many Indians and even some Indian Americans were (and are still) caught in the trap of gender discrimination. That simply wasn't true of my parents. Both my father and mother really wanted to raise girls, even though the world around them kept saying that if they were lucky, they would have a boy. When my mother was pregnant with me, especially given that she already had my sister, people would say very pityingly to her, "*Koi bat nahin, chota munna ayega*" ("Don't worry, a little boy is coming"). In fact, people used to say it so much that my three-year-old sister insisted on shouting, "*Munna ayega, munna ayega*" ("A boy is coming, a boy is coming!"). When I was born my nickname was Munna, even though that means little boy! It's the name that old family friends call me by to this day.

Some of my parents' attitude to women likely came from the overall attitudes to women in our home state of Kerala. Although I was born in Madras—now called Chennai—in the neighboring state of Tamil Nadu, my family is proud of our Kerala roots. Kerala prides itself on being a matrilineal society where property and name were, and are, handed down through the mother's side. Historically ruled by maharajas who were exceptionally open-minded in their view of education for all, regardless of gender, Kerala had one of the highest literacy rates in the country for both men and women: 96 percent for men and 92 percent for women, according to the 2011 census.[3] Kerala's public health system is excellent, long touted by the World Health Organization and other international development agencies as a model.

The strong peasant and labor movements of the 1920s and 1930s led to the formation in 1934 of the Congress Socialist Party in Kerala. After later splits, the Communist Party was formed in 1956 and came to rule in the state. As a result, Kerala has some of the country's strongest worker protections, like pensions and higher wages.

My own family's history had plenty of its own contradictions. My grandmother on my mother's side, who I called Ammamma, went to college and made it through three of the four years before being married off to my grandfather. She always regretted that she was not allowed to finish her college degree. Although Ammamma was too often browbeaten by my grandfather, she had a wicked sense of humor and strength. She was also apparently a great athlete, rumored to hitch up her sari and play a mean game of tennis. She also swam well (unusual for women in that age), and she was fiercely competitive even when we were just playing games. Ammamma was a devout Hindu and I loved lying in bed in the morning and listening to her chanting her prayers. Her sister, P.K. Devi, became renowned as one of the first women ob-gyns in the country, who co-authored the main academic text that is still used in medical schools across the country and devoted her life to reproductive healthcare for poor village women. She was said to have performed complex procedures to help women who had survived rape and many other challenges. In the 1990s, when I returned to live in villages across India on a fellowship, I was stunned to see village women fall to their knees and touch my feet in reverence to her when I mentioned her name.

My grandfather, meanwhile, was known for his strong integrity and work ethic. He went into the police force and served under the British, eventually becoming a chief of police—stern, strict, and absolutely incorruptible. When my mother got married, he refused to allow her to accept a single wedding gift from anyone in fear that it would be construed as a bribe. He was deeply critical of all the corruption—big and small—that he saw in the police force and he made it known that he would not tolerate any of it. He was a strange mix of the creative and intellectual. He absolutely adored words and the English language. He bought every dictionary available and every morning, on his morning walk, he would memorize the meanings of five new words and endeavor to use them all that day. He also loved to sew, which was certainly countercultural at the time. He sewed some of his own shirts, designed jewelry for my mother's wedding, and drew up his own plans for the house he built. The opposite of my grandmother when it came to religion, my grandfather was an atheist. He revered education and ensured that each of their four children got not only bachelor's degrees but also master's degrees: my mother (the oldest) in English literature, my older aunt in medicine, my uncle in business, and my younger aunt in social sciences.

I didn't really know my grandparents on my father's side: his mother died young before I was born and his father, who I met a few times, was a taciturn man who worked for the Indian railways his whole life. My father's oldest brother was the second in charge of the Labor Department in Kerala, with similar politics to mine, it seemed. My father regularly sent money to support his youngest brother, who struggled with alcohol addiction and was found dead in a train when I was a teenager. What I do know is that my father often felt mocked by his siblings and even his father. Perhaps that pushed him even harder to succeed himself and to want the same for his daughters.

My parents primed me to believe I could do anything I wanted—but that was still within the context of their notions of success. To my dad, only three professions were worthy of his ambition for me: doctor, lawyer, or business person. His particular dream was that I would one day become the CEO of IBM, which was at that time a cultural icon of uniquely American success. Weighed down with money issues his whole life, he wanted me to have the kind of secure future he felt had escaped him. When it became clear that I was not interested in medicine as a career, he determined that my major in college would be the steady, intellectually appropriate field of economics that would give me a pathway to anything else I might want.

The problem was I didn't really *like* economics. I was reasonably good at and interested in macroeconomic theory, but the rest of it seemed boring.

My sophomore year of college, I used my annual call home from the dorm hall phone to tell my father that instead of economics, I was going to be an English literature major. You can imagine how that went down! I had to hold the phone away from my ear as my father yelled at me: "I didn't send you to America to learn how to speak English, you already KNOW how to speak English!"

But I refused to back down. I loved English. Like my grandfather and my mother, I loved the words on the page. I loved the rhythm of sentences. I loved reading aloud and hearing the ups and downs of a great story. Reading made me feel whole, taking me to places and introducing me to people that I could almost see and touch as they came out of the pages of my books.

Economics attempts to explain the world according to the relative accounting of who has what or who does not have that same thing. English attempts to explore the world by piercing into the nooks and crannies of the heart and the head. The highest expression of the English language occurs in the moving of others to feel and, sometimes, even to act. I didn't know then how English would serve my intentions, but I had writerly instinct enough to simply trust that this was the realm in which I wanted to plant myself.

I want to be clear, too, that I got what I needed from economics: I can ingest or absorb a spreadsheet and its implications very quickly; I can apply economic thought to inequality or other issues I am dealing with as a member of Congress. However, it will always be in service to some much larger goal of helping to move us together to the next better place.

To assuage my father—and because the truth was at that time, I didn't really know what I would DO with an English major—I promised him that I would still get the same job with a major in English that I would have gotten with an economics major. When I graduated from college in the 1980s, the top jobs were with Wall Street investment banks or management consulting firms. For a new college graduate, the jobs and salaries were princely, highly competitive, reserved for the supposed "cream of the crop." If you made it into one of those firms, you were said to be set for life—a very wealthy one. I decided I would fulfill my promise to my father by parlaying my liberal arts degree and English literature major to the top investment banks in New York City as the foundation of any other success: "A liberal arts degree taught me to *think*," I peddled to my interviewers. "An English degree taught me the power of words, how to speak and write articulately. Everything else can be learned." I do think I actually believed this, too.

During the interview process with investment banks, I was horrified by the clear gender discrimination. I interviewed at a top firm with two young male associates in their thirties—who put their feet up on the desk. One of them said to me, "Let's say you're in a meeting and you're the only woman in the room. Someone turns to you and says, 'Honey, go get me some coffee.' What would you do?" Anger flooded into my veins, making my head throb. "I'd do exactly what I'm about to do now," I said, as I stood up, thanked them for the interview and walked out. True to the Wall Street ethos at that time, I got a call that afternoon from one of the men, raving about my performance. "That's the kind of killer spirit we want!" he exclaimed. "You're the kind of girl for us—we'd like to move you on to the next round!"

I politely declined.

Shortly thereafter, I ended up at the investment banking firm, PaineWebber, where I was eventually placed in the leveraged buyout department. There, I built complex spreadsheets and became comfortable with financial statements and numbers. It was the mid-1980s when the financier Mike Milken was at the height of his fame. Nicknamed the Junk Bond King then, Milken was later jailed for racketeering and corruption.

I quickly realized I was doing things that no twenty-year-old should have even been allowed to get close to, much less manage. For example, overseeing bankruptcy proceedings for a long-time shoe company that had been sold a load of lies about how taking on enormous debt would be good for their expansion when the company clearly couldn't sustain that level of debt. These kinds of experiences felt completely wrong to me and led me to question what I was doing and who was benefiting. There seemed to be far too many highly leveraged, risky deals across Wall Street where a lot of people were laid off—and the only people who seemed to benefit were the investment bankers and lawyers.

After two years, I was clearer than ever that investment banking was not the place for me. I needed to get up in the morning and feel good about what I was doing—and for all the skills I had attained and the big bonuses I received, I didn't feel fulfilled at all.

Even though I was unhappy in the moment, I later realized that the skills I had gained turned out to be invaluable as the executive director of a nonprofit organization, and later when I served on the budget committee in the U.S. House of Representatives. To this day, if you put a spreadsheet in front of me, I can find a numerical error in under five minutes. This experience also gave me firsthand insight and credibility that helps me take on the excesses and greed of Wall Street in Congress.

Most important, I learned what was key to my own core values.

Perhaps this is the great gift of the wanderer: you appreciate the opportunity for what it can teach you about the next step, the next marker in the road ahead. I often share with young people who I mentor today that learning what you *don't* want to do is as important as learning what you *do* want to do. Take every experience, get as much training as you can from it, and learn what you do and don't like, and what you do and don't do well. Then, if you're still not fulfilled, move on—with no regrets. My experience on Wall Street just made the journey forward that much clearer.

When I left PaineWebber, I didn't really know what to do next, so I did the next most expected thing, given the trajectory I was on so far, and applied to graduate business school at Northwestern University's top-ranked Kellogg School of Management just outside Chicago.

That's where the serendipity happened.

During my first year of business school, I started tutoring kids at the Cabrini Green Housing Project on the South Side of Chicago—a world away from Kellogg's wealthy Evanston suburb. I felt somewhat suffocated

by the very white community where I lived and I was still consumed by a
desire to do something that mattered. Cabrini Green back then was considered by too many people as drug- and gang-ridden and dangerous—it
was later torn down completely—and many of my friends thought I was
ridiculous to venture there. But I liked it. My presence, for the sweet children I tutored and their parents, seemed to matter and that was what I
was looking for.

Chicago's South Side was interesting to me. It was extremely diverse.
And it had been the home of Saul Alinsky, the author of *Rules for Radicals*
(a great community organizing handbook) who many considered the
founder of modern community organizing. Alinsky died in 1972, so he
was long gone by the time I arrived in Chicago in 1988, but his book was
instructive for me—and his work lived on through numerous organizations and activists who followed his path to fight poverty and racism.[4]

Somewhere along the line, I heard about the redevelopment efforts of a
community bank in the area called South Shore Bank. I read what I could
find about them, and then boldly called up the bank's co-owner, a woman
named Mary Houghton, to see if she would agree to meet with me.

She said yes and it changed my life.

Prior to Houghton and her partners taking over the Bank, South
Shore Bank had been engaged in common-for-the-time racist redlin-
ing practices—either denying services to the primarily black residents of
South Chicago or charging them far more than white customers. Now
that they had taken what they could, they planned to desert the area and
move to a wealthier white neighborhood where they could make more
money. Houghton and her partners were not going to let that happen.
They successfully petitioned to keep the bank from moving and then took
it over, turning it into the nation's first and most successful community
development bank. For a time, they were able to help facilitate some revi-
talization in the South Side of Chicago, bringing in grocery stores and
helping to provide jobs and affordable development financing.

It was Mary who first helped me to see that I could use my business
skills for social good. She encouraged me to think of economic develop-

ment as a new area where I could apply my skills. I invited her to speak at Kellogg, and eventually the school instituted a new economic development concentration. It was Mary who encouraged me to turn down another summer job in consulting or investment banking and find something in economic development instead.

In the summer of 1989 between my two years of business school, I made my poor father's heart palpitate again when I moved, with two other women classmates, to Thailand for a three-month internship. I was working for The Population and Community Development Association, Thailand's largest nonprofit organization. I spent a lot of my summer along the borders of Laos and Cambodia, where I counted chickens and tried to figure out how rural economies operated. I also had the unexpected opportunity to go to Site 2, the largest refugee camp along the Thai-Cambodian border and—for many years—the largest refugee camp in Southeast Asia.

In 1989, Site 2 held almost 150,000 people in just three small square miles. That population continued to increase to almost 200,000 people by 1991. The United Nations Border Relief Operations (UNBRO) had established Site 2 with the assistance of the Thai government as a single, centralized relocation site where services could be more easily provided for a number of camps that were destroyed by military action. Just four miles from the Cambodian border, Site 2 also faced its own direct and indirect bombing attacks. In April, just a few months before I arrived in Thailand, Cambodian government troops launched an attack just outside the camp, killing thirty-eight people and wounding forty-two others. Around the same time, Vietnamese troops fired four artillery shells into Site 2, severely wounding three people.

I had never seen or experienced anything like what I saw in Site 2. It was my first exposure to the travails, trauma, and the dire situations that cause migration. People were crowded into tents by the dozens. Aid organizations unloaded the food they had to the sound of running feet as people swarmed to get what they could. Because this was to be a temporary shelter, very little beyond the basics were provided in the early days of the camp. UNBRO had just convinced the Thai government to begin providing some education for the children, but it was minimal and constantly disrupted. The shelling and constant artillery fire meant no one felt safe. Many of those who were living in the camp had gone through pure hell to even be in the camp, and they had lost sons and daughters, husbands and wives, mothers and fathers along the way. There was a sadness in the eyes of many I met, a black hole of memories that couldn't be forgotten no matter how hard they tried. And yet, there was also the resilience that would come to characterize so many of the immigrants and refugees I ended up working with many decades later.

My stay in Thailand was life-path adjusting. It was the first time I understood that vocation and avocation could, in fact, be the same thing; that you could fill your life doing work that felt truly meaningful, not just as a side interest but as your job. My work was not easy but every day was a reminder about the work that still needed to be done and the small role I might be able to play in doing it. I felt everything deeply—the pain, loss, and suffering of people whose lives had been uprooted; they lived with so much fear and violence and yet still found the courage to continue. It was a deep lesson about how the most meaningful work is that which is connected to others, especially when they are enmeshed in meaningful experiences of their own and often overcoming suffering through sheer determination. It was impossible to be in a place like Site 2 and not think about how those in power were obligated to find new and better ways to address the horrific situation and conditions of refugees. I started to see then how direct service work and policy are linked. Looking into the eyes of those most affected, being in relationship with them is something all policy makers ought to do. I may not have thought about it exactly like that then, but Site 2 sent me on that trajectory.

Let's be real: it takes a lot to get rid of the pressure and expectations of your family and the mainstream world. Back then, in the world I was in, people with two degrees from relatively fancy schools were not generally going off to try and change the world. My father was worried about my financial situation and so was I, so I decided I would try to find work at a company that sold some sort of necessary product that actually helped people. Maybe this could be a happy medium between earning money and feeling fulfilled. I found a Seattle-based company called Physio-Control that sold cardiac defibrillators. I was hired into a new program, designed to groom MBAs for senior management, that rotated recruits through all the different departments within the company.

Everyone had to start with a year in the field, in sales. I was shipped out to Cincinnati, Ohio, where I was the first woman and the first brown person ever in the district. It was clear the rest of the guys didn't want me there—medical equipment sales was lucrative, and they had worked hard to get there. They did not appreciate a brown woman with no official sales experience waltzing in, and they assumed I was going to bring down the district's sales numbers, which helped determine everyone's compensation.

I was determined to prove them wrong.

My territory covered most of western Ohio and eastern Indiana. I drove a blue Ford Aerostar van in which I could barely see over the steering wheel. There were no back seats in the van, so my foldable cart piled high with different types of defibrillators could be stashed there, then pulled out and wheeled through all the big hospitals as I peddled my wares to doctors and nurses. I also sold to paramedics and firefighters at a time when fire trucks were just beginning to have automated external defibrillators (AEDs) on board. Some of these fire departments were all-volunteer and located in rural areas. When I walked in with my brand-new portable AEDs, all eyes would be on me.

"Where you from?" one of the firemen grunted at me suspiciously.

"India," I said with my sweetest smile.

"Where in Indiana?" came the response back.

I had to smile, even as I wondered if I would ever sell a defibrillator to these folks who seemed to have so little in common with me.

That was to be my next lesson on my wander-path: no matter how different we might seem, there is a place—a human place—to connect. That time in Ohio and Indiana taught me so many life lessons. I learned how to work with and talk to anyone, regardless of how little they seemed like me or seemed to like me. I learned to look for the similarities in values around family or the basic things we all wanted in life. I was curious about them and their lives and I discovered they were curious about me—that was a good place to start.

I found myself an urban loft apartment in a converted warehouse in downtown Cincinnati near the main downtown fire station where the busiest and biggest paramedic crew was based. I parked myself there and made friends with the medics. I wanted to get to know how the equipment was actually used and I convinced them to let me ride with their unit on Friday nights—they were disbelieving and then charmed that I would ask to do so! Lt. Mike Uphus taught me how to run an IV and allowed me to tag along with his crew on all the tough and easy rides. I sold lots of equipment, yes—but, more importantly, we also became friends.

I flew through my sales quotas, but I still remembered Mary Houghton's advice. In Thailand and South Chicago, I saw broken systems and poor people whose voices were not sought out or even heard. I saw people who wanted more for themselves, wanted more for their communities and families. I saw that I could climb higher and become a novelty—a single brown woman in a sea of white faces, not having really helped anyone but myself—or I could actually work to fix the structures so that *everyone* could have real opportunities and real choices for their lives.

So I stayed in Cincinnati just long enough to break all the sales records and prove myself.

And then I left.

I met Alan Preston the first week of orientation at Kellogg and we started dating soon after. He had worked on Wall Street as well—and strangely we had encountered each other during a service day where investment bankers went and volunteered around New York City. We had both been painting a shelter and he and his friend even gave me a ride, but it was not something that either of us put together until long after we met again at Kellogg. We had similar views on life and when we were applying for jobs, we both decided to apply for the job with Physio-Control—and we both actually got the job. When I was placed in Cincinnati, Alan was placed in Milwaukee. Both of us wanted to leave and so we did, moving back to Seattle to get married in November 1990 and then spending some months traveling in Africa and India. Somewhere in those travels, I realized I needed to leave the private sector for good and find work that made my heart sing. I had no idea what that meant; I knew the money would not be good and my parents would be disappointed in me. But I listened to myself and there it was: the inner voice that we are so often told to ignore telling me that there really was no other choice.

We returned to Seattle in early 1991 and I began working for PATH— Program for Appropriate Technology in Health—a Seattle-based nonprofit that worked on improving health, particularly for women and children, around the world. Today, PATH acts almost as the operating arm of the Gates Foundation's global health work, with 1,600 employees in more than seventy offices around the world. But at the time, PATH had about 120 employees, mostly in Seattle, with a few offices in other countries including India, Kenya, and Thailand.

I was hired into the department that handled the business development side of simple but effective technologies that could work in low-resource village settings: ways to keep vaccines cold; birth kits to deliver babies safely; and birth control methods. Soon after starting, I was promoted to run a loan fund that helped invest in health projects in countries that simply could not get financing anywhere else, from manufacturing injectable contraceptives in Mexico, to running nonprofit clinics in rural Gambia, to social marketing in Indonesia to fight the spread of HIV/AIDS. We took no collateral and processed very little documentation, but we did our due diligence and had a stunning 99 percent repayment rate.

I thought I had died and gone to heaven. The people I worked with were talented public health officials, smart people who cared about the world and wanted to make it better. The work was exciting and challenging, and I was allowed to grow and experiment with the fund I ran. But I was noticing something: at the time, there were few people in senior management who looked like me. I was one of just a handful who had

actually grown up in one of the countries in which we worked. Most of
the country directors were American. I began to feel more and more out of
place. The job involved staying in five-star luxury hotels in poor countries
and feeling the dissonance of then going to look at projects to get people
out of poverty. Solutions still seemed to come from the top when they
needed to come from the bottom to succeed. This realization would hold
throughout my life and career and would be a hallmark principle of both
my organizing and my legislating.

After four years of that, I realized I wanted something even more: to go
back to my birth country, live in villages myself, forge real relationships
with people over time, and learn from their deep wisdom and perspectives
on the world.

It was time to go back to India.

In 1995, I was awarded a two-year fellowship from the Institute of Current World Affairs to live in and write about villages and small towns in
India. The institute gave me a lot of freedom to define what my fellowship
would look like and what I wanted to do with my time. Alan generously
agreed to leave a job he loved, working to get some of the most vulnerable
women into jobs, to move to India with me for the fellowship. He arrived
about six months after me, so that I would also have some time on my
own. I spent a month in Kerala, my birth state, and another six weeks in
the stunningly beautiful, mountainous and then-isolated area of Ladakh,
in the perpetually politically charged state of Jammu and Kashmir, where
the land had been fought over since Partition. Those trips gave me a sense
of the vastness of the country. But what I knew was that I wanted to get
to know the northern part of India, and specifically to live in the northern
state of Uttar Pradesh, where poverty was high and I felt I would learn the
most about what grassroots development looked like.

I wrote about a wide range of topics I found compelling and often challenging: child labor, education, women's issues, spirituality. I also wrote
about my own personal experience of returning to India as an adult and
what it felt like to go back and reconnect with that part of me. I learned to

speak Hindi and sing Indian *bhajans* (folk songs). I fell in love with India all over again, even with all her complexity and shades of gray, which felt so different from the United States where everything seemed black or white.

I knew when I returned to India that part of my reason for going was that I needed to explore my own identity, ground myself in who I was and where I came from, to stop—I hoped—living in the hyphen. Perhaps here I would finally figure out if I was Indian, American, or something else altogether.

One morning, while I was working at a women's dairy cooperative in Kerala and staying with a host family in a small village, one of my hostesses and I sat on the veranda talking. Suddenly, I saw twenty pairs of eyes focused on me. Their owners, a group of young girls, leaned against the flimsy gate of wood and wire, crowded together like sardines, hanging over each other's backs to get a glimpse of the woman who had come from America. Embarrassed at first, I stared at the coarse red mud between the gate and the house, then at the coconut trees around us. Finally, I looked over and smiled, only to be met with stares. Twenty pairs of black eyes opened wider, staying focused and expressionless. I stared back until my eyes began to dry up from concentrated looking. I blinked and the stillness broke.

One young girl opened the gate, and the young girls poured toward me like an ocean coming to shore. They took hold of me, several on each limb, and pulled me down to the ground tenderly, curiously, determinedly. I sat in the middle of a circle as they draped themselves around and on me. I felt fingers in mine, hands stroking my hair, arms pulling at my neck.

They were asking me questions in a great rush of words in Malayalam, the language of my ancestors, a language I understood but no longer spoke well. They asked me why I wore a sari if I had come from America, where was my *pottu* (the dot on my forehead), where were my bangles? If I was from America, they asked, why did I look so much like them? They were disappointed, they told me. Why was I not wearing gold jewelry? Surely I must have enough money to buy lots of it? They disdainfully fingered the dangling silver earrings I had bought in a street fair in Seattle. They said you were from America, they repeated in disappointed voices. I explained in a strange, halting mixture of Hindi, Malayalam, and English that I only lived in America but had been born in India just like them.

They began to laugh, but insisted: "You're not like us, sister. Living in such a rich place and you are wearing only one thin gold chain!" Now they were serious, trying to understand.

They were asking me what I often asked myself: to explain who I was, why I seemed to be neither from here nor there.

I suggested we go for a walk. We walked for hours barefoot on dirt paths, through coconut tree groves. As we walked, we talked: about marriage, about children, about America, about Madras where I was born. They held on to my arms as if they would never let go, and as I felt their warmth around me, I remembered both the familiar and the unfamiliar of this place and these people.

Being back in India changed me. I met women who were saving forests, fighting the early impacts of climate change, and standing up to violence. I saw government and nongovernmental efforts mired by corruption and indifference; as well as projects and people steeped in compassion and excellence. I questioned injustice and inequity. I connected to a deeper spiritual power that I had not really acknowledged before then. But every day, that same belief was put to the test by the sheer unfairness, overwhelming poverty, and unbearable sadness that wrapped around millions of Indian villagers. At the very same time, it was there in those villages that I also learned about love, generosity, and resilience; about community and fellowship; about the tools of nonviolent movements for peace and truth and justice. I had tapped back into my heritage of powerful Indian women leaders: my mother, my grandmother, my great aunt, the forest-saving village women, these young village girls. I was reconnected to a power that would be so central to my identity long into the future.

It was also in India where I learned that, no matter what we imagine, we simply cannot control everything. We just have to take life as it comes to us.

I was still not a U.S. citizen. Although I'd been married to a U.S. citizen since 1991, I had been ambivalent about transitioning from being a permanent resident (otherwise known in immigration-speak as "having a green card") to becoming a citizen. Since coming to the United States in 1982, I had spent almost a decade on an alphabet soup of student and work visas. Marriage afforded me some permanence, but the truth was I was somewhat ambivalent about having to renounce my Indian citizenship since India and America did not have a dual citizenship arrangement. My parents still lived in India and I still wondered if perhaps down the road, I might want to move back to be with them.

As a permanent resident, I was required to return to the United States once a year just to keep my status current. The institute did not typically accommodate this—they liked you to stay at your post for the whole two years of your fellowship—but they made an exception in my case, bringing me back to the United States for a brief visit before the first year of the fellowship ended.

Alan and I had decided that after the fellowship was the perfect time to have a baby. In our ideal world, I would get pregnant at just the right time, so I could spend my first two trimesters finishing my fellowship in India and then return to the United States for the third trimester and birth—which would also be just in time to keep my green card current.

My plan was completely on track until two weeks before we were scheduled to come back to the United States. Suddenly, at just twenty-four weeks pregnant, I developed a leak in my amniotic sac. After a harrowing couple of weeks, it was not resolving and I had to urgently fly to one of only two neonatal intensive care units (NICU) in India to deliver my child.

Janak was born at 26.5 weeks and weighed just one pound, fourteen ounces. By all accounts, they never should have survived.*

I was now faced with a dilemma. In order to preserve my permanent

---

* Janak identifies as nonbinary and uses they/them pronouns. See Chapter 6.

resident status, I needed to return to the United States within weeks of giving birth. But returning to the U.S. would mean leaving my baby, who faced down death every single day for months. Janak was so tiny and in such critical condition that they could not fly, and I refused to leave their bedside knowing they might die. By virtue of Alan's U.S. citizenship status, Janak was automatically a U.S. citizen. But I, married to a U.S. citizen and mother of a U.S. citizen child, had lost my green card—and with it, my ability to return to the United States with my family. Even as we fought to keep Janak alive every single day, I now also had to worry about how we could keep our family together and whether I would be able to return to the United States with Alan and Janak. These visceral emotions stayed with me for decades after, often recurring as I was dealing with the plight of immigrant moms who had been separated from their children or families that could not be together.

There was also the enormous worry of Janak's medical needs. They were the size of my hand and needed a total of seven blood transfusions. At one point, we had no blood left that we could spare so our pediatrician and neonatal doctor, Dr. Mahesh Balsekar, who had by then become a friend, gave his blood. Although he had no formal training in an NICU, Dr. Balsekar had done fellowships in NICUs in America and elsewhere. He was brilliant, compassionate, and deeply skilled and he worked all the time, responding to patients at all hours of the day and night. But as Janak's situation developed additional complexities, we faced real challenges. The Indian hospital's technology, equipment, and even some of their knowledge about low-birthweight babies was still new and limited. When Janak developed water in the brain, a serious condition, we knew we needed to return to the United States for the necessary care.

In the end, my institute was able to use some of their connections in order to help me return to the United States. My permanent resident status was restored, but all the years that qualified me for citizenship were stripped away and I had to start again from scratch. I was so much luckier than many others, and the time was a radically different one than the one we are in today where the Trump administration has no quarter for compassion.

I vowed that I would get my U.S. citizenship as soon as I was eligible. I could not imagine going through the fear of being separated from my child again. Because I had lost the years that qualified me for citizenship, I had to wait another three years until I was eligible—which took me to the year 2000.

It was time to become an American.

2

Becoming an American,
Becoming an Activist

IN THE SUMMER OF 1997, ALAN, JANAK, AND I RETURNED TO AMERICA. Janak's health still presented many stresses: pneumonia every year that required visits to the emergency room, seizures in the early days of our return, and developmental delays that kept us on edge.

After living in the hubbub of India and a community that had so much more time, America felt cold and isolated. No one dropped by for tea. Alan went back to work almost immediately, and most of my friends I'd made before I left for India had lives that were in full swing without me by then; their time was limited for a friend with a brand-new sick baby. I drove on enormous roads filled with cars that contained just one person, filled gas at automated gas stations, and shopped at markets with automatic checkout counters. It seemed so strange that, after two years of living in crowded places in India where there was no privacy, I could now go days without talking to a soul. For the first time, I also was not working, staying home to care for my miracle child. I knew how incredibly lucky we were that Janak was *here*, on this earth despite all the odds. But somehow, I could not shake the deep sadness I felt. Only much later, after I began to see a therapist, did I realize that I was experiencing some combination of post-traumatic stress from the terrifying birth, and postpartum depression.

Even today, neither of these conditions is widely acknowledged, much less discussed. I felt adrift and alone—and terribly unfamiliar with how to navigate the straits of depression and the shame of feeling what I felt.

I began writing in those moments when Janak was asleep or in the early mornings when the first light was just coming up. I had decided I would try to parlay the essays I had written during my fellowship into a book about my time in India, titled *Pilgrimage to India: A Woman Revisits Her Homeland*. I found a wonderful independent women's press to publish the book and it came out in March 2000.

That same month, I finally walked into the cavernous hall at the old location of the Immigration and Naturalization Services (now called U.S. Customs and Immigration Services) south of downtown Seattle. I was prepared to simply undertake a business transaction: citizenship finally, so I would always be with my child. I was neither prepared for the emotion that came with citizenship nor the future that would unfold with my citizenship.

There were hundreds of others at the ceremony from all over the world, and you could hear so many languages from every continent spoken. We all carried small American flags. Grandparents clutched grandchildren, moms and dads held hands. As we took the oath of citizenship, the weight of the moment came crashing down on me. Tears welled up and rolled down my cheeks. I was here to stay, far from my parents. I would never again be separated from my child but I was now renouncing any allegiance to my birth country of India where I had been a citizen for thirty-five years.

It was time, with all the mixed emotions of the moment, to embrace this country as it had embraced me as a sixteen-year-old who had come here by myself, with nothing in my pockets, in order to study. Time to build a life of better opportunity.

America, a country built on the idea of being a refuge for those in need, "the tired masses, yearning to breathe free."

America, a country that has always celebrated itself as a nation of immigrants even when its actions often contradicted that very notion.

In that moment, as I took my oath, I realized how lucky I was. I had waited a long time for the privilege of becoming a U.S. citizen: eighteen years. And now, even though I was making a choice to live on a different continent from my parents, who had sacrificed so much to send me here, I knew that my future had opened up, that citizenship would offer me the unique freedom to seek opportunity and to enjoy the freedoms of our democracy. I knew, too, that with those freedoms and opportunity came enormous responsibility: to do everything I could to preserve and build our democracy, to vote, and to use my life to pay it forward and ensure opportunity for others.

Even as I found newfound freedom, I experienced a new separation.

Toward the end of 2000, Alan and I finalized a painful divorce and had to work through all the attendant questions of joint parenting—an arrangement that was far from common at the time. Almost all the books on divorce we could find were locked into the idea that the mother would have primary custody and the father would have the child over weekends or for holidays. Alan was a devoted father—then and always—and would never have been willing to settle for that arrangement. So, we worked out a mediated settlement that allowed us to have an even split of time with Janak each week. That meant each of us would be single parents for the time we had Janak. In the pain of divorce, the sad truth was we pushed one another's buttons and there was no space to be anything but angry with each other. (Today, Alan is one of my closest friends, but it took us years of hard work. I often say that having a good divorce is as difficult as having a good marriage.) The consequence, though, was that in those early years of our divorce, we talked to each other as little as possible and only to make arrangements for Janak. When Janak was with me, I truly felt like a single parent and everything I did in the years to come was in that context, even as I came into my activist life.

It was time to move into a new house and begin a new life.

The date was September 10, 2001.

Friends came to help me move into my new house and we celebrated the fresh start that evening with beer and pizza. I spent my first night in my new home on a mattress on the floor in the midst of boxes piled high in each room.

At 5 a.m. on September 11, the phone rang, waking me from a deep sleep. It was a friend from the East Coast. "Have you heard?" she said urgently. "There's been a huge incident . . . "

Many people that I have spoken to since September 11 said that they first heard the news from others in this same sort of way. We didn't really know how to comprehend what was happening. Planes flying into buildings, "incidents" not "attacks" in those first few moments.

My thirteen-inch television was piled haphazardly in my bedroom. I pulled it out and hooked it up to watch in horror as the first pictures replayed over and over.

Surrounded by boxes, I sat numb. Unpacking felt trivial, as did just about everything else. The chaos in my house seemed a reflection of the chaos in the world.

Within twenty-four hours, I had received the first fearful calls from individuals in the South Asian community who were being attacked simply for wearing turbans. On September 13, a man armed with a gun and a tank of gasoline targeted a mosque in North Seattle, trying to fire at Muslims as they were coming out of prayers in the evening. He doused cars in the mosque's parking lot with gasoline and, when he couldn't get his gun to work or to start a fire, he jumped in his car and drove around the block and smashed into a telephone pole.

On September 15, 2001, the first Sikh American was murdered in Mesa, Arizona. Balbir Singh Sodhi owned a gas station and had come to America from India some thirteen years earlier to escape the persecution and killing of Sikhs in India following Indira Gandhi's assassination. He was killed because his killer thought he looked like Osama bin Laden and therefore should be held responsible for the terrorist attacks. As the killer was being taken away by the police, he was shouting, "I stand for America all the way."[1]

The mosque attack and Sodhi's death reminded me of a death twenty years before in Detroit, Michigan. In the late 1970s and early 1980s, the American automobile industry was suffering. Japanese automakers had swept into the market with high-quality, less-expensive cars, leaving American manufacturers reeling. Thousands of American workers were laid off, and Detroit in particular fell into deep economic despair. Vincent Chin, a young man of Chinese descent, was out at his bachelor party in June of 1982 with some friends, when he was accosted by laid-off autoworkers who beat him brutally and fatally. They believed him to be Japanese and believed Japan to be responsible for the downfall of the American auto industry. As Chin was dying, his last words to a friend were, "It isn't fair."[2]

There was a profound *lack* of knowledge about race and culture in the racist violence in Seattle, Detroit, Mesa, and across America following September 11. If you wore a turban, you were a terrorist. If you wore a *hijab* (head covering for Muslim women), you were a terrorist. If you wore a head covering at all (Hindu women often cover their heads also), you were a terrorist. In fact, if you "looked different" in any way, you were suspect.

For the first time while living in America, I felt scared. Many of us kept our children at home. The situation felt like a powder keg and if something set it off, everything could explode. When I went out, I could feel the tension in my body as I eyed those around me. Would someone attack me? Would someone say something to me? A few occasions arose when I would normally have worn my Indian dress—*salwar kameez*—but I chose not to put it on. Instead I dressed in skirts and pants, as unobtrusively as I could.

My fear was compounded by the stories I heard. Because I had been doing consulting work in the immigrant and refugee communities in the previous year, I was well connected. Every day, I received calls from people telling me more horrible stories about the discrimination and violence that they and their families had been experiencing in my own city: Muslim women who had been harassed on the streets and had their *hijabs* pulled down (tantamount for many of these women to being stripped naked on the streets); young girls who were too scared to get on the school bus to go to school; a Somali woman who was stabbed in a gas station in West Seattle; a Sikh taxi driver who was beaten at the airport.

What was happening to us? What was this insanity? The Sikhs and Arabs and Muslims who were being harassed on the streets around me had nothing to do with the people who had flown the planes into the twin towers—and yet, here they were, being targeted because of what they looked like, whom they prayed to, or where they were born.

Days after the attacks, President Bush made the proclamation, "You are either with us or with the terrorists."[3] For many Arab, Muslim, and South Asian communities, the stark language seemed directed at us. It is hard to overstate the psychological impact of those words: they instilled fear in all of us who felt we could just as easily be perceived as "them." They broke the world into black and white, drew out false patriotism, and cemented division. Most of all, they left many of us wondering where we stood when it seemed to be increasingly evident that the only way to be "with us" was to look the same as "us."

Subsequent policies and programs from the Bush administration and the Department of Justice would make it very clear that they had divided the world by skin color, religious beliefs, and ethnic origins. Those same policies and programs, cloaked in national security rhetoric, laid the groundwork for very similar policies from the Trump administration, decades later, that legitimized racial profiling and created a set of discriminatory policies targeting particular populations of people.

On September 15, a friend who taught in a public school in my ethnically diverse neighborhood called me in tears. "Pramila," she said, "This is the third Muslim family that has withdrawn their kids from school because they are too afraid to even get on the bus or go out in public. What have we come to?"

When I hung up the phone, I wept. I wept for the lives that had been lost in New York and Washington, DC. I wept for the insanity that had raged through the country in response to the attacks. I wept for the people who suffered not just the terror of the first attacks but now of recrimination from their own neighbors and friends and schoolmates. In tears, I called my friend Paul in San Francisco, who was a well-known environmental activist and no stranger to organizing for change. "I have to do something," I said to him. "I can't just sit here and watch this happen." He listened and then said, "Maybe you should do something like what San Francisco did—they passed a resolution declaring the city a Hate Free Zone."

It was a start. It felt like it would be meaningful to make a statement about Seattle's values and who we were as a community.

I dried my tears, went on the internet, and found reference to the resolution that the San Francisco Board of Supervisors had passed in the days following September 11. Paul had told me that the nonprofit group, Global Exchange, had been instrumental in the passage of that resolution, so I called Medea Benjamin, the co-founder of Global Exchange who I had met the year before, on her cell phone. She was delighted that we were thinking of doing something similar in Seattle, and directed me to their website, which offered a copy of the resolution and some other materials.

Then, I called my closest friend, Aaliyah Gupta, who was the executive director of Chaya, a nonprofit organization based in Seattle that provided services to South Asian survivors of domestic violence, where I served on the board. South Asians were being targeted mercilessly because of the head covering they wore (both Hindus and Muslims) and the color of their skin. Aaliyah immediately understood the need to take action, left her kids with her husband, and came over. This is a perfect example of who Aaliyah has been for me time and time again, to this day: she was supremely capable, incredibly compassionate, and absolutely ready to roll up her sleeves and do what needed to be done.

We cleared space on my cluttered dining room table and began to talk about what we should do. "Why just Seattle?" I asked. "If we're doing a Hate Free Zone, shouldn't it be for the whole state?" We agreed that this should be our goal, but we needed an elected official to take the lead. We made a list of politicians who could help us lead this effort and then began looking them up in the phone book and making cold calls. It was Saturday and we were only getting answering machines, so I called another acquaintance, Akhtar Badshah, who ran an organization called Digital Partners. It just so happened that Akhtar was going to a reception with Congressman Jim McDermott the next afternoon. "I'll bring it up to him and see if I can set up an appointment for you," he said. True to his word, Akhtar called the next day and said that Congressman McDermott would see me on Monday morning at 10 a.m.

This may have been my earliest lesson in crisis organizing and in how political movements start. I had an idea and no real knowledge about where to go from there, but a determined activist is not deterred by such trivialities! I called in my troops (Aaliyah, in this case) and then began using any and all contacts I had to get me the help I needed. I had never spoken to a politician in my life, but I knew that if I was going to try to get that Hate Free Zone resolution passed, I needed to find someone who would help move my cause. And yes, why think small when the problem was so big? Seattle wasn't sufficient; we were shooting for the whole state.

The weekend passed in a blur. I continued to call around to various people to see what they were doing and talk about the idea of declaring the state a Hate Free Zone. People were interested—but how? And what did that mean? I didn't know myself. I knew passing a resolution was a symbolic act only—but an important one. It seemed essential to tell those who were staying home in fear that the politicians stood with them and against hate. It is also well documented, I learned later, that when elected leaders speak out against hate, the frequency of hate crimes does go down. Some people do listen.

On Sunday evening, I could not sleep. My meeting with Congressman McDermott the next morning would be my first with a U.S. congressperson. I was nervous about the meeting and felt I needed to hand him something written, something more than a request to declare Washington State a Hate Free Zone.

At 11 p.m. that evening, I pulled my computer out of one of the many boxes still piled around my new house and began typing at the top of a file in bold capital letters: "HATE FREE ZONE CAMPAIGN OF WASH-INGTON." Underneath that, I wrote a very broad vision statement about making the state a welcoming place for everyone and denouncing hate, and then underneath I came up with a plan of four distinct areas that we needed to work on if the state was truly going to be hate free: First, providing direct support through a helpline and direct care to those who were the victims of hate crimes. Second, working to pass legislation like city and state resolutions and ordinances that supported the idea of a hate-free environment. Third, working in the schools and with the public to educate people about the cultures and religions that were now an integral part of the American fabric. And finally, engaging in a communications strategy with the press to ensure our messages could be heard far and wide.

When I was finished with my one-page document, it was 2 a.m. and I collapsed into bed.

The next morning, I arrived at Congressman McDermott's office as he was holding a staff meeting around his conference table. He invited me to join them all there. I introduced myself and told him we needed to do something to push back against the hate crimes and discrimination. I handed him my one-pager that I had written just a few hours before. He responded positively immediately—"Yes, we must do something"—and then he pulled out a poem by Martin Niemöller that he kept in his jacket pocket:

> First they came for the socialists, and I did not speak out—
> Because I was not a socialist
> Then they came for the trade unionists, and I did not
>   speak out—
> Because I was not a trade unionist.
> Then they came for the Jews, and I did not speak out—
> Because I was not a Jew.
> Then they came for me, and there was no one left to speak
>   for me.

Congressman McDermott turned to me and said, "So, what should we do?"

"Let's pull together a press conference," I said spontaneously, "with you and the governor and every major elected official we can get and declare our state a hate-free state."

"What a great idea!" he said, with genuine enthusiasm. "When should we do that?"

I shot back immediately, "How about tomorrow?"

I'll never forget that moment. Congressman McDermott turned to look at me with a perplexed look on his face and said, "Who ARE you?"

I knew what the expression meant: pulling off a press conference in twenty-four hours with the governor and every major elected official in attendance must have seemed like an outrageous idea.

"I just think we have to do this right away," I pressed. "Tomorrow will be one week since September 11 and people are suffering. They need to hear from our elected officials. We need leaders to say that we will not tolerate hate."

After a moment of shocked silence, Congressman McDermott jumped into action, telling his staff to begin calling around to other elected officials and getting a space for the press conference the next morning. A Seattle City Council member, Judy Nicastro, picked up the idea of the resolution and said they would get it passed the next morning before the press conference.

On Tuesday, September 18, at Seattle Center, we had the most incredible press conference with the governor, mayor, King County executive, labor leaders, and of course, Congressman McDermott to declare Washington a Hate Free Zone. Seattle City Council members attended and read their resolution, which mirrored the one from San Francisco.

I stood off to the side, both bemused and delighted at the speed with which everything had moved—and my role in making it happen. McDermott saw me standing there, motioned me immediately into the center and began introducing me to people as "Pramila Jayapal from Hate Free Zone

Campaign of Washington" as his staff handed out copies of my one-page document—a rough draft I had never imagined would be made public.

"Congressman," I said quietly and urgently, "there IS no Hate Free Zone Campaign of Washington. That was just an idea!"

He looked at me with a tiny smile and said, "Well, then, you better get to work!"

I got to work.

For my first experience with a U.S. Congress member, it was a damn fine one. Jim stood by us, time and time again, in support of Hate Free Zone of Washington (renamed OneAmerica in 2008). As we took on the U.S. government in some of our bleaker days and stood up against discrimination and abuses of civil liberties, Congressman McDermott supported the organization and me, helping us grow our power through the years.

Through this experience, I saw how the platform of elected office could be used to lead with conviction and courage, to stand up for people whose voices were not being listened to, and to drive a message that was different from what we saw around us. I saw what real leadership in an elected office looked like.

Fifteen years later in 2016, as the congresswoman elected to replace McDermott upon his retirement, I held another press conference at the very same Seattle Center. It was one month after Donald Trump was elected, and a new but remarkably similar fear was permeating our communities. According to the Southern Poverty Law Center, there were nearly nine hundred reports of harassment and intimidation in the ten days following Trump's election; many of those invoked Trump's name during the assaults.[4]

I invited our whole Democratic congressional delegation, Washington State Governor Jay Inslee, and a number of my long-time community and union leader allies from the coalition I had helped to build over the past decade and a half to this press conference.

There onstage, we remembered what had happened in 2001 and now again, we reaffirmed our commitment to being a hate-free state. I felt more prepared than I ever could have imagined to represent my district at a time of such injustice.

"Here in Washington State, we refuse to succumb to fear-based politics. We know using fear to advance an agenda is an old and practiced tactic," I told the crowd of several hundred people. "We come together today to say we will fight injustice and policies rooted in racism and will condemn hateful rhetoric. . . . Together we say we respect women, we value Muslims, we value Black lives, we stand with LGBTQ community members, and with immigrants, refugees, and people of all faiths. We value workers of all abilities, and we will fight for dreamers of all kinds, immigrant and Native-born."[5]

Looking back at September 18, 2001, that pivotal day when we declared Washington State a Hate Free Zone, I had no idea that our nation's path would unfold as it did, that my desire to just do *something* would lead to fifteen years of organizing and advocacy, and that in 2016, it would all come full circle again.

In the months following September 11, 2001, Congressman McDermott had laid out a challenge for me to turn my idea of Hate Free Zone of Washington into reality. Hate crimes were spiking, so I worked with the Seattle Office for Civil Rights to start a hate crime–reporting line. A host of attorneys who wanted to help formed a pro bono legal group to help address what were now becoming civil liberties abuses by the U.S. government. The Patriot Act had passed within ten days of the September 11 attacks, with little attention from either Democrats or Republicans to the enormous problems it created for civil liberties and privacy protections for all Americans, but especially those most likely to be targeted. Congress was in a frenzy to "do something," and the Patriot Act was it: a dusted off-the-shelf piece of legislation that had been waiting for a moment like this. It was soon clear that few members of Congress had even fully read the legislation, and we would end up spending the next two decades essentially trying to fix the problems of a bill that never should have been made law.

Volunteers and organizations who wanted to do something were starting to gather, from the Asian Counseling and Referral Services to the King County Labor Council, AFL-CIO, to the Church Council of Greater Seattle. I realized I could no longer run everything from my kitchen table; we needed to have an actual organization and headquarters. I quickly wrote a few grant applications to raise a small amount of money to rent a small office space blocks away from my home for the newly established Hate Free Zone Campaign of Washington, a nonprofit organization whose mission was to uphold the fundamental principles of democracy and justice, particularly for immigrants targeted in the wake of September 11, 2001.

On the morning of November 7, 2001, agents from the U.S. Treasury Department's Office of Foreign Asset Control raided Maka Mini Mart, a small Somali market just blocks away from my home and our new Hate Free Zone Washington office. The entire Somali community relied on this market for their groceries. The raid also included two neighboring businesses, one of which was a franchise of the international Barakat Wire Transfer Service. The federal raid was conducted under the auspices of a new Executive Order, issued by President George W. Bush, that authorized the blocking of assets of any persons or entities that provided funds to foreigners alleged to be supporting terrorism. The Treasury Department contended that Barakat was skimming portions of the money transfers for illegal purposes connected to terrorism. Although the agents were after the assets of the money-transmitter business, they raided all three businesses because they occupied the same premise. They did absolutely nothing to minimize the impact of their presence on any of these community-owned businesses that were central to the community's well-being.

Abdinasir Ali Nur, the managing partner of Maka Mini Mart, testified later that he received a phone call at 8 a.m. that morning telling him about the raid. Nur rushed to the store and was personally searched by an officer. He watched in disbelief and fear as the agents took most of his inventory, including frozen meat from two large, well-stocked meat lockers, coolers, toilet paper, gift items, furniture, cash from the register, and shelving, threw it into their trucks, and hauled it away. Nur learned later that the agents threw out all perishable items, including the meat, and stored some of the rest of the property in a warehouse. The agents left Nur with an empty store and a notice on his door shutting down his business. Nur was never told by the agents why the raid was taking place, nor whether he was charged with anything.

"It was Ramadan," Nur told me some months later. Ramadan is the most important month of the Muslim year, the time of fasting and religious reflection. "This is the peak time for our business. Our freezers were stocked with meat, because we must cook big meals at night when we break our fast. Without my store, people had to go to different places to get their foodstuffs. We lost a lot of money, especially because it would have been our busiest time of the year."

Community groups and neighborhood activists held rallies in support of the businesses, and an attorney from the Seattle chapter of the ACLU stepped forward to represent Nur and the owners of the other businesses. We quickly learned that raids similar to these were happening across the country, all targeting Muslim money-transmitter businesses allegedly connected to Barakat. Meanwhile, in the wake of 9/11, the newspapers were not waiting to see if the stories were true. Their front-page headline blared the assumptions that the businesses were linked to terrorism and the U.S. Department of Justice was successfully nailing terrorist financiers. Some six months after the raids, in April 2002, a small item tucked on the inside pages of the *New York Times* reported that the U.S. government had been unable to find any connection between Barakat Wire Transfer businesses and terrorism.[6]

I closely followed everything that happened at Maka Mini Mart. Less than a month after Maka reopened in December 2001, Nur and the owners of two other Somali grocery stores received identical letters from the U.S. Department of Agriculture. All three letters were worded exactly the same way, even though they were addressed to different owners of different stores. The letters charged that the owners of the stores (one of whom was Nur) had engaged in food stamp trafficking. Because of that, the USDA suspended the stores' ability to accept food stamps. For Nur and the other two stores, this was tantamount to shutting the business down, since most of their customers were low-income families who depended on food stamps for their grocery purchases.

I had been alerted to the letters in January 2002, when a Somali-American journalist named Mahdy Mahweel came into the Hate Free Zone (HFZ) office brandishing copies of them. "Something is not right," he said. "The community is in a panic. There is a meeting tonight of the owners, some community leaders, and other people who want to help. Can you come?"

Ibrahim, an Arab-American community leader I had hired to work with me at HFZ, and I agreed immediately even though we had no idea what we would do. I made phone calls to two people I thought might be helpful: Amy Kratz, the then–legal director for the Northwest Immigrant Rights Project (NWIRP), the only nonprofit organization in the state providing pro-bono legal immigration services to those in need, and John Tirpak, who was with another nonprofit organization and said to be an expert on food stamp issues.

The meeting was at the Somali Community Services Coalition office, located on the second floor of one of the Rainier Avenue buildings, above a Vietnamese restaurant. Several Somali community leaders were already gathered around the long table, coats still on to beat the chill of the January evening, when Amy and I walked in. John Tirpak was there, as was a woman who worked at the City of Seattle and was instrumental in pulling together assistance for the stores.

Stopping Maka and the two other Somali grocers in the area from accepting food stamps devastated community members, who were dependent on food stamps and would be unable to purchase their meat and supplies. Maka was one of the oldest Somali grocery stories in the area and its main business was the sale of Halal meat—meat that has been slaughtered in accordance with Islamic law and is the only kind of meat Muslims are allowed to be eat. In fact, as the case dragged on, public health officials at the local schools began to report health deficiencies in Muslim children who were not getting enough to eat.

After the community meeting, I got in touch with one of the pro bono attorneys who had signed up after 9/11 to help in any way possible. Susan Foster was a senior lawyer at Perkins Coie law firm, and she and her team agreed to take on the case for Nur. Over months of working with Foster and her team, we came to the conclusion that the government analysis of the food stamp transactions was based on faulty understanding of the Somali community's shopping habits and culture, and likely was an attempt to target the business owners simply because they were Muslim.

The USDA said that Maka had very high transactions compared to an American mini mart of the same size, the most common of which would be a food mart at a gas station. But Maka was completely different. As small as it was, Maka functioned as the main meat market for the Somali community; the store had meat slicers and grinders and often sold an entire goat that would be cut up and frozen in a family's freezer. The typical Somali family consisted of eight to ten people, and because they often did not have cars, they tended to go to the shop once a week to buy all of their groceries for the week.

The Perkins attorneys were dogged; they clearly saw the USDA's charges as part of a larger attempt by the U.S. government to target and close down Muslim shops around the country. The fact that it was happening across the country and to stores that were located right next to the wire-transfer businesses implied that the government had specifically targeted these stores and were trying to put them out of business. Hate Free Zone became the bridge between the community and the attorneys; the community trusted us and that was incredibly important. We helped communicate information from the lawyers in a way that was culturally competent and we also organized the larger community as necessary to fight back and learn about what the U.S. government was doing when they targeted the Somali community.

The lawyers filed paperwork to request administrative review of Maka's disqualification from the food stamp program, and after nearly five months, Nur was notified that the USDA had reversed its decision to disqualify Maka and two other stores. This was a huge victory, and it was also Hate Free Zone's first high-profile attempt to stand up to the U.S. government.

While Nur was pleased with the outcome, he was deeply worried about this attack on his reputation and the challenges of getting Maka back on its feet. "Where I once ran a successful small business, I now struggle to make ends meet," he told me. "I have lost months' worth of revenue and find it difficult to cover my expenses. In addition to these financial costs, my family and I have paid an emotional toll in the aftermath of September 11. I have now been accused twice of wrongs that I have not committed, and this feels very bad to me."

For Nur and so many others, the pain and turmoil of being targeted by the U.S. government cost him and his community dearly, some members in unimaginable ways. Unfortunately, this was not to be the end of the suffering.

A year after 9/11, Hate Free Zone and a coalition of community organizations decided to hold the first ever Justice for All town hall in Seattle as a way to document and lift up the voices of affected communities. The idea for the public hearing emerged in the basement of the local Wing Luke Asian Museum at a meeting that I had called with approximately thirty people from the Somali, Sikh, Arab, Latino, Muslim, and Japanese American communities to discuss how to commemorate September 11 and its aftermath. Although Hate Free Zone had been working with all of these immigrant communities in the year since 9/11, most had never met each other. As each spoke about what their community was experiencing, it became crystal clear that they had in common a terror of speaking out and a sense of being isolated and unwelcome in America.

Devon Abdallah, an Arab American, and Jasmit Singh, a Sikh American, said they wanted an event where "we can stand up and talk about what is really going on" not just a surface-level coming together. The idea for the public hearing came from Karen Yoshitomi, who was the director of the Pacific Northwest District of the Japanese American Citizens League. Karen suggested we hold a hearing modeled on the redress hearings held in the early 1980s to address the injustices of the internment of 125,000 Americans of Japanese ancestry. "Let's not wait forty years this time," Yoshitomi said passionately during the meeting.

That meeting became the first of many organizing sessions that we convened every week that were attended by twenty to thirty people from different ethnic communities. In the end, more than a hundred people from thirty different organizations joined together to work with a consuming energy and excitement over two short months to pull off what would be one of the most amazing grassroots organizing efforts I have ever been involved with. Our goal was to have six hundred to eight hundred people in attendance and to get top elected officials to function as "commissioners" for the hearing, sitting and listening to the powerful stories of those directly affected.

The magnitude of what we planned to do was tremendous. First, because drawing together a coalition of such diverse communities—many of whom had never been involved in speaking out politically—was quite novel across the country; and second, because putting directly affected people up front and center was not done often back then. We were also asking people to take a huge risk by coming forward to testify about being targeted by the FBI and the U.S. government, which had been unjustly questioning, detaining, and even trying to deport them or their family or community members. People were terrified to speak out for fear that they would be further targeted by the government. It was then that I saw how false patriotism and fear together are such a powerful combination to suppress dissent from any corner.

The week before the hearing, we were still collecting testimonies, which had to be translated and transcribed. The organizing logistics were endless: securing buses to bring immigrants who did not have cars; printing a preliminary report with the testimonies to distribute to the elected officials; coordinating media releases, interviews, and volunteers, including a peace-keeping force of over thirty-five people. Somalis, Arabs, Muslims,

and Sikhs were still fearful of coming forward. It had also been difficult to secure confirmation from the commissioners that they would be
attending. We heard unofficially that several of the elected officials we'd
invited felt it would be "too controversial" to participate. Others apparently did not believe that immigrant communities of color could really
pull together something of this magnitude.

In the end, our panel included then-Congressman (now Washington
State governor) Jay Inslee and Congressman Jim McDermott, as well as
top officials from the FBI, Department of Justice, Immigration and Naturalization Services (now called US Customs and Immigration Services),
and some state and local elected officials. We were able to secure as a
moderator for the hearing a highly respected Washington State Supreme
Court justice, Charles Z. Smith, the first African American on the court,
with a long history of working to ensure civil rights.

Now, only one question remained: would people come?

The day of the hearing, September 21, 2002, dawned sunny and gorgeous. By 8 a.m., Seattle's Town Hall was bustling. Our video crew was
there. Fifty-some volunteers had their instructions. The peacekeepers were
standing guard. A local television news crew and reporters from the *Seattle
Times* and the *Washington Post* arrived. The commissioners arrived. And
yes, the people came.

Over 1,100 people began streaming into Town Hall, filling the venue
with one of the most diverse audiences Seattle has ever seen: Somali wom-
en in *hijab*, Sikh men in colorful turbans, Japanese Americans, Cambodi-
ans, Muslims, Arab Americans, and white allies who understood that the
hearing was about the rights of all of us.

When the attendees came in they seemed tentative; after all, for many
of them, this was the first political event they had ever attended. But as
they listened to the testimonies—stories of people from their own communities told by community members themselves—they sat taller. They
became defiant. They radiated beauty. "We want to testify, too," they
started whispering to us. "I want to tell my story, too!"

USE THE POWER YOU HAVE 43

Those onstage testified about FBI harassment, hate crimes, discrimination: Aziz Junejo, whose car was doused with gasoline at the North Seattle mosque days after September 11; a Sikh taxi driver who was beaten for supposedly looking like Osama bin Laden; children who were bullied and hit in school; women denied jobs because of their *hijabs*; Latino airport workers swept up in raids; and a lawyer for a Tunisian man who had been in detention for a year simply because a woman claimed to have heard him say he was going to blow up a bridge.

The final testimony came from Mako Nakagawa, who had lived through the Japanese internment camps herself. "We have been through this all sixty years ago," she said, her voice breaking with tears. "Not again, please, not again! Haven't we learned anything?"

The commissioners listened for almost two and a half hours. They stayed for the whole hearing and they did not speak until the end—both extremely unusual for elected and appointed officials. Some of them were defensive. The head district counsel for the Immigration and Naturalization Services, Dorothy Stefan (who later became a good partner on a number of issues), said, "You have to understand that we are simply government servants. We just carry out the policies."

But others found it difficult to back away from what they had heard. Bruce Miyake, a Japanese American himself and the assistant U.S. attorney for Western Washington (now also a friend of mine), was there representing the Department of Justice, which was directly responsible for many of these policies.

"Part of me doesn't want to be here because I don't want to be identified with the stories I have heard today," he said. "But we have to be accountable. We have to hear the effects of the policies that are being enacted . . . I intend not only to brief the U.S. attorney for Western Washington but also to send a letter to President Bush and to Attorney General John Ashcroft about what we have heard today."

The crowd jumped to their feet, roaring with applause, tears running down the faces of many in the audience who felt—finally—as if they were being heard, made powerful through their storytelling.

That hearing taught me much about successful organizing, what it takes to build coalitions, and the power of ordinary people coming together for storytelling. We did not wait to be invited to participate. We did not wait to be given power, because we knew that marginalized communities rarely are given such power. We took power ourselves by raising our voices to show the strength of collective action. One NPR reporter who covered the event put it so well: "Over one thousand people that we often take for granted are showing us that democracy works."

In June 2003, about nine months after the first Justice for All hearing and at the request of the late senator Ted Kennedy, Hate Free Zone held another hearing called "Justice for All: Selective Enforcement in a Post-9/11 Era"—this time in the U.S. Senate. It was my first real brush with Congress in the nation's capital.

The goal of the hearing was to dispel the myth that these issues only affect a small group of people in specific places. We wanted to show the universality of the narrative of discriminatory policies through the coming together of different peoples, in the same way that Chinese and Filipino and Japanese laborers came together to strike against injustice in the early 1900s. We wanted people to understand the extent of civil liberties and civil rights abuses, and we wanted people with power to do something about it.

Since this was a national hearing, we put together a coalition of national organizations, including the ACLU and the American Immigration Lawyers Association, as well as community groups working with affected people all over the country. Our panel of witnesses came from around the country and included Latinos, Haitians, Iranians, and Syrians. We highlighted people who had been secretly detained, shackled, and put on planes in the middle of the night by federal immigration officials and sometimes the FBI. We also had people tell their stories who had been forced to register and get fingerprinted in what we now think of as the precursor to Trump's Muslim Ban, a program called the National Security Entry-Exit Registration System (NSEERS), or Special Registration. Implemented by Attorney General Ashcroft in November 2002, Special

Registration was a program designed to register and fingerprint foreign visitors from twenty-six countries, twenty-five of which were Arab and Muslim. (The twenty-sixth country was North Korea.)

The hearing was powerful and moving, and despite our fear that no members of Congress would come and listen, many did. These Justice for All hearings became a model for other groups across the country. We would do one more a year later, in collaboration with our own U.S. senator Patty Murray.

At Hate Free Zone, we were being pulled into more and more work on an even bigger scale. Our work with the Latino community had highlighted the need to get engaged in the longstanding issues of comprehensive immigration reform, helping to organize immigrant communities across our state to fight for federal reform so that we could bring 12 million people out of the shadows, reunite families, and ensure that immigrant workers would have rights on the job.

In 2003, I was asked by Steve Williamson, the head of the King County Labor Council, to co-lead the Seattle Coalition of the Immigrant Workers Freedom Ride, a national organizing effort of the national AFL-CIO—modeled after the Freedom Rides of the 1960s—to bring immigrants from two dozen cities on buses to Washington, DC, to advocate before Congress for comprehensive reform and then to end our journey with a giant 250,000-person rally at New York's Flushing Meadows Corona Park, site of the 1964 World's Fair site. While the effort was officially supported by the national AFL-CIO, four primary unions were driving it: UNITE HERE, SEIU, United Food and Commercial Workers, and the Laborers' International Union. Each of these unions by then had large numbers of immigrants within their membership ranks. Immigrants were changing the AFL-CIO from within. It was that organizing from those key unions that had, in fact, led the AFL-CIO in 2000 to revise its official position on immigration reform from opposition to support, a powerful 180 degree reversal. This would be the first major nationwide campaign led by labor, since that reversal, to push for comprehensive immigration reform and it was significant.

Our Freedom Ride coalition worked for over nine months to pull together the coalition, find immigrant riders with powerful and diverse stories, and raise the money we needed. We had to deal with all the challenges of multi-ethnic organizing, but in the end, our bus had forty-two people speaking twenty-four different languages, traveling together across the country for ten days. It was one of the most diverse buses in the country and it was a remarkable journey.

When we got to the World's Fair site in New York where the final rally was being held, I was given the opportunity to speak on the mainstage just before a hero of mine, Congressman John Lewis, spoke. "Forty-two years later, the freedom riders of 2003, you, are going to win," Lewis thundered. "We are one people, we are one family, we are one house and we are not going to let anybody turn us around. We've come too far."[7]

I will never forget what it felt like to be onstage looking at a quarter of a million people, immigrants from all over the world and allies who remembered their families' own immigration histories, holding signs that read "No Human Being Is Illegal" and "Justice Now," chanting and singing "We Shall Not Be Moved." And as I came offstage and shook Congressman Lewis's hand, I never in a million years imagined I would one day have the honor of working side by side with him in the U.S. Congress.

In the fall of 2002, President Bush, Vice President Cheney, and Secretary of Defense Donald Rumsfeld began laying the groundwork for an invasion of Iraq. This came out of an Authorization of Use of Military Force (AUMF) passed into law by Congress and signed by Bush shortly after 9/11. The AUMF granted the president the authority to use all "necessary and appropriate force" against those whom he determined "planned, authorized, committed or aided" the September 11 attacks, or who harbored said persons or groups. The only member of Congress to vote against the AUMF was Congresswoman Barbara Lee, who criticized the AUMF as being a blank check that gave the president unlimited power to wage war without debate.

Now, Bush, Cheney, and Rumsfeld were laying out the purported reason for the invasion of Iraq: that Saddam Hussein had weapons of mass destruction. In convoluted logic, the Bush administration made the case to an international coalition of allies and to the American people that somehow, Saddam Hussein was connected to the September 11 attacks, and that invading Iraq was an act of self-preservation without which America could be attacked again by Saddam's weapons of mass destruction.

In October 2002, Congress passed a resolution authorizing use of military force against Iraq. All of these events led to months of large-scale anti-war protests involving some 36 million people across the globe. In Seattle, Hate Free Zone was asked by Not in Our Name, Seattle, to participate in an anti-war rally there. (Not in Our Name, or NION, was the main organizer of protests across the country, along with the Sound Nonviolent Opposition to War or SNOW.) We proposed that the rally and march should explicitly connect the war in Iraq to the war on immigrants at home in the wake of 9/11. NION was excited about this, and asked that I also speak at the anti-war rally. I agreed to do so, and also to help find other speakers.

We had no idea what the turnout would be. Our hope was that at least five to ten thousand people would attend. Imagine our elation when over five solid miles of people lined the streets! Estimates were that fifteen to fifty thousand people marched, making it the largest rally and march in Seattle for decades, until the 2017 Women's March.[8]

I spoke at the Seattle Center rally just before Congressman McDermott. Together we argued that going to war with Iraq would be a devastating and disastrous mistake. The march started at Seattle Center, went through downtown Seattle, and ended at the INS building where immigrants were detained back then, just south of downtown.

Everything we had feared seemed to be coming true, abroad and at home.

One day after the invasion of Iraq began in the spring of 2003, the Justice Department announced that it would be interviewing approximately eleven thousand Iraqis and Iraqi Americans living in the United States. The very next day, the newly formed Bureau of Immigration and Customs

Enforcement (BICE) sent out a press release stating that the Justice Department had also authorized FBI agents to act as immigration officials, and that the FBI and BICE would start a program aimed at arresting Iraqis with immigration violations.

At Hate Free Zone, we began receiving calls from people of Iraqi descent immediately following the announcement. The FBI was going to interview people of Iraqi origin in their homes, often unannounced and during the day when only women or children who could not speak English were home and they were terrified. The FBI offered neither interpreters nor lawyers. When Iraqis said they felt nervous to answer questions either because they didn't understand them or because they wanted to consult with someone else, they were made to feel as if this was an admission of guilt. The FBI's questions ranged from information about other family or friends in the area as well as in Iraq, to whether people sent money home to Iraq (considered illegal because of the sanctions), to what an individual's views on the war and Saddam Hussein were. Many Iraqis felt trapped by these questions, because although they were vociferously against Saddam Hussein, they were also resolutely against the war.

I was put in touch with the head of the federal public defenders in Seattle, who immediately said his office would do everything they could to accompany Iraqis to their interviews with the FBI. Pro bono immigration attorneys also organized themselves to participate to ensure people did not unknowingly implicate themselves in any way. If the FBI started on a line of questioning that could be harmful to the client, the questioning was shut down by attorneys. We were extremely lucky to have the support of attorneys in Seattle—across the country, the large majority of Iraqis who were interviewed did not have access to attorneys or translators.

The Iraq war caused trauma for Iraqis across the country. At a meeting we arranged in Seattle with the FBI special agent-in-charge and the U.S. attorney for Western Washington, the director of the Iraqi Community Center communicated the hurt and fear his community was feeling.

"We came here to escape Saddam," he said. "More than you, our families have been tortured by him. More than you, we have been put in jail by him. This is our home now. We want to do everything to help. But when you destroy relationships by suspecting us, questioning us, making us afraid, then we are the ones who have to fix that, not you. The problem, however, is that you have the power and we don't."

At the very same time that the anti-war protests were beginning, in the fall of 2002, Hate Free Zone was overwhelmed with another crisis.

In November 2002, I was contacted by leaders in the Somali community because five Somali immigrants were picked up by the INS and told that they were going to be imminently deported. Working again with attorneys from Perkins Coie, we filed a temporary restraining order in the courts and won, staying the deportation. Word about this success spread like wild fire through the Somali community across the country. We started getting inundated with calls from Somalis nationwide who were seeing community members being picked up, put into detention, and in some cases, flown out within days on special night flights.

I called an emergency meeting of some of the top immigration experts and federal public defenders, and a crazy idea emerged: we would file a nationwide class-action lawsuit on behalf of about five thousand Somali detainees across the country. We would use a barely known provision that said you could not deport someone back to a country that can't accept them, and we would show that Somalia had no functioning government at the time to accept detainees. As we were preparing to file the lawsuit, people said, "You can't sue the INS! Nobody has ever done that." And I said, "Let's try. The worst that can happen is that we won't win."

In federal court, U.S. government attorneys argued that these deportations were necessary in order to protect Americans, because Somalia was a hotbed of terrorism. U.S. District Court Judge Marsha Pechman asked the government why, if these people were suspected of being capable of terrorism, would the government want to send them back to a place the government itself described as a "hotbed of terrorism"? The government attorneys had no answer, and stunningly, we won again in district court! The government appealed the decision to the Ninth Circuit. We won again.

Today, almost two decades after September 11, 2001, we are still connecting the dots and seeing the reverberations of the actions taken after 9/11 (most with support from both sides of the aisle) that would affect the future of immigrants for decades to come.

It seems inconceivable that Hate Free Zone could have built what we built in such a short time and taken on the struggles we did. There were so many leaders in the community who came forward in those early years to help establish the organization, leaders of other organizations and people who had been justice seekers in the community for decades before I came along. I will never forget their generosity, mentorship, friendship, and lack of ego as a new organization—and, I, a new leader—came into being.

I also learned one of the most important lessons of organizing: that strength emerges in times of crisis. You don't know what is possible until you are tested. Even more important: *you don't need to know everything before you start!* You just need to be willing to follow every thread to its conclusion and build your coalition of allies and experts, people who can help you get what you need and help build the movement that raises the alarm bells so everyone understands what is at stake.

I knew very little when I started, but I learned how to build movements and apply political pressure. Our organization grew, becoming the largest immigrant advocacy organization in the state and one of the largest in the country. We engaged on the national level with federal policy reform while also growing our presence in the state capitol in order to bring about some of the most innovative pro-immigrant policies in the country. We built new relationships and alliances with labor, business, and faith communities locally and nationally and, in 2008, Hate Free Zone changed its name to OneAmerica to better reflect the positive vision we were working for.

When we felt like elected officials weren't paying enough attention to us, we came up with new strategies that would force them to pay attention: we ran the largest voter registration drive in the history of this state, registering over 23,000 new immigrant citizens to vote. We realized we needed some "legitimacy," so we worked with the governor to establish a

Governor's New Americans Policy Council and with the mayor to establish a Seattle Office of Immigrant and Refugee Affairs that could be filled with allies who understood the needs of immigrants and would work with us to change policy. At the federal level, we worked to coordinate our work and our activism with others working on the same issues, helping to lead a national coalition of organizations convened by the Center for Community Change called the Fair Immigration Reform Movement.

I also educated myself on the minutiae of policy. Too often, organizers want change but when they are let in the door, they have no real policy proposals to put forward. I have learned through the years that, if we are going to advocate for change we need to understand the policy and be able to say what we want. In the leadership role I was in, I cared both about the substance of the policy and the organizing that would make it possible for that change to occur. This ability to understand the details and the big picture has been extremely helpful to me as I have grown in leadership, and is a critical part of my work in Congress now.

One of the biggest lessons of those organizing years was the recognition that we would be most powerful if we broadened our coalitions. Too often, we have a tendency to compete in a sort of "Oppression Olympics," fighting a "hierarchy of oppressions" that says "my oppression is worse than yours." What I have found is that we must to lift up the horror of all types of oppression, because we need everyone at the table and need to recognize that the hierarchy only serves those who seek to divide us.

I learned how to build real relationships and understanding of our collective struggles between diverse immigrant communities, and also to find the intersections with labor, faith, and what we called "unlikely allies." In the case of immigration reform, that meant some of the agricultural business owners who desperately needed workers but needed to be brought along on key issues. Sometimes the problem with us on the left is that we want people to agree with us 100 percent on everything: not only the desired outcome, but also steps one through ten of why we want the outcome and how to get there. This can be the death of a successful coalition with unlikely allies. My belief is that we can all come to the goal differently, as long as we do no harm along the way. I believed legalization of undocumented immigrants was the moral thing to do, that there were human rights violations that needed desperately to be addressed. The agricultural business owners, however, did not necessarily agree that it was a matter of civil rights and fairness to legalize immigrant workers; they just wanted them legalized because they did not want to have to find new, unskilled workers each year and they needed permanent workers— not guest workers—for their businesses to succeed. We wanted the same thing in the end and that was good enough for me to be able to work with them and build bridges where we could.

One of the places where I got the most energy and inspiration was in building youth leadership. Young people are some of our most fearless leaders, bringing creative energy and new organizing techniques to the movement. We organized and built leadership with thousands of young people across our state who participated in direct actions, storytelling, lobbying, and many other forms of advocacy both outside and inside the government. Many of these students were also undocumented, living in a world where papers defined their ability to live free and full lives. But they were unafraid. They rose up and they spoke out, calling attention to the impact of our policies and prejudices on their families, naming what it meant for them as American kids to see what our country was doing to their communities. It was their energy, organizing efforts, and courage that eventually led our state to pass a Dream Act.

The more work we did on immigration, the more I understood what it meant to be intersectional, to know that our movements for economic, social, and racial justice are deeply intertwined. I adapted a wonderful phrase from my friend, Jackie Payne, to fit me: "I am not a woman on Monday, an immigrant on Tuesday, a worker on Wednesday, and a mom on Thursday. I am ALL of those things ALL of the time."

This understanding led me to broaden Hate Free Zone's work beyond immigration. In 2003, Hate Free Zone became one of the first signatories to an amicus brief to support domestic partnerships in our state and then spent a decade organizing in immigrant communities to support marriage equality for LGBTQ communities. We worked with labor unions to help pass Seattle's paid sick days ordinance and to support collective bargaining efforts everywhere. In 2010, OneAmerica (renamed from Hate Free Zone in 2008) signed on to the ACLU's request to the Department of Justice to investigate misconduct by the Seattle Police Department, which ultimately led to a federal civil-rights investigation of the police department by the Department of Justice during President Obama's administration. We took on the issues of economic inequality, building strong relationships with labor unions, joining picket lines and doing deep organizing and education around the need for unions within our immigrant communities. We would also play a major role in the movement that led to the Fight for $15 (see Chapter 15) and, in 2014, I was appointed to serve on the mayor's Income Inequality Committee, which led to Seattle to become the first major city to pass a $15 minimum wage. We also challenged the mainstream environmental community early on to think of climate justice, not just climate change, and to put low-income communities and communities of color at the center of the policy proposals we put forth.

We were trying to put into practice what it meant to be truly intersectional. That often meant challenging the way things were, redefining the importance of bringing the voices of affected communities to the table, and forcing our way into the rooms where we had not been before. As Frederick Douglass said, "Power never concedes anything without a demand." That is true when we are facing off with the forces that stop progress on the outside, but it is also true when we are doing the work we need to do within our own movements for change. As challenging as it was, that deep work—including working through our own issues within the progressive community—and the relationships I built with leaders in multiple movements would ultimately also be a key part of my success when I ran for office years later.

What marks fundamental change? What are the characteristics of an event that you know you can look back on in ten or twenty or thirty or even one hundred years and see that it was a turning point in history? For me, the unfolding of a movement is best expressed in this quote from the poet William Stafford: "A divide comes in a life. At first you don't know, and then looking back you see before and after. That's what they mean when they say you can't go back home: it's the same, but half-closed eyes have opened."

My activism was shaped in the crucible of September 11, 2001, when I could not abide by what my own government was doing in my name. Some of our work—then and much later in the age of Donald Trump— was to sharpen the contradiction between what is true and moral to who we are as a nation, and the deeply contradictory way society was acting in our name. To do this, there are moments that call for something more than a protest rally, a march, or petitions. These tactics register disagreement but they do not always cut through the noise, particularly in this day and age. They are easier to execute as tactics, partly because they do not require any particular risk for the majority of people taking part in them. The Justice for All hearings were powerful for two big reasons: they required risk of the people who were engaged in speaking out, and they spoke directly to those in power, forcing them to listen. There was real fear on the part of participants that they could be targeted following those hearings, and there was an agreement from the community that should that happen, we would be there to support them.

The next step in sharpening the moral contradictions and challenging power would be to use nonviolent civil disobedience. I was introduced to the concepts of nonviolent civil disobedience through the life and work of Mahatma Gandhi, who has influenced so much of how I see protest, resistance, and justice. Gandhi used the Hindi word *ahimsa*, which means non-injury or nonviolence, to describe a central belief of his work, leadership, and philosophy. *Ahimsa* combined with civil disobedience became a signature of the successful Indian resistance against colonialism and the fight for Indian independence. Nonviolent civil disobedience was the unifying force of famous actions such as the 1930 Salt March when Gandhi led a defiant 241-mile march to the sea to make salt from seawater, in defiance of British policy that prohibited Indians from collecting or selling salt. Gandhi called this mass civil disobedience *satyagraha* or "adherence to truth." Nonviolent civil disobedience called on people to openly disobey an unjust, immoral, or unconstitutional law as a matter of conscience, and to accept the consequences, even if they included imprisonment.

I am an unusual elected official, in that I have been arrested three times for leading and participating in civil disobedience. I count among my leaders and mentors the great civil rights leader Representative John Lewis, who has been arrested dozens of times; was beaten on the Edmund Pettus Bridge in Selma, Alabama, in the 1960s; and continued to participate in civil disobedience actions even in Congress, actions he has called "causing good trouble." For me, Lewis has been a moral north star and teacher on the strategies, tactics, brutality, and successes of deeply planned and prepared-for mass civil disobedience that was part of the civil rights struggles in the United States.

The first time I led a mass civil disobedience action was in Seattle in 2010 to protest unfair immigration policy. We prepared for the action for months, and we trained the participants in what to expect and the deep moral grounding of what we were doing. I admit that I was afraid of being arrested myself as a new citizen of the United States, and I felt weighed down by the responsibility for all those who made their own decisions to participate. Contrary to a lot of our protest tactics where we try to exercise power to make change, here we relinquish power to bring about change. True civil disobedience requires you to make the choices at each moment to relinquish control, to steadfastly adhere to complete nonviolence even in the face of potential violence or brutality from those seeking to enforce the laws, and to bring with you a moral center of peaceful acceptance in your resistance. That civil disobedience action in 2010 was the first time I landed in jail with a few dozen others, and the bonds of struggle with leaders and volunteers carried us far into the future together. Jennifer Chan, my legislative director in Congress, and Yasmin Christopher, who was my legislative aide in the state senate, were both arrested with me in 2010. So were some of the city's great civil rights leaders, such as Diane Narasaki

from the Asian American community and King County Councilmember
Larry Gossett.

In 2013, then as co-chair of the We Belong Together campaign for
women and immigration reform (a wonderful campaign led by the
National Domestic Workers Alliance and the National Asian Pacific
American Women's Forum), I helped lead another mass civil disobedience protest, this time outside the U.S. Capitol, and this time with 105
women. What was remarkable about this action was that twenty-two of
the women who took part in the protest were undocumented and stood
to be deported if arrested. Again, we prepared for months for this massive
action, working with everyone in our group to understand the consequences and the power of what we were doing, to prepare for the logistics,
and to provide training in nonviolent principles of resistance. It was, by
far, the most beautiful and moving action I have ever had the privilege to
lead or be a part of. All 105 women joined hands and formed a giant circle
in the middle of the road, blocking all four roads to the Capitol. We sang
and chanted together, and refused to move. Within our group were even
some generations of women from the same family, taking enormous risks
together: daughter, mother, and grandmother. We had made intersectionality more than a buzzword: white women leaders sat with immigrant
women leaders from multiple countries; LGBTQ leaders sat with union
leaders and immigrant leaders.

In an article in *Feministing.com* after I had been released from jail, I told
the reporter this:

> In terms of a moment that was really powerful, it was watch-
> ing that circle of women, knowing that everyone was taking a
> risk, but knowing that those 22 in particular were taking so
> much more risk. I'm just getting goose bumps thinking about
> it because it was just one of those moments where you see
> women coming together, across races, ethnicities, immigration
> status. It was a moment of complete power and togetherness as
> we claimed that intersection. And you could see that visibly in

the women. You could see it as they were chanting or as they were sitting there quietly, but there was this surge of power through this circle as we showed Congress what it looks like to have courage and to act for the good of millions of people across the country.

We have been in this place for many years. We are both so close and so far. We're always told that it's not the right time for the issue . . . There are still 2 million people being deported since Obama took office and the fact that those deportations are happening in an increasing rate.

We are dealing with those deportations in the field every day as women and children see the effects play out in their lives. [Our] demonstrators were moved by the urgency they feel because we know that immigration reform needs to happen this year. You build leadership, you continue action, but there are these moments when it feels like the stakes are so high and you are ready.[9]

Later still, in 2017, I became the only member of Congress to participate in another mass civil disobedience action with over six hundred women in the U.S. Capitol over the separations of families. And while I recognize I am unusual, I also recognize the tremendous privilege I have and the fact that the risk I take in getting arrested for blocking traffic is nothing akin to the risk of the undocumented women who were arrested with us, or that of the courageous Dreamers who built a whole movement around their courage to come out of the shadows, leading marches and protests knowing they too could be deported.

In each of these actions, our goal was to open the awareness, hearts, and minds of those who have the power to make change happen. The courage of those who put their bodies on the line to take real risk is juxtaposed with the notion of nonviolent protest against the violence of a system that oppresses people with its policies, sharpening the contradictions in a powerful way. Nonviolent civil disobedience becomes, then, not just a tactic but a force; the more deeply we adhere to its principles, the more powerful that force is.

To learn about this, we can also look to the incredibly courageous movements across the world that have taken to the streets with organized, principled, and sustained mass nonviolent actions against brutal regimes in China, Egypt, and, most recently in 2019, Sudan, among others. Many of these movements have been led by women; and all have endured violence and death en route. They have been both planned and unplanned, but none have succeeded without the deep grounding in the principles of nonviolent mass civil disobedience.

As I write this with Donald Trump as president and a democracy that struggles to push back against the forces of corporate power, racism, and outdated institutions, I am beginning to feel that we again need to go beyond rallies and protests. It may be that we, too, in America need to relearn the lessons of our past movements and of the global responses to oppression, to develop the courage it takes and the risks required to take on our own oppressive systems of government that undermine and even shred our democracy.

I know that sometimes we feel powerless, and we despair at our seeming lack of power. But we do have options and choices that we don't always exercise. Nonviolent civil disobedience is a deeply grounded force, aligned with a deeper set of truths about who we are as human beings. Our mission is to explore this deeper force, and how we use the power we have. We have shining examples around the world and those of us both inside and outside government must constantly study those examples and school ourselves in how we continue to sharpen the contradictions of injustice and morality to fully use the power we have.

3

Why Not Me? Running for Office

I NEVER THOUGHT I WOULD RUN FOR OFFICE. FOR TWENTY YEARS, I HAD been an activist pushing for change from the outside. I had used every tool I could think of in my toolbox to advocate for positive changes on issues from immigration to environmental justice to economic inequality. I had led voter registration drives, rallies, marches, even nonviolent civil disobedience actions where I was arrested twice. I deeply believed that organizing, advocacy, and storytelling by real people were what made change happen.

Truth be told, I was quite cynical about elected officials. Over the course of my two decades of organizing, I saw too few who were willing to use their positions to exercise leadership, particularly when an issue was seen as "controversial." The things I had seen—government incursions into civil liberties post-9/11, Islamophobia, and anti-immigrant sentiment, among others—regularly required people who were willing to speak out *before* an issue was popular. And yet, too many elected officials were inclined to wait before speaking out; they followed rather than led. Even in my state, where we did have some champions and some successes, it took enormous amounts of pushing and in some cases years to get the attention of elected officials.

I was also deeply frustrated at the lack of diversity and representation I saw among those who held elected office. Low-income people, people of color, immigrants, women, and other marginalized communities were simply not represented. I had to explain for too long, too hard, and too loudly about what seemed like obvious problems to me. Many in government had been there for a long time and did not seem to understand what life was actually like for the huge number of their constituents who had very different backgrounds and experiences from them.

Even in the Democratic Party, few elected officials were willing to talk about race or class, or take on stereotypes that were baked into the policies that even Democrats proposed. Perhaps this struggle around race and monied interests should not have been surprising to me or any other student of history: just look at slavery and the Dixiecrats; President Lyndon Johnson's "War on Crime," which increased the incarceration of black and brown people; and President Bill Clinton's promise to "end welfare as we know it," which led to cutting aid to poor people, as well as his draconian 1996 immigration bill, which criminalized immigrants and expanded detention and deportation without due process. As an activist, I had even taken on President Barack Obama for being the "Deporter-in-Chief," a still unpopular but in my view necessary critique of an otherwise extremely popular president. I had taken mental note of a long list of times when Democrats said talking about race was "divisive," or that we shouldn't focus on institutionalized racism because it would push away white voters, or that certain policies to rectify the wrongs we saw would be counter to our interests in some false analysis of national security or safety.

When I first began organizing after September 11 around the detention and deportation of Muslims and Arabs, there were very few elected officials willing to stand with me. "National security" concerns triumphed over civil rights and civil liberties, because once again communities of color were treated as the suspicious other. My congressman, Jim McDermott, was an exception, as was our only black county councilmember, Larry Gossett. When I began organizing rallies outside mosques to protest the lack of due process for Muslim Americans and for Arab Americans who were being secretly detained and deported in the middle of the night, it became even more difficult to find elected leaders who would stand with us.

Our message fell on more sympathetic ears with locally elected officials. Although our city council knew very little back then about the circumstances of immigrants, they were much more open to the concerns of their diverse constituents. There were organizers on the council like councilmember Nick Licata who believed in people's voices being at the table. Working with him, we passed one of the first ordinances, now called Sanctuary City ordinances, to prevent local police and city officials from asking about immigration status.

The higher the elected official rose, the harder it seemed to get them to take a stand that might be seen as controversial. Back then, immigration reform was far from popular and it took years to convince our congressional delegation to boldly embrace humane and just immigration reform. It was only after I worked to organize the hearing with Senator Ted Kennedy in Washington, DC, that we were able to move one of our own senators to participate in a Justice for All town hall in Seattle.

My first light bulb moment about how to build greater political power for immigrants came in 2004. I was frustrated that the immigration issues we were focused on were not getting the attention they needed. Too few elected officials were willing to work to reverse policies like Special Registration, speak out against Islamophobia, or champion immigration reform.

I realized that elected officials seemed to care only about two things: first, money from donors and corporate lobbyists, which seemed to work to block courageous votes or action, and second (sometimes in this order), the votes of their own constituents. We didn't have money, but couldn't we organize existing voters, maybe even register new voters? Could we mobilize those voters to build the political power of immigrants and demand that politicians respond to our communities' needs?

The truth was too many immigrants had lost faith in government and they didn't vote. Like me, they didn't see elected officials who represented them, who looked like them, or who understood their lives. Some even just sat out the elections, because they felt cynical about the people who were running and their desire to really serve them and make a difference. Many had also not received the kind of civic education that even allowed them to understand the basic processes of voting in the United States, which are far from simple for a new American in this country. Could we get them to care about and trust the power of the vote?

I decided to try an experiment: Hate Free Zone partnered with the brand-new Seattle chapter of the Council on American-Islamic Relations (CAIR) to implement a new pilot project designed to get Muslim Americans educated about and registered to vote, and then encourage them to turn out to actually vote. It was a small project, implemented just months before the 2004 election. We went into mosques and community centers and registered some three hundred new Muslim American voters. They were well aware of the terrible things that were happening to their communities in the years after 9/11, and so our job was to convince them that their voices and their votes would make a difference. This required a lot of conversation, education, and ultimately mobilization to get them to the polls when it was time to vote. In the end, 98 percent of them voted!

Armed with a successful pilot project, we began a much larger voter registration drive in 2005 and 2006, ultimately registering over 27,000 new American citizens to vote. It was the largest voter registration drive in the history of the state, and it caught the attention of elected officials. At approximately the same time, we began a big statewide campaign to push Washington's governor Christine Gregoire to establish a New Americans Policy Council and to fund a massive program to help legal permanent residents who were eligible get their citizenship. Because of our voter registration work and growing political power, in 2008, we were able to establish the first-ever state level policy council and get funding for the New American Citizenship Program. If I had ever questioned what it really means to build political power, I could see it working now.

And yet, we still were not where we wanted to be. For example, in spite of all our work on immigration, we fought frustrating battles to get elected officials to come out and support us, particularly against unjust and cruel enforcement measures against immigrants. I've come to believe that the term "progressive" really just refers to the people who advocate for justice on an issue first, before it is popular. Back then, even some of our Democratic congressmembers who are out front on immigration issues today were not particularly strong on those issues then, sometimes voting for anti-immigrant bills or just staying silent at critical times when we desperately needed their voice and leadership.

All of this contributed to my own distrust of elected officials and kept me away from the idea of running for office myself. Community members would often mention the possibility to me, but it is notable that nobody from the Democratic Party machine asked me to run. I was not part of "the system." I was pushing people hard for what I believed was necessary, and I was not wealthy or well-connected—all viewed as negatives to the party machine that had a lot to say about who would run for office, or at least who would get the needed early support.

I did have some heroes in elected office: Jim McDermott, who had been so influential in the start and success of Hate Free Zone in the early days and Congresswoman Barbara Lee, for her vote against the 2001 Authorization of Military Force in Iraq, for starters. I had also read Shirley Chisholm's book, *Unbought and Unbossed*, with rapt attention. Later, in 2013, I met Stacey Abrams, who at the time was the minority leader in the Georgia State Senate. She talked to me about how important it was for us as women of color to run for office and to be in office.

It was months after that conversation, in late 2013, when the longtime state senator for my district announced that he would not seek reelection. Immediately, a whole host of candidates declared themselves. Some friends reached out to me and asked if I would consider a run for the seat. My state legislative district at the time was the largest minority-majority district in the state, and I had the distinct honor to live in what was often cited as the most diverse zip code in the nation. But I said immediately that I was not interested. Most of my recent work was at the federal level, with Congress, and the state legislatures at the time were not the focus of much activist work. I also just wasn't convinced that elected office was for me.

But over the next month or two, as I watched the wide slate of candidates who stepped up to run for the open state senate seat talk about why they were running, it slowly became clear to me that I had been thinking about elected office all wrong.

As activists, we were critical of the way government worked—and yet, at the same time, we turned our noses up at the idea of running for office ourselves. I realized that in our own judgmental way, we were ceding important political space to others, instead of occupying it ourselves. What if we began to think about running for office as a way to organize more people, to connect people to the government, to bring organizing from the outside to the inside, to have the proverbial seat at the table but use it to lead not just follow?

It was the beginning of the formation of my new theory of change.

For years, I had believed that if politics is the art of the possible, then our job as activists is to push the boundaries of what is possible—but from the outside. Why couldn't that pushing also occur from the platform of an elected office? An elected office could be the biggest organizing platform yet! Perhaps part of the problem was that there weren't enough of us on the inside to do the pushing, and I realized you really needed people working from both the inside and the outside for change to happen as quickly as necessary.

I was starting to see that elected office could be a new platform for building a base of supporters, systematic organizing efforts, and progressive policy development. We don't get a more responsive government unless we systematically run organizing campaigns to change the way government works. We don't understand what we are really dealing with or how to change it unless we know exactly how it works now. We don't get a more powerful and progressive group of elected officials unless we insert ourselves into the equation. And we can't organize on the inside if we have no organizers on the inside. In other words, we don't get a more representative government unless we run it ourselves. As my experience serving in an elected office would confirm, you really need to organize on the inside just as hard as you organize on the outside. We needed both.

I was now ready to try out my new theory of change and, to do it, I decided—in just a week of talking to family and friends—that I would run for the Washington State Senate open seat. Many of my activist friends thought I was crazy. SEIU 775 president David Rolf told me it would be a waste of my skills. My immigrant friends were mixed—they pursed their lips and said they needed me to advocate for them in the field, not in Olympia, the state's capital—but then they also said it would be deeply meaningful to them to see someone like me in elected office representing them. Other organizer friends said the sacrifices were too many—state office paid hardly anything and was supposedly part-time. However, the reality was that being a senator was actually full-time work and you had no time to hold another full-time job. Many incumbents had sweet deals where their employers paid them full-time salaries, despite spending months each year in Olympia. We movement leaders transitioning into state legislatures had no such cushy rides.

I listened to all of the advice and comments, but in the end, I decided it was an opportunity for me to try out my theory of change, to find out if elected office could be another important organizing platform that we could utilize to build our movement. I told myself what I tell so many other people who agonize over life choices: if I didn't like it, I could always leave. For now, it was time to get to work and win the campaign.

This story would not be complete without a discussion of the person who has stood by my side and whose life has been intertwined with mine in the most beautiful of ways for the past fifteen years.

In the early years after my divorce from Alan, I had also fallen in love. No good political story is complete without a love story! I met Steve Williamson in the days after 9/11 when he was the elected head of the King County Labor Council, AFL-CIO. He had been one of the conveners of a meeting with the Washington Association of Churches the day that I met Congressman McDermott and planned the press conference at Seattle

Center. Truth be told, I was too engaged in the work in front of me to notice him much, but he was helpful at the time, providing Hate Free Zone signs that his labor council staff had used earlier to fight a white supremacist rally. In 2002, he had asked me to co-lead the Immigrant Workers Freedom Ride with him and some time after that, we fell in love, first moving in together in 2004 and then getting married in 2007.

When I first met Steve, I'll be honest that I had unfair stereotypes about white labor guys. But as I came to know him, I was completely bowled over by his strength, compassion, and kindness, on top of all his other political and organizing skills. Steve was from Pittsburgh, raised by an adoring single mom, an older sister, and an aunt who lived next door. His dad had committed suicide when Steve was six, and so he knew hardship of a different kind though he never, ever asked for sympathy for what he had been through. He had wild stories to recount of cross-country adventures and the rebelliousness of youth. He was able to go to college at Pennsylvania State University only because of his dad's Social Security survivor benefits combined with the very low state-tuition costs in those days. After college, he moved across the country to Colorado, beginning as a union apprentice on his way to becoming a journey-level bricklayer and marble mason. From there, he worked his way up into union leadership, working first for the Machinists organizing manufacturing workers, then for SEIU organizing healthcare workers, and finally for the Teamsters organizing transportation industry workers. In 2000, Steve ran for and was elected as the head of the King County Labor Council, representing 125,000 workers across multiple sectors. We met shortly after that in 2001.

One of my favorite Steve stories was from when Nixon resigned after Watergate in 1974. Steve was seventeen at the time, with long hair down to the middle of his back. He was at a major tennis match in Pittsburgh in a crowded stadium when the match was stopped to play Nixon's speech. Steve was deeply against the Vietnam War and had watched the impeachment trial all summer on TV. He detested Nixon, who he saw as a corrupt, immoral, and lying president, unworthy of the office. When Nixon finished his speech, the stadium was so quiet you could hear a pin drop.

In the midst of that quiet, Steve stood up and loudly began clapping, eventually inciting others to join him in cheering and clapping at the idea that Nixon had finally been brought down. Every head had turned toward him but he didn't care. That was Steve! He brought that rebelliousness and sense of fairness into everything he did, but in the ensuing years, he also built and brought real leadership, strategic thought, and a deep sense of all the tools of organizing—including nonviolent protest—to his labor organizing work.

We were a great team and we weren't afraid to take on each other's stereotypes: he taught me a tremendous amount about unions and I taught him about the politics of race and immigration. He worked hard at recognizing his privilege as a white man, and he listened carefully and learned from watching and listening to me what it meant to not have that privilege. For a man with relative power in his position, he ceded space to me day after day, year after year. I learned from him how to navigate power and how to be comfortable demanding it. Over the fifteen years we have been together, I could not be more grateful for the love and support he has given me, as well as being my number one adviser and a true partner in every way. Steve was a fantastic campaigner and we were absolutely a team. This campaign for state senate was going to be no different.

I was late to the field; lots of people had already declared their intent to run for the senate and had a month or two head start on me. On top of all that, I felt the pressure of my particular candidacy. If I won, I would be the ONLY woman of color in the state senate and the first South Asian American ever elected to the Washington State Legislature.

How I ran the campaign was a part of my theory of change too. I wanted to run a different kind of campaign, one that countered traditional political advice like, "Don't spend more than two to three minutes at a door talking to people," or "Don't waste money on yard signs," or "Don't emphasize your own immigrant story because you might scare off white voters." These were real things I had heard before and they all angered me. I knew we could do something different.

First, I wanted this to be a people-powered, field-driven campaign. I planned to recruit hundreds of volunteers and I, personally, was going to spend most of my time at the doors, talking to voters and getting to know them and their lives. I wanted to know what they were feeling and experiencing, and I wanted them to see that I was a different kind of candidate who would fight for them.

One of the things I had seen clearly was the way in which candidates for office targeted only "likely voters" for their door knocking or other voter contact. A "likely voter" was someone who had voted in three of the last four elections or more. Think about it: that meant that the vast majority of voters never got contacted by a candidate! Mail, doors (if they were being knocked), and phone calls were all directed at a tiny slice of voters, the rest be damned. Candidates were narrowing the field of voters they engaged with each year, giving in to the myth of the likely voter instead of the truth of every voter. If you didn't vote or if you moved (because then, you showed up as a new voter at your new address and it would seem like you hadn't voted in previous elections), you were out. Consultants got paid big bucks for sending out mailers and producing and running expensive television ads because it was money for them and it allowed the candidate to stay cooped up in a room, dialing big donors for dollars. Even if campaigns built door knocking into their plans, they seemed to be doing it just to *say* they had knocked on doors, not really that they had listened to the people they were talking to. That's why candidates were urged to only spend a minute or two, at most, talking to each voter they encountered.

I had a different theory. I wanted to expand the electorate—go to everyone, emphasizing folks of color and young people even if they hadn't voted recently. Most consultants thought this was a waste of time, but to me it was central to the kind of campaign we wanted to run. We needed to talk to voters, convince them that they should vote. I knew it wouldn't be easy, but it was necessary.

For me, knocking on the doors of real people was a miracle and a privilege. In an increasingly technological and disconnected world, door knocking offers this incredible moment when someone you have never met opens the door to you and sometimes tells you their deepest hopes and fears. The stories I heard were invaluable. I learned new things about the challenges people faced, and it sharpened my understanding of the issues and helped me bring the issues to life on the campaign trail with stories of real people. I also believed that if I spent more time at the door with someone who really wanted to talk—say, five minutes instead of the minute that I was being told was "efficient"—it would pay dividends. That person would share with their neighbors and friends that this candidate had stopped by and really listened, and that momentum would matter.

Second, I thought about basic pieces of the campaign differently. For example, I wanted my yard sign to reflect that I was a different kind of candidate, and I wanted to use my signs differently. We made the sign a bold mustard and red color—no red, white, and blue. (Later, I would hear from other candidates of color who ran that they modeled their colorful signs on mine—no more standard boring colors!) Because my name was so hard, we decided to feature "Pramila" as the main part of the sign. I figured if potential voters could just remember that part, it would be sufficient. Plus, using just my first name conveyed the kind of accessibility that has always been and will always be a calling card for me, a sense of real-ness that is often missing from elected officials.

Political pundits at that time generally believed yard signs were a waste of money. I didn't agree, particularly if they were in people's yards and not on the thoroughfares. I felt it was part of what we, in organizing speak, call a leadership ladder—the idea that there are steps an individual can take to engage with an issue. If someone asked for a sign, they were taking one more step of engagement on the leadership ladder. In doing so, they were more invested—my candidacy was their candidacy. These people were proud to be Pramila supporters—we called our growing group of people who wanted yard signs to put in their front yards our "yarmy" (for "yard sign army"—hokey, but people loved it). The proliferating number of signs helped with the strangeness of my name, while at the same time, offering the opportunity for neighbors who hadn't met me to see people they knew and trusted feeling strongly enough about me that they wanted to display a sign. To me, this was worth spending money on.

Third, and relatedly, I wanted to be fully me in my campaign. I decided to make my immigrant story a central part of my campaign, instead of brushing by it out of fear that I would be "too different" for voters to vote for. Despite years of training and encouraging others to tell their stories, I had not told my own very much. My work had never been about me. Now, the campaign had to be about me because people would be checking my name on the ballot box. I was uncomfortable with this focus on me, but I realized it was important. Still, how could I take that immigrant story and make it not just about me but about more than me?

That led me to the fourth principle of my campaign: it wasn't about me, it was about the movement we were building—together. I wanted to engage other activists and leaders in this campaign too. I wanted this to be a campaign that put their hopes and dreams in the center, that lifted up leadership that came from volunteers, that showed momentum for a movement that was far bigger than just one candidate. My slogan—which I would use again later in my run for U.S. Congress—was, "This campaign is not about ME, it's about WE!" Adopting this grammar faux pas ("It's about WE") was challenging for my English major self, but the value of the inclusion principle overrode the grammar! It really was about everything we could do together to create a better world for all of us.

I wanted the campaign to change how people thought about politics and about people who were running for office. Many activists who worked on my campaign told me that they had never been involved with a campaign that was so diverse and engaged so many new people who had never been involved in politics before. To this day, I hear stories about young girls of color who came with their parents to volunteer and who began to think of their futures differently because they saw me running and, through that, saw the possibility of a different future for themselves.

One of my favorite stories from the campaign is about two young Indian American teenagers who used to take the bus over from Bellevue every day to volunteer for the campaign. In the beginning, they were a little shy and didn't want to say much. But by the second week, one of them sidled up to me and said, "Do you think I could run for office one day?"

I have no doubt that she will! In fact, many years later, when she was going to college to get her political science degree at a university in Washington, DC, she interned in my congressional office for a semester. She is definitely going places, and I take enormous pride in the fact that her vision for her own path changed because she saw someone like her doing something she hadn't been told was possible before.

It was a transformative campaign and it gave me great hope that my theory of change could start from the very place of running for office, regardless of whether or not we won.

There's that phrase from the movie *Field of Dreams*, "If you build it, they will come." We built it together. Collectively, we knocked on over 25,000 doors and recruited over 300 volunteers, including many young people, women, and people who had never participated in an election campaign before. They felt deeply that they were a real part of the campaign and they were excited about the possibility of having an organizer and an activist in office—and yes, the first person of color to represent the district in the state senate.

Unlike a lot of first-time candidates, I had a tremendous amount of experience in organizing and I had strong relationships with numerous groups who were excited about my race. Campaigning was hard but fun too. Still, I came to see clearly the barriers to running for office that so many people face. I had stepped down from OneAmerica by then, but I was running a national campaign on women and immigration called We Belong Together, a collaboration between the National Domestic Workers Alliance and the National Asian Pacific American Women's Forum. I found that it was impossible for me to run for office and run We Belong Together at the same time, because campaigning is a full-time job and I don't like to do things halfway, so I decided to leave that job to focus on the campaign. Luckily, Steve had a great union job with benefits, but this challenge haunts so many lower-income people and people of color who want to run for office.

We got a storefront office in my district, right in the midst of the South End, in Rainier Valley, where I lived. The office had a giant pole outside with a huge oval signboard that we were allowed to use, so a friend of mine who ran a print shop and whose kid went to preschool with mine did an in-kind contribution of two enormous "Pramila for State Senate" signs for me—one for the side of the office and one for that sign post. I hired a smart campaign manager who had some organizing experience and understood field programs but had not run a campaign before, so Steve and I stayed heavily involved in strategy and obsessed over every detail.

When we came up against barriers, we found creative ways around them. The rules were often not set up to benefit those who had not been part of the system, but we needed to figure out a way to make the rules work for us. One example of this was the role of the local Democratic district organizations. I had been so busy running OneAmerica that I had never participated in the Democratic Party organizations. In fact, most of those district organizations were quite homogenous, and at the time were structured in ways that were not conducive to engaging diverse communities—with arcane and rather strict rules of order, late meeting times that made it impossible for families with young kids to participate, and little outreach or a foundation of trust with many communities of color. (Democratic district organizations have since improved on many of these issues.) In spite of those challenges, however, these district organizations still gave important endorsements in these races and—depending on the district—had the structure of precinct committee officers who could help with voter turnout. I felt like the support of the Democratic Party organization in my district was an important endorsement and getting it would help my campaign show momentum. The problem was that the organization was filled with people who had been there a long time and were more inclined to endorse some of my opponents who had a longer history with that organization, though not necessarily in the community. Steve and I decided that our strategy would be to change the composition of the organization itself to bring in more of my supporters—which meant signing up new members who knew me, getting them to pay their dues, and then most importantly turning them out for the big endorsement vote.

We worked that strategy like we worked everything else and, in the end, we dramatically expanded the membership of the organization. I won the district's endorsement and my strategy became a new playbook for other candidates running for office. In some cases, it expanded beyond the sometimes exclusive atmosphere of those organizations, leading to the engagement of more folks of color and a building of new trust and relationships, though the underlying structures and leadership still need more deep-rooted change.

Two stories stand out to me from that state senate campaign.

One Sunday evening, I was out door knocking in a neighborhood pretty close to where I used to live: modest homes, many in various states of disrepair, some unkept gardens, mostly people of color. I came to a house with a few black folks sitting on the porch, shooting the breeze. When I told them who I was, a couple gave small laughs and one of them said, "We don't have any use for politicians. You're wasting your time."

I could see from the walk sheet I had that the people in this house had not voted before. One man—probably in his thirties—came over and I sat with him on the porch steps. I did a lot of listening and not too much talking. By the end, we were having an intense, deep conversation about the world, the injustices and inequities of it—about racism and the criminal justice system, about the lack of representation in the halls of power, and the belief he had that, really, nobody cared what he thought; the system was bought and paid for by the wealthy. He wanted no part of it.

The sun was setting and I realized I had been at the door for more than half an hour—definitely not what the consultants would approve of. But this conversation felt really important to me.

"You're all right," he said, looking sideways at me. "Hold on a second."

He went into the house and came back with his ballot. "You know, I've never done this before. Can you walk me through what I need to do if I want to vote for you?"

I showed him that he had to fully fill the oval circles, then put the ballot into the first envelope and then the second, then seal and sign the envelope.

"Thank you," I said, as he shook my hand.

He shook his head. "No, thank YOU. You know, when you walked up here, I was fully and completely convinced that you knew absolutely nothing about my life and I would be wasting my time talking to you. But I was wrong. And you know what? You've given me just a tiny shred of hope that perhaps we can make change happen, that maybe someone like me really matters."

I looked at him and saw a tiny tear in his eye.

He dropped my hand, turned around, and went inside the house. I checked the voter rolls much later, and he did turn in that ballot to vote for the very first time.

The other story came from a much more suburban part of my district, a blue-collar working-class area called Skyway. One of my favorite things about door knocking is that you never know what or who you are going to get. Truth is, we all have our biases and walking up to a door, seeing the person you will engage with brings some of that out.

It was a gorgeous sunny Saturday morning and I was visiting voters who were listed as independents or moderate Republicans. Washington State has a "top-two primary" which means that the top two who get the most votes—regardless of party—advance to the general election. Since my district was a largely Democratic district, it was me and another Democrat who had made it to the general election. This meant that Republicans and Independents would either have to sit home or vote for one of us—why not me? I have never been afraid of talking to people who disagree with me—especially after years of going on conservative talk shows on Fox News and conservative radio, but also working with moderate Republicans and unlikely allies on immigration reform. I decided I would go talk to Independents and moderate Republicans—either way, it would be great for me to hear from them.

The house that I walked up to was a well-kept ranch-style house with a wide, slightly sloping driveway. In the driveway were two big burly Caucasian guys with heavily tattooed arms, busy cleaning their Harley Davidson motorbikes. I admit that I had a little catch in my throat—how would this go? What would they think of this strange immigrant woman approaching them?

I needn't have worried. They were engaged, and as we began talking, I was amazed that they were in complete agreement with me on a number of issues, including a $15 minimum wage, immigration, and the injustice of regressive taxes.

The conversation was going well and it was time for the close. But one of the voters had one more question for me.

"Okay, so now, what about guns?"

"Guns?" I said, thinking, *Uh-oh, this may be a problem.* "Well, to be honest," I said, "I don't like guns."

I watched his face start to close up. "Aw shit, you're one of those liberals who wants to take my guns away," he said disgustedly.

"Look," I said. "My husband used to hunt and had guns in the house." (I didn't mention that he was now a Buddhist and a vegetarian at that). "I'm not trying to take people's guns away, I just think we should have restrictions around guns so that only responsible people like you can have them."

I could see I wasn't getting very far. We talked for several more minutes until it became clear that we were not going to agree on this. It was time to move on.

"So, I gotta go," I said. "I see we're not going to agree on this issue, but can I still count on your vote?"

"Nah," he said, somewhat diffidently now. "Too bad, I really liked you until we started talking about guns. I just can't vote for you."

My heart sank. All that time, and it had been going so well. I looked past him and saw the woman that he had earlier introduced to me as his wife. I decided to take one last try.

"I understand," I said. "Listen, how long have you and your wife been married?"

He stopped for a second, looked at her, then me, and replied, "Twenty-three years, why?"

"That's wonderful," I said. "And do you and your wife agree on 100 percent of issues?"

His face broke into a smile and he guffawed. "Ha! Of course not!"

"Well," I said, with my sweetest smile, "You married her. I'm just asking for your vote!"

For a minute, he looked at me and froze—then started laughing and laughing, reached out his hand, took mine, and said, "You know what? I like you. You're real. You don't run away and you say what you mean. We need more of that in politics. Okay, you've got my vote! But listen, if you start to take away my guns, I am going to be on your ass, got that?"

"Absolutely," I said. "That's what democracy is!"

It was one of the best mornings of the campaign and I've never forgotten it.

I went on to win the primary election with over 54 percent of the vote in a six-way race, and to win the November general election with 71 percent of the vote.

I became the first South Asian American ever elected to the Washington State Legislature, the state senate's only woman of color, and one of only four people of color in the senate. A couple of months after I was sworn in, an article about my move to elected office blared the headline: "From Handcuffs to Elected Office: Washington State's Rabble-Rousing Senator."

My campaign had opened up all kinds of possibilities for me, my volunteers, my community, and my movement colleagues. We wanted to run a different kind of campaign and we did, emphasizing a strong field campaign, authentic engagement with voters, and coalition-building strategies in our volunteers and allies. We showed too that diverse candidates who can speak authentically to a diverse electorate will expand that electorate.

Some of the things we did in our campaign would still take more than four years to be seen as winning strategies. The old structures and theories of change were not easy to push out, even though our little campaign had shown a different way. It would take the election of Donald Trump to show how badly our democracy was failing and to bring about new kinds of candidates and campaigns that all seemed to mirror many of the things we had tested and found to be true in my 2014 campaign for state senate.

It seemed I was on a path, and only time would tell whether I could take this same theory of change into my role as a newly elected senator in the Washington State Senate.

4

State Senate: A Proving Ground

I LOVED MY DISTRICT, THE THIRTY-SEVENTH LEGISLATIVE DISTRICT IN Washington State, where I had lived for more than twenty years. It was the most economically and racially diverse district in the state at the time, a place where over one hundred languages were spoken. Black Americans had made their home here when other parts of the city redlined them out, and poverty and wealth, entrepreneurship and struggle, openness and difference were all woven together in a giant tapestry of life.

But the elation of being elected a state senator quickly gave way to the many barriers to doing the work I had imagined. I was going into the state senate at a time when Democrats were in the minority. The legislative bodies had entrenched power structures, weak staff infrastructure, and, of course, few brown and black people.

I had already seen the barriers to running for office for low-income people and women, but now I faced the problems of serving in office, too, starting with money.

Like most state legislative bodies, the Washington States Senate was supposedly a part-time gig, with a salary (in 2014) of $42,000. The theory was that, annually, you only serve for a 90-day or 120-day session, depending on the year. But in the recent fiercely partisan times

with split Democrat-Republican legislatures, we had additional special sessions during both of the two years I served before running for
Congress—meaning that the legislative session would be extended
by months, even sometimes running through July. The schedule was
extremely unpredictable, making it near impossible to fit another job
into the mix.

Even when you weren't in session, the reality was that you didn't stop
being a legislator the day the legislative session ended. If you cared about
doing your job well, you were on call, day and night, responding to constituents, attending community events, and planning your bills for the
next legislative session. If you really wanted to be a "people's politician"—
the only kind I was interested in being—you had to be available all the
time, not just when the Senate was in session.

Every state legislature has different rules, but in Washington State, there
was no prohibition on serving in the legislature and working a full-time
job in either the public or private sector. Industry groups used this to their
own advantage: they put out brochures stating that businesses could put a
legislator on their payroll by essentially creating a job with no real requirements and paying a full year's salary, thus ensuring that those lawmakers
were beholden to their interests. Those of us who refused to take that road
and wanted only to be beholden to our constituents had to figure out some
other way of supporting ourselves.

Depending on where a senator lived, physical distance was a problem
too. Olympia, the state capitol where the legislature operated, was about
one-and-a-half hours from Seattle in traffic and further from the north,
south, and eastern parts of the state. That meant most people had to get
an apartment in Olympia for the workweek. The state legislature reim-
bursed daily expenses during the legislative session, but the rate wasn't
quite enough to cover food and an apartment. On top of that were issues
of practicality for parents with young kids. I was fortunate in that Janak
was now in their senior year of high school, so I could stay in Olympia
during the week for a few days, if necessary. I rented a room in the house
of two public school teachers so that I had a place to crash if needed, but I

still tried my best to make it back and forth to Seattle every day whenever possible so I could have dinner with my family each night.

I realized, too, that using my platform for organizing was not going to be easy, given the lack of staff provided for senators. At OneAmerica, while we always felt understaffed, I had grown the organization to eighteen employees by the time I left, plus interns, volunteers, and community coalition allies. In the state senate, we got one paid full-time legislative aide who stayed with you for the year, plus one session aide and two interns (usually college students) who were with you just for the session. The senate Democrats also assigned each senator in our caucus a communications staffer who was split among several members. The legislative aide ended up being a Jill-of-all-trades, handling everything from scheduling to policy to legislative research and constituent services. There was no time in either of our schedules to do the kind of organizing with outside groups and coalitions that we really wanted to do to help move major bills forward or generate resistance to bad proposals that popped up. I tried as best as I could to use the relationships that I had with the major advocacy groups to help build momentum, but it was an enormous amount of work with little time or support behind it.

Money, logistics, and distance were challenges I could overcome. But learning how to use my state legislative platform for organizing was a hurdle of a different order. Before me, there had been very few organizers elected to the state legislature. In fact, at that time, the state legislature was not seen as a particularly prestigious place nor was it the focus of much of the outside organizing by the broad and diverse coalition that had helped elect me, with the exception of the public sector unions who always needed to bargain their contracts with the state. Too many activists had written off elected office as an effective way to make change, and Republicans were far ahead of Democrats in terms of recognizing the power of state legislatures to push effective policy change.

I had been elected by a coalition, but once I got to Olympia, most of the institutional support dropped away. The organizations that did have a presence in Olympia were extraordinarily siloed: everyone was advocating almost exclusively for their own piece. The women's organizations mainly focused on reproductive choice; the labor unions primarily on their contract bargains, workers' compensation, or regulations; and then a few scattered racial justice groups, including the organization I had built, advocated for immigrant rights. The proactive, strategic coalition building I was used to simply didn't exist there. Nor was there much attention at all to the necessity of rapid response to the bad bills that were coming up in our Republican-controlled Senate. Nonprofit organizations were focused on whatever they were funded to do—and not necessarily on the same timetable as the legislature. That meant any work Democrats in the senate did was largely proactive work drafting bills as placeholders for when Democrats regained control of the Senate or on budget items the party knew would be coming up.

Because I was one of the few organizer leaders who was elected to the senate, there was also a strange dynamic where now I was seen to be on the "inside" and not part of the "outside" movement. In the beginning, that meant I was suddenly automatically excluded from the organizing coalitions I had previously participated in. This seemed ridiculous to me. Now that I was an elected representative of the district, wasn't it even more important that I sat at those tables and that we strategized together? Of course, I had to be careful of not sharing certain things that were said in private rooms in the Senate, but still there was a lot of strategizing that needed to happen *together*. Our movement had become so accustomed to our own form of internalized oppression: we were not part of the power structure and so this was a continuation of that "us" versus "them" mentality. Having our own people in positions of power required both a mental shift and a restructuring of the way we did things.

Finally, at that time, I was the *only* woman of color in the state senate and one of just four people of color in the senate. Many of my colleagues were good people who cared about racism, criminal justice, and immigration rights, and I was able to build some strong allies for the fights I took on. But the truth was, it always felt like a push because there just weren't many senators who came from the communities most directly affected by these issues or who were willing to fight against the mainstream on difficult issues. Their awareness of racial equity was not particularly high, and I often had to be the person who challenged a particular perspective on legislation we were discussing or the one to put forth different ways of analyzing the problems and the solutions. Turf was a big issue as well. I was the newbie so others felt ownership of some of the very issues that I intended to work on. I had to navigate those dynamics carefully but fiercely given my own expertise.

I also had to get to know my Democratic colleagues, most of whom I had never met. I decided I would also set up introductory meetings with all my Republican colleagues, a gesture that won me many early points—though the amicability didn't last long once I started speaking up about my priorities. I used a strategy I learned from organizing called power mapping to help me understand each of the Republicans, their districts, and what moved them. I reached out to a former OneAmerica staffer, Jennifer Chan, who was now in graduate school in Chicago and had volunteered to help me on specific projects, to ask her to put together a power-map analysis for each of the Republican senators.

A power map allows you to create a profile of each person that details their priority bills and interests, what the composition of their districts is, and personal details including religious affiliation, where they went to school, where their kids went to school, as well as identifying their biggest donors. All this information taught me what made them tick and helped me look for areas of common ground that I could use to start some relationships. Power maps also tell you who has power *over* a person, in other words, who would be a good influencer. For example, we found that a Christian member who was extremely religious may be influenced by the Church Council's or Association of Churches' position on immigration. These power maps were very useful tools that allowed us to look at the spread of power and utilize it for strategic organizing.

I undertook my new role with a deep commitment to making the most of my role. But during my first few months in office, I constantly had this "Now what? " thought. With few staff members in the Senate, I felt lonely and missed my relationships with OneAmerica staff, colleagues, and movement allies, which had been tested through struggles and built trust through both defeats and victories.

I decided to start with broader coalition building, focusing on the idea that all these progressive people who were in Olympia working in their siloes needed to be helping each other, working toward a shared, collective agenda. When I say that these coalitions didn't exist, I should add that various connections had been made over the years long before I came to town. But what was missing, I felt, was a permanent infrastructure of the left in Olympia of the sort that existed in Seattle. Folks had talked about building such an infrastructure over the years, and now that I was working on the statewide scene, I saw and felt exactly what they were referring to: the ongoing and institutionalized infrastructure of the left was nothing compared to the permanent infrastructure of the right at the state legislature.

I began by calling a meeting of the diverse progressive groups that I playfully called the Blue-Green-Pink-Brown-Black-White Coalition, a play on the BlueGreen Alliance started some years before between labor and environmentalists. These groups were of course used to working in coalition in Seattle, but somehow they had not thought to do this in Olympia. OneAmerica had been instrumental in forming a racial justice coalition that involved many different racial justice groups, but beyond that, there was no broader progressive platform of environmental, labor, women's, and racial justice groups who met on a regular basis to build the likelihood that we could win on a whole slate of progressive priorities. The hardest group to engage was the environmentalists who, at that time, were still largely white and worked separately from the rest of the organizations. Still, the majority of groups liked the idea and were willing to try it. Together, they wrote sign-on letters and helped mobilize rapid response around a whole range of issues.

Some groups like NARAL Pro-Choice Washington understood the charge so deeply that they took it even further. Their new executive director, Rachel Berkson—who had spent a decade as a community and political organizer working for the Working Families Party in New York and then SEIU and Washington Community Action Network in our state—decided to create an expanded legislative report card that would institutionalize their belief in an intersectional agenda by adding priorities like immigrant rights and raising the minimum wage. The idea that raising the minimum wage was an economic issue that deeply affected the ability of women of color to have reproductive choice was exactly how I felt we needed to be framing things. It meant that some of the legislators who claimed to be pro-choice would have to contend with not getting a good score from NARAL if they opposed an increase in the minimum wage. Years ago, Steve and I and others had framed the immigrant workers freedom ride this way to bring labor and community together—immigrant rights are worker's rights and worker's rights are immigrant rights. Now we were trying to bring that same idea to the state capitol.

It is a fitting coda to this story that two years later, when I got elected to Congress, I hired Rachel as the district director of my congressional office and she has been a key strategic partner who has been by my side every step of the way since then.

I knew I wanted to be a different kind of elected official. That meant regularly organizing town halls with hundreds of people in attendance and telling people what was really happening in the state legislature. It meant strategizing with my advocacy friends and helping to plan how we would get our progressive priorities through. It meant taking on thorny subjects like race. And it also meant keeping a year-round organizing operation active on the campaign side, knocking on people's doors just to check in and see how they were doing and what they were thinking even though I wasn't up for reelection for another four years.

I still remember how, a few months into my first term, I gathered a few dozen volunteers and we went door knocking. People would open the door and their jaws would drop to see me. "Didn't we just elect you?" they would ask. I would laugh and say, "Yes, you did! Thank you! But I am here to check in and see how you are doing and what you want me to know about your priorities." I was talking to them about what they wanted in their lives, not just trying to get a vote when it suited me.

I also wanted my office to be different; I wanted it to be the refuge for folks of color who came to Olympia and rarely saw anyone who looked like them. When it was time to hire my only full-time staffer, the Senate Democratic staff gave me a stack of résumés, but not a single person who had any appropriate experience was a person of color. I desperately wanted someone who knew some of the ins and outs of Olympia and the state legislature, but I also felt that I needed to be true to my beliefs in hiring a person of color who could help me to represent the diversity of our district and understood *why* I was in office and what I was trying to achieve.

I recruited Yasmin Christopher, a brilliant, young, mixed-race South Asian American woman who had just finished law school and had volunteered for me at OneAmerica. Yasmin was a part of our civil disobedience action years before, when we were arrested and spent the night in jail together. We like to joke that we got to know each other in a jail cell. She had never really thought about working in politics before, but she was drawn to the idea of working for an activist and the first South Asian American woman in the legislature, so she jumped at the chance.

Yasmin had become a powerful activist herself, some of which she credits to her experiences volunteering at OneAmerica where she learned the power of the personal story. Born in Bangladesh to a fourteen-year-old Bengali mother and a forty-seven-year-old American father, Yasmin entered this world as a product of human trafficking. When she was four years old, her father falsified travel documents for Yasmin, her mother, and seven other Bangladeshi family members. He brought all of them to America and kept them confined to a farm in Washington State where they raised cattle and goats to sell as halal meat in Seattle. Yasmin says they worked from "sunup to sundown and he isolated and enslaved everyone." While Yasmin and her baby sister were spared from her father's abuse, he terrorized all the others physically, sexually, and mentally. It was this horrific abuse that finally brought a detective from the sheriff's office to the farmhouse and ultimately led to the freeing of Yasmin and her family. Yasmin's father was ultimately charged, convicted, and sentenced to four years in prison, though he served only eighteen months.

When I found out about Yasmin's experience, we talked many times about the pros and cons of sharing her story. She didn't want to be pitied, she didn't want people's sympathy—but she did want her experience to help change the law, draw attention to the issues of human trafficking, and make life better for others. When she went to law school, she found other supportive resources in professors and student associations that gave her even more courage to think about how she wanted to use her own story to make a difference. In 2013, the year before I got elected, she agreed to go public with her story as part of the county-wide campaign to raise awareness of trafficking, which included ads on two hundred Metro buses, a public service announcement, and a front-page story in the *Seattle Times* on her experience.[1]

Yasmin's courage, smarts, and resilience were what drew me to her, and when she agreed to be my legislative aide (or "LA" in lawmaking-speak), I was thrilled. Yasmin understood exactly what I was trying to create: a diverse, generous, and inclusive office that made elected office a part of movement building. She hired a driven young black woman as a session aide and a couple of people of color as interns. She herself became a strong mentor to other people of color who began to get hired, starting meetings for the few nonwhite staffers, increasing diversity in hiring in other offices, and turning our office into a safe organizing space for other POCs.

Because Yasmin and I were both new to Olympia, we had to learn everything together, which meant we fumbled around a lot more than was comfortable, experienced extra stress, and put pressure on ourselves to work harder and smarter than everyone else. That's the immigrant story, right? So much rides on an immigrant's success or failure—which means failure just isn't an option. In the midst of a largely white male legislature, we dealt with what felt like constant slights, racism, and injustices in the broadest sense. Yasmin had adopted from the writer Sarah Hagi what Hagi called her Daily Prayer to Combat Imposter Syndrome: "God give me the confidence of a mediocre white dude."[2] We made it our morning prayer as well, laughing and crying simultaneously over both the serious-ness of institutionalized sexism and racism and the need for some humor to keep us sane. Yasmin's brilliance and fortitude took her, with my proud blessings, from being my legislative aide to becoming the only person of color on the policy staff of the Senate Democratic Caucus and then to being legislative director for our popular state attorney general.

Training, mentoring, and providing space to other women of color was movement building, too, and I loved it.

One reason representation matters is because the conversations are differ-ent when we are at the table, as women, as people of color, as immigrants, as low-income folks, or LGBTQ people. We bring our different perspec-tives and experiences to everything we do. We craft different legislation. We chair hearings differently. We tell stories differently and we tell dif-ferent stories. All of this means that, in the end, we bring a deep, inher-ent wisdom and perspective to the policy agenda and the crafting of the legislation itself, making it that much better at the end.

I understood early on what this representation meant to the rest of the communities of color. A group of older black women had come to see me in Olympia. "Senator Jayapal," one of them began. "Oh, call me Pramila," I said immediately, wanting to maintain that sense of accessibility. The woman stopped in her tracks and looked at me with the kind of look that my mother used to give me when I had done something really wrong. "No, no, no," she said sternly. "Do you know how long we have waited to have our people in these bodies? Do you know how much we have done to get you here? You claim that title and you own it and the respect that comes with it."

In that moment, I understood all over again that this wasn't about me, it was about our communities and our collective voice. *They* deserved the respect that the title conveyed.

Two years later, after I was elected to Congress, my mother related another story about how people across the oceans in India saw my elec-tion. The gentleman who delivered newspapers on her street came up to her and asked excitedly if she had seen the big article and picture of me in the local Kannada language paper. She told him apologetically that she didn't read Kannada so she had not seen it. The next day, he arrived at her house with the paper to present to her, and translated the entire article into English for her. She thanked him and asked if she could pay him for the paper. He looked at her with a faint sense of outrage and said, "*Ai-yo, Amma*! Isn't she *our* daughter also? We are so proud."

This sense of pride and ownership other people of color, in particular, feel is humbling and reminds me constantly that I have a responsibility to represent with authenticity, fierceness, and grace for the millions of others out there who see themselves reflected in what I do and say. It's a tall order but one I take seriously.

There really wasn't an issue I worked on that didn't touch on race or racial justice, and I knew that part of what made me a different kind of elected official was that I was going to keep race central in everything I did. Too few lawmakers and even too few progressives were ready to do that. But as an immigrant rights leader, the only woman of color in the state senate, the first ever South Asian American to be elected to the state legislature, representing the most diverse district in the state, it was never a question for me that this focus would be central to my work.

A month after I was elected, I called a meeting of some leading black pastors and black activists in our state to ask for help in putting together a legislative agenda that would begin to address these critical issues of race and racial justice, specifically from the perspective of the African American community, which was prominent in my district. The painful and traumatic deaths of Michael Brown and Eric Garner were dominating headlines, and I wanted to just listen and think together about how we could really work on addressing the institutionalized racism that was prevalent everywhere. None of us had answers, but it seemed that even talking about the problem and committing to work together toward solutions was rare.

In the privacy of our Senate Democratic Caucus, I often had to argue for the concerns of people of color that were not at the table. During a debate over the body cameras bill, I argued forcefully that the bill as drafted could actually hurt communities of color in many ways; they could be used against the very people we were trying to help if the footage was not considered seriously or used selectively. It was a tense debate and, as I left the room, a longtime senate staffer came up to me and quietly thanked me. "I've been here a long time and I just have never heard these perspectives voiced in these rooms," he said. "Don't give up, these are discussions that must be had no matter what the result is."

The legislation I worked on often centered on racial equity as well. While at OneAmerica, I had been among the first to endorse and organize around an effort by some civil rights attorneys to draft a Washington State Voting Rights Act based on a similar California law drafted by one of those very same attorneys, who was based in Seattle. Although the bill was not mine in name, when I got to the Senate, I took over much of the negotiation with Republicans to try to get it to the floor. The bill would have, among other things, transitioned city and local elections in the state from an "at-large system"—where voters in a jurisdiction elect members from anywhere in that jurisdiction—to a "districted election system"—where you elect someone to represent you from your neighborhood, or district. This would theoretically allow for the election of a more diverse body, ensuring that those who represent you actually look like you and share your life experiences.[3] But the power of the bill showed in the opposition: because of the very nature of transitioning power, every single Republican opposed the bill, in fear of giving too much voting power to growing communities in their districts who could vote them out. We organized hard and we made it a Democratic priority, holding rallies at the capitol, targeting different state legislative districts by bringing constituents from those districts to visit their senator, and then engaging Republicans in a real negotiation that I helped to lead. We got extremely close that year to getting it to the floor for a vote, but it would take a Democratic majority in the Senate the year after I went to Congress to win a major victory and actually pass the Voting Rights Act.

I also took on drafting an Automatic Voter Registration bill, similar to legislation that was beginning to pass in other states around the country. In Washington State, this was complex. Some legislators were racing to introduce the bill without understanding the particular situation in our state. Thanks to the work of OneAmerica and the coalition we had built, Washington State was one of only three states to allow immigrants to have driver's licenses without proof of citizenship. That was great, but it meant that legislation crafted in other states that automatically registered people to vote upon getting a driver's license could not work in our state, since you cannot vote if you are not a citizen. Working with immigration attorneys and the broader Voting Justice Coalition, we crafted a bill that navigated this challenge carefully to ensure only U.S. citizens were registered, and at the same time, expanded the pool of people beyond just those with driver's licenses. I worked hard on attracting Republican support, and successfully got our Republican secretary of state to sponsor the bill and a former Republican secretary of state to testify on behalf of the bill. Like the Voting Rights Act, this bill was passed and signed into law a year later when Democrats took control of the Senate and I had already gone to Congress.

Centering on race and equity in everything became an obsession to me because it felt so urgent and I recognized I was one of the few in the chamber doing this work. Sometimes I knew the bills would not pass, but I proposed them because we needed a way to start the conversation and begin organizing around an issue. One example was a bill I introduced that would require an equity-impact analysis to be conducted on all education policies *before* they were implemented. It didn't pass but I ended up including a portion of it in the budget that we passed, and it helped an important discussion surface that our communities could organize around. I also wrote a bill to ban the use of the military weapons handed down by the federal government to local police departments, and participated in early discussions around taking on the issue of use of deadly force that was roiling communities of color across the state.

Many of these policies were far from popular, even among Democrats, and it often felt alienating to be the one putting them forward. But I was always willing to speak up for policies I believed in on the senate floor.

"She has to speak about everything," Republicans would joke, somewhat nastily. But even some of them privately admitted to me that they wished I wasn't . . . *so articulate!*

After I gave a speech against charter schools that focused on how we needed to have good public education so EVERY child, including kids of color, would be able to thrive, one of the older white Republican men came up to me and said, "You know, the problem with you is that you're just too believable, too earnest, and too good, dammit!"

Imagine that. An older white man, who'd been doing his job forever, telling me that I was too good at mine because I really believed in what I was saying, and I didn't lose too many opportunities to call out injustice when I saw it. I do think it really bothered him that I had authenticity on my side—it wasn't just the politics that bothered him; it was that what I said came across as true. Perhaps in politics, that was somewhat of a rarity.

I learned early on not to discount those who ridiculed me. As a minority—both in terms of my party's representation in the state senate and as a woman of color—I never had that luxury. And despite my repetition of Yasmin's morning prayer, I too suffered from my own insecurities. Was I being too shrill? Should I not always be the one to raise the issue of race? When should I step back and let something roll off me? A couple of times, I got so angry that I teared up and I hated the feeling that those tears signaled weakness—even though I spent hours telling younger women that feeling emotion is good, it brings us closer to our own values and conscience.

Truth be told, it was damn tiring to be one of very few people in the room who would always speak up for racial justice and equity. It was tiring to even have to think about when it was just not strategic to raise the issue of race. It was tiring to do so without a real pack to travel with. And it was tiring that everyone assumed that I would raise the issue, so that even if they thought about it, they never raised it themselves.

Women of color ask me all the time how I deal with racism and sexism. I tell them that I really do have to pick my battles. Because if I took on every single injustice, I'd be exhausted and ineffective. I also did not want to be pigeon-holed as someone who only focused on gender and race or constantly "played the race card." This was a constant dilemma for me because the phrase itself made me bristle. It reflected the unequal power dynamic of white folks who essentially control politics and certainly the legislature. When they use this phrase, I feel like they have missed the whole point. We women of color aren't "playing the race card or the gender card," we're just talking about the discrimination that is so real around race and gender that it desperately needs to be called out. The problem is that we're still educating others on the fact that it exists and, more often than not, people just don't want to see it. And therein lay the problem: if I wasn't careful, I would get categorized and dismissed, so in spite of my bristling, I had to recognize that this dynamic was a real possibility.

At the end of the day, I wanted to speak my truth powerfully and also be taken seriously for everything I brought to the table. It was a difficult balancing act, one that I got better at with time but still work at every single day. I think it's important for young women to know that even now, even where I am, I sometimes feel plagued with the very same insecurities and I have to remind myself that institutionalized racism and sexism are so powerful because they burrow their way deep into our own psyches, despite ourselves. We women of color have to unlearn our own internalized oppressions. Same goes for men of color and for women generally in many ways. I speak about it most often as being something that women of color confront, because—let's face it—women of color confront racism and sexism daily on both fronts.

The other thing I have learned in talking about race is that you have to call people in as well as call them out. Most white people run as far as they can from any conversations having to do with race or racism. As a result, they have way too little experience talking about race and are deeply uncomfortable even acknowledging that they themselves may be racist. Legislative colleagues on both sides of the aisle have said to me that they are afraid to talk about race because they will get "pounced on" if they say something wrong. It can be bit of a counterproductive cycle but we desperately need to have these conversations. I often encourage my enlightened white friends and my own husband to take on talking to other white people so that they can start to gain that experience without brown and black folks having to take on the burden of constantly being the teachers.

I had failures, too. There were times when I tried to moderate my anger in order to uncover pathways forward that never materialized. One example was the debate over racial impact statements. State legislatures use these to score proposed legislation in terms of whether the effects of a bill will hurt marginalized groups or whether it will affect all citizens equally. It shouldn't be something that's controversial: other states use this system, and it's common to score bills in terms of budgetary or even environmental impact.

But my Republican colleagues didn't like any of this. The most vocal among them was a seventy-eight-year-old, been-in-the-Senate-forever man from Yakima, Washington, named Jim Honeyford. During a discussion about racial impact statements, someone had brought up crime. In the course of his response, he said: "It's generally accepted that the poor are more likely to commit crimes. And generally, I think, accepted that colored people are more likely to be poor."

Racial justice advocates were outraged at both the term "colored people" and the stereotypes. The media was on it immediately and there was a firestorm brewing. Many were calling on me to immediately put out a statement condemning what had been said, and I had to decide whether to do that.

Jim Honeyford was one of my staunchest opponents in work I was doing to get several million dollars in funding to support pre-apprenticeships for people of color and women in the transportation sector across the finish line, and he was also one of the biggest opponents of my efforts around the Voting Rights Act. He was a strange anomaly. He represented a huge Latino constituency, but they weren't voting, in part because of the way the voting districts were drawn and the lack of representative candidates. As a result, he was reelected over and over again. On the other hand, he had a big Filipino constituency in his district, and he had backed an effort to get a big chunk of state money appropriated for a capital campaign for the Filipino Community Center that happened to be in my district. In fact, that year, both he and I were honored at the same ceremony—a rather surprising occurrence! Jim bristled at the idea that we should do anything different for people of color. Perhaps he really didn't believe in the politics of race, or perhaps he didn't believe that HE was racist. Either way, he was not really a friend or an ally, at least not from what I had seen.

In the end, I didn't put out a statement. Out of some inexplicable sense that perhaps he would listen to me, I tried to go and talk to Jim. I wanted to explain to him why a racial impact statement made sense, to explain what life was like for the many people of color in his state and, indeed, in his district, given its Filipino population.[4] I have had this approach work before; I've found that it often disarms people. Most of the time, they don't expect someone who completely disagrees with them on something as sensitive as race to go and talk to them about it. In short, they are often far more comfortable responding through a media sound bite than if you just step right up and talk to them. I thought maybe Jim would be disarmed, too. Maybe there would be some opening that would help us to develop a relationship and even move the Voting Rights Act forward.

I've always said that you have to be an optimist to be an activist. That was certainly the case here. Jim didn't listen at all. In spite of my diplomatic phrasing, he knew what I was trying to do and he was still mad at being called out. He did what happens all too often when someone is called out on their racism or racist assumptions: he told me why he could not possibly be racist. It made me feel only slightly better that, because of the media firestorm, he did ultimately apologize to the public, though my talk with him probably had little to do with that.[5]

Looking back on it now, I do wish I had put out a statement. I probably should have known that talking to him would get me nowhere, and it felt like it was probably more important to support the communities that were feeling the same pain of racism and stereotyping that had been going on for so long. Defeats like this—when my strategy of face-to-face reasonableness fell short, when someone on the other side was shortsighted—were never easy. But learning is never about doing everything right, it's about doing things that don't work and then recalibrating. My failure with Jim didn't sour me to using the same strategies again, but I also became more realistic about when I could expect change and when it was highly unlikely. And that became an important skill in determining strategy for just about anything when I served in Congress.

In almost every way, it was a hundred times easier to take on the opposing party than to take on your own side. When I came into the Senate, Washington State had some of the toughest regulations on predatory payday lenders. These are companies who provide consumers quick cash to pay their bills on time, then charge interest rates as high as 400 percent (no, that zero is not a typo!).[6] It had become a big business in the wake of the 2008 financial crisis. I firmly believe that this type of payday lending preys upon low-income citizens who don't receive regular paychecks and are short on cash when the rent or car payment comes due. It exists in the vacuum of a lack of regulation on these lenders and a lack of other affordable options for people who are desperate and simply not earning enough to pay their bills, often even if they are working a full forty-hour week.

In 2009, the Washington State Senate—led by Senator Sharon Nelson, who was also the Democratic minority leader during my tenure—tightened restrictions on payday lenders, setting stricter limits on the amount of time borrowers have to pay back loans, the amount of loans, and the amount of interest a lender can charge.[7] My immigrant rights organization was part of the broad coalition that pushed for those changes, led by the Statewide Poverty Action Network.

Early in 2015, my first year in the senate, Sharon got wind that a few of our fellow senate Democrats were introducing a bill to essentially roll back the progress that had been made on payday lending. They wanted to allow payday lenders to offer loans that customers could stretch out over a whole year. Under their proposal, borrowers could borrow $1,000 per month for an entire year, but interest would accrue so that a $700 loan would ultimately cost a borrower nearly $500 in fees after the first half of that year.[8]

Why did they do this? Because Moneytree, a payday lender, had contributed to their campaigns, of course.

I was familiar with the payday lending industry, both through my own finance background and my activism work. Sharon was an ex-banker who felt a real anger toward payday lenders and rightly saw the existing payday lending restrictions as her victory. She enlisted me and another state senator with a financial background, Mark Mullet, to help fight the proposed rollbacks, which we knew would disproportionately hurt people of color and low-income citizens.

It felt like Whac-A-Mole, as Stephen Colbert once put it in a pointed segment on payday lending, to fight the industry and see them come back again to lobby in the legislature.[9] They would always have a new way to talk about it, to get around the rules.

To her enormous credit, Sharon was willing to help lead the fight on the Senate floor even though she would be coming up against a couple of other Democrats who were sponsoring the bill for the payday lenders. She, Mark, and I got together and penned an onslaught of amendments to stall and attempt to kill that bill, which, of course, meant directly opposing our own colleagues.

One of the Democratic sponsors of the bill removed his name from the sponsors list when we raised our objections. In fact, in a particularly emotional exchange in my office, he apologized profusely to me for co-sponsoring the legislation, saying that he had been wrong to support it. But the other prime sponsor stayed stubbornly on the bill.

Sharon, Mark, and I knew we didn't have the votes to kill the bill in the minority. When you're outnumbered by Republicans and you lose some of your own members, you lose. But our play was to create a huge fuss in the Senate, show that we were willing to fight to bring down the bill and also set it up so the Democratically controlled House would see that there would be hell to pay if they passed the bill. An organizer in her own right,

Sharon called up a group of activist nuns who were organizing up around the issue in the districts represented by the Democratic sponsors of the bill and asked them to turn up the pressure. Faith community pressure, it turns out, can be some of the most effective! I planned town halls and we pushed reporters to cover what was going on. As I would come to find out again and again, reporters were only too happy to report on a story that was about fissures within the Democratic party!

The night of the floor fight on the bill, our proposed amendments stretched late into the night. Sharon, Mark, and I stood up over and over again, arguing amendment after amendment and seeing each one voted down by opposition led by one of our own Democratic colleagues. It was disheartening and excruciating to watch, and the Republicans were gleeful at having divided us. It was my first major fight on the floor against some of my own colleagues.

When the final vote tally on the bill came in, it was around one a.m. The vote was 30–18 in favor of passage. Through the haze of my frustration and tiredness, I noticed that one Republican senator, Kirk Pearson, had voted with us against the bill.[10] I was stunned to see his vote—against all of his colleagues.

I had never interacted with Pearson before, but on an impulse, I went over to his floor seat.

"I know you don't really know me, and I have no idea why you voted the way you voted," I said, "but it really means so much to me and I just want to say thank you."

He looked up at me from his seat, then put his head down in his hands, shaking it from side to side.

He paused a moment, then said, "It would have really hurt people. I just couldn't vote for it."

He went on to tell me that his town, about thirty miles northeast of mine, was predominantly poor. "My people sleep in their cars and often don't even have a home with a hot shower," he said. "I try to look out for them." (Later, I found out that Pearson was one of the few Senate members who did not even have a cell phone.)

"I'd love to find something we can work on together," I said.

"Well, if you really want to be hated," he said, "you and I should take on the usury credit card interest rates.[11] That's killing people in my district."

"Deal," I said. "I'm ready when you are."

In spite of the brutal fight on the floor, I was walking away with a tiny smile. I had been reminded of another great lesson that night: always be ready for surprises. My long-time instinct to never completely count anyone out was vindicated again that night. People can surprise you and you never know where you might get support.

The payday lending bill did ultimately die in the House. By the time it got there, our voices on the floor of the senate, combined with some serious community organizing at town halls and in the media, had made plain to the public and the House speaker that it would, indeed, hurt people and would not be well received by a Democratic majority.

Together, even in the minority, we got some things done to benefit people of color, immigrants, and other marginalized people in Washington State. One of the things I'm most proud of is my role in funding the Southeast Economic Opportunity Center, now known as the Othello Square project. When I ran for state senate, several advocates in communities of color as well as the Rainier Valley Chamber of Commerce were talking about how we needed a real economic engine in Southeast Seattle. The idea was to incorporate a one-stop shopping center into a transit-oriented development next to the new light-rail. The development would combine some government service offices, affordable healthcare services, retail space, an early childhood center, a business incubator and—best of all—mixed-income housing that would allow Seattle's poorest residents (too often displaced by the effects of gentrification) the opportunity to apply for home ownership. And we'd create tons of good wage–earning jobs in the process.

Nothing like this had ever happened in Southeast Seattle. We had too few bus and light-rail stops, too few hospitals, and too few affordable housing options. Communities of color were rapidly being pushed further and further down south and out of Seattle. We needed jobs, health centers that didn't require multiple bus rides, and some hope. Our area needed a boost and a giant one, at that.

The idea had been circulating for a while, but when I heard about it during my Senate campaign, I loved it. It was huge and ambitious, but it was just what we needed in the district. We deserve this, I remember telling people on the campaign trail. If other parts of Seattle could receive such investments, why not us?

I made this project a key focus of my first two years. I had a fantastic ally in House Speaker Frank Chopp. Frank was an organizing machine and a force to be reckoned with. He noticed everything and valued hard work, which he saw in my work ethic. Frank cared deeply about low-income people and housing, and he loved the idea of the Southeast Economic Opportunity Center. With his support, I was able to secure $1.5 million in state funding to purchase a property from a somewhat reluctant Seattle Housing Authority, who would have preferred to sell it to the highest bidder instead of keeping it for affordable housing. I also wanted the developers to be people of color from the community, so we tapped Tony To, a local Asian American community developer, to help put together a coalition from the area to help lead the project.

The next step was to get more money from the City of Seattle. When I went to the city council and told them the vision for the center, I was told by one of the councilmembers, "That's way too ambitious! Why not scale it down some?"

Why is it that anytime we want to do something in the center of communities of color, we are told we are too ambitious? I refused to back down, and thanks to the politics of elections, I was able to get the council president to back a significant match from the city—which then led to more money from the county.[12]

In 2019, the project, now called Othello Square, broke ground. Few people remember the start of it, but I am filled with pride to know my role in building something that will benefit the lives of so many in South Seattle who need to know that they are valued and see opportunity in this new project.[13]

What leads to the successful implementation of legislation? My favorite saying—if politics is the art of the possible, then it is our job as activists to push the boundaries of what is seen as possible—resonated for me both inside and outside elected office.

Before taking office, I had been frustrated at the way elected officials often waited until an idea was popular before jumping on board. Too much importance was given to some notion of being "practical"—proposing ideas that would pass with ease in the moment. It seemed equally important, if not more important, to draft legislation that could help movements organize for what was actually *necessary*, not just possible.

I am firmly convinced that being a progressive just means being first to the best, most just idea. If often means being ahead of your more cautious elected colleagues, and then working to build the movement for acceptance of the idea. What is possible is not static. It changes and can be changed by multiple factors, including elected officials who are trusted by those who elect them to use their platforms to help change the conversation, to help lead not just follow. I wanted to use my platform to the fullest, and that meant sponsoring legislation that was necessary and using my platform to help make the case for it even if it didn't seem possible right at that moment.

Bills I introduced that were called crazy at the time became law after I left. Ideas that I and other progressives fought for became mainstream in just a few short years. While major newspapers like the *Seattle Times* did not even cover my efforts to push for free community college because apparently it was a crazy idea when I introduced it in 2015, just a few years later, they wrote an editorial praising Seattle's mayor for introducing the same idea.[14]

Our coalition of progressive activists fighting for a broad progressive agenda had to build momentum and create a tipping point, but you never knew exactly when that tipping point would arrive. Every time we introduced legislation it gave us an organizing opportunity. Every organizing opportunity allowed us to build momentum. And eventually, our ideas would become mainstream.

When I introduced the $12 minimum-wage bill in 2015, on my first day in the state senate, businesses fought with us and said that was too high. Take it now, I advised, otherwise you'll be paying more if activists decide to file a ballot initiative, an alternative to the legislative process outlined in our state constitution that allows a group of voters to gather signatures on petitions to qualify an initiative or referendum to the ballot. The business coalition wouldn't listen and came down on our minimum-wage coalition with a vengeance, calling us Seattle liberals who didn't understand the rest of the state and putting forward doom-and-gloom prognoses of the consequences of the $15 minimum wage we had just passed in Seattle. After more courageous organizing by fast-food workers, our coalition of progressive allies got a $13.50 minimum wage plus paid sick leave on the ballot two years later and it passed overwhelmingly across the state. Three years after that, I sat on the House of Representatives Education and Labor Committee as we passed the federal $15 minimum-wage bill through committee and then on the floor of the House with 228 Democrats and three Republicans voting for it.

Momentum. It builds achingly slowly sometimes, but it does build. And you always have to be ready for that tipping point moment when it becomes clear that all the organizing work has finally paid off.

I don't believe anything truly significant that we've accomplished would have happened if we'd played it small or listened to those who said the political will wasn't there. I ran for office because I saw how broken the system was and how many people were suffering deeply and had been largely ignored. The scale of the crises people faced were enormous and our solutions needed to match that scale in boldness. If I was going to stay in elected office, I wanted to make damn sure I kept my vision big and honed my ability to pay attention to my instinct and my conscience, two things that are too often beaten out of us as women of color, in particular. They had served me well until now and I believed they were the basis of my success. I just had to keep fighting the pressure to give those up for more temporary successes or promises of power.

My decision to run for the state senate was a good one: it gave me a real opportunity to test my theory of change, see what worked and what didn't, and understand the challenges and the opportunities of change at the state legislature level. People who want to run for office are often interested in immediately running for Congress. This is certainly not out of the question and it can happen! But too many people overlook local and state offices, which are far easier to run for and win and also serve as an important place to gain an understanding of what being an elected representative requires.

I also was able to shine a light on the importance of state legislatures, and work with numerous groups—from the Women Donors Network to progressive state allies—to understand the barriers to elected office for women of color in particular, to rethink the need to support progressive organizers to office, and to build real structures that could leverage this new form of power. These were all newer ideas at the time, but in the wake of Donald Trump's election in 2016, they began to take off and get more attention.

Serving in the state senate opened my eyes to the importance of the issues that state legislatures deal with and the major decisions they make each year that affect millions of people. I had honed my skills, tasted humility, and had a few victories. I take my hat off to all elected officials for the sacrifices they make. Particularly in these supposedly part-time state legislatures, the legislators from the left end of the spectrum are fighting righteous fights against a highly organized and resourced opposition. I understood even more fully what we needed to do to build the infrastructure for real progressive change, and I was more than ready for whatever would come next.

5

Congress: Testing My Theory at the Highest Level

STEVE AND I HAD SPOKEN BEFORE ABOUT WHETHER NATIONAL OFFICE would be in my future, and Steve's advice was always, "Stay open. You never know what opportunities will come up." Most of the issues I had worked on—from immigration reform to international health to foreign policy—were really federal issues, so political office at the national level seemed more appropriate to my background, but Olympia was where opportunity had presented itself and where I had landed to test my theory of change.

When it came to next steps along a career path, I had never been one to decide where I wanted to be in ten years and then position myself in such a way that I could climb the appropriate rungs on the ladder to get there. I was still the wanderer, throwing myself into the task at hand but always paying attention to what my heart said and what opportunities unfolded in front of me. I was unafraid (or at least not afraid enough) to leave things if they weren't right for me. I believed there was no choice that was permanent and that everything taught you something about what you should be doing next.

In January 2016, U.S. Congressman Jim McDermott of Seattle announced his retirement.[1] Jim had been my congressman for almost the entire two decades I lived in Seattle. Jim was mostly beloved in the district: in addition to the strong role he had played with me in those days and years following September 11, 2001, he had a great pro-labor, anti-war, progressive reputation. Still, he had been in office for twenty-eight years and there was a feeling among some that it was time for him to retire and make room for the next generation.

That hunger for new leadership was foreshadowed just a few months before, when a young state house representative named Brady Walkinshaw announced that he was going to challenge McDermott. Brady had been elected to the state House just two years before and was among a small group of progressive legislators I had gotten to know and with whom I periodically got together to strategize. A number of people had been positioning themselves for years to run for Jim's seat in anticipation that he would step down, but Brady was the first one of notable political stature to actually challenge Jim directly. I considered Brady a new friend, but when he told me he planned to challenge Jim, I said I would not be able to support him given Jim's progressive record and everything he had done for immigrants in his work with me after September 11.

Even if Jim had stepped down and the seat had been open, it never would have occurred to me that I could run in that district because a few years earlier, in 2012, redistricting split up Seattle and had redrawn our home just outside of the congressional district that Jim now represented. As a result, I now resided in the Ninth Congressional District, only twenty blocks away.

On January 1, I flew to New York for a meeting on a national project called the Women's Economic, Social and Political Action Network (WESPAN) that I was co-leading with a wonderful feminist activist named Dorothy Thomas. The next day, we were sitting around a conference table with the women we had pulled together for the meeting, when I suddenly noticed my phone blowing up with texts and phone calls. Curious, I looked at the phone and saw the first text from Ilya Sheyman, the national co-director of MoveOn.

"McDermott has stepped down. Are you going to run for Congress?" he texted. "You should run! We're all talking about you running! Run!"

Now completely distracted from my meeting, I looked at the list of texts and calls coming in: they included a former state senator, national immigrant rights advocates, labor union friends. *What was going on?*, I thought.

"I can't run, I don't live in the district," I texted back to Ilya.

Ilya texted back immediately: "You don't have to live in the district."

I didn't have to live in the district I would run to represent? This was news to me. I looked it up. Ilya was right! To run for Congress, according to the Constitution, you have to be at least twenty-five years old, have been a U.S. citizen for at least seven years, and live in the state where you are running for office. But there is no requirement to live within the exact boundaries of the district you represent.

To be perfectly honest, I thought this was very strange. But at that moment, it suddenly occurred to me that I had an opportunity to run for Congress, a chance to test my theory of change on a much bigger platform. Congress!

The women I was with noticed my sudden preoccupation with my phone. "Is everything okay?" one of them asked. "What's going on?"

I had known most of these women for years. They were activists, philanthropists, and colleagues who had done deep work in the activist community and had fought for justice for most of their lives. Even though they had never been drawn to elected office themselves, they had been thought partners with me along my journey and believed wholeheartedly in what I was trying to do and in me. During my state senate campaign, they had organized fundraisers, given generously themselves (often for the first time), and even come out to stand on street corners with me and wave signs on election day. I trusted their judgment and I needed their advice.

"Ladies, I've got some thinking to do and need advice." I responded. "People are asking me to run for Congress—can we go have lunch and discuss?"

Lunch was filled with amazement, followed by enthusiasm, then caution, then pros and cons and more conversation. It was cut short by my scheduled flight to Seattle. By the time I got to the airport to fly home, I realized that I was serious enough about this prospect that I needed to alert

Steve immediately. I was—in truth—nervous about how he would react. A couple of years back when someone had suggested that I run for Congress, Steve had hesitations, mainly because of what it would have meant for our family. Janak was in high school at the time, and the demands of Steve's job meant that he would not have had much flexibility to deal with my travel schedule. He also knew—even from my limited experience of being in the state senate—that being in office, travel, and stress could take a real toll on personal relationships, especially as this would entail living in DC for half the year. I had largely agreed with him. I had my own strong desire to be available for Janak in the last years before they went off to college. But now, Janak was about to graduate from high school and the reality of a congressional run seemed more possible.

I called Steve from the airport. "Babe, Jim McDermott just announced his retirement and lots of people are telling me I should run. Turns out I can run for that seat even though we were just redistricted out of that district. I feel like I have to think seriously about it and I want to talk to you about it when I get home," I said, somewhat nervous to be breaking this news so suddenly.

There was a long pause on the other end. I need not have worried. Steve has always been my biggest champion, strategist, fundraiser, and love-supporter. He believed wholeheartedly in me and what I could do.

"Come home," he said. "That's an incredible opportunity. Let's talk about it."

When I got home, we ran through all the things we had to think about: loss of salary while I campaigned again and the enormity of a congressional race, among other things. We had only about a week to make up our minds about this monumental life-altering decision.

I didn't think living outside the new boundaries of the district was insurmountable, because I had lived in the same place for so long and, through all my activist work, done so much that covered the geography of the district. In some of my brief conversations with others, a few people had advocated that we move into an apartment in the district, or other such ideas. These did not seem like honest solutions. Steve and I decided that we would just publicly pledge that, if I won, we would move into the district. The voters deserved a congressmember who lived in the district, in our opinion. But we didn't have the money, nor did it seem right, to pick up and move right then or to engage in other less-than-honest shenanigans. This was a huge deal—giving up the house and neighborhood we had loved and lived in for decades now—but we figured we would worry about that all later if I actually won.

The other big discussion that stands out to me was not a discussion about winning, but about being willing to lose. Steve reminded me of the discussion we had had when I ran for the state senate. We had agreed then that running for that office was only worth doing if I was willing to lose, if in losing I stood my ground on core principles. If I could take that—losing because I stayed true to my principles—then the pressure to win would ease a bit and I was free to run with all I had. That had worked in my state senate race and when I became a senator: I may have made mistakes and learned from them, but I never, ever felt that I betrayed myself, my principles, or my people.

Now, I had to answer the same question as I decided whether or not to run for Congress: was I willing to lose, as long as I didn't budge from my core principles, and I put everything on the table during the race? My belief is that people get into trouble when they want to win more than they want to stay true. We see it all the time, whether it involves actual corruption or just selling out or doing nothing out of fear of not getting elected or reelected.

My answer was almost instantaneous. Yes, I was willing to lose if the voters didn't want what I stood for. I could accept that, even if it would be a very public loss. It would still be a very rare opportunity to advance my values and principles, to put forward my theory of change. I was all in, and so was Steve.

There is real freedom in making such a decision. Time stood still for a moment as the calmness of making the decision washed over me, even as the interminably long to-do list was unfolding.

Everything unrolled quickly from there.

Within days, multiple other people announced their run, including a county councilmember named . . . *Joe* McDermott. He was no relation to Jim, but conventional wisdom was that with a name like that, the race was his to lose. Within a week, there were six candidates who had declared their candidacies. Brady had also raised a remarkable $233,000 in just the one month after he had announced, a testament to his fundraising ability.

I began by making calls to people I trusted, people who understood politics, understood me, and would tell me honestly what they thought. Steve and I discussed who we could talk to and Steve came up with Jeremy Bird's name. Steve knew Jeremy from his work on the Walmart campaign.[2] Jeremy had been the national organizing director for the first Obama campaign, and was known as a whiz kid on organizing.

Jeremy responded immediately and, remarkably, he said he would get on the first plane out to Seattle so we could talk it through. He was hugely helpful in the process and I am forever grateful for his faith in me and his early work to get me started when few others were doing so.

Meanwhile, there were some prominent women leaders who approached me and essentially told me not to run. They felt that it was "not my turn" and I wouldn't be able to raise the money I needed. Apparently, they were recruiting another well-known, well-placed, well-funded white woman who would be able to run and win in this seat. And this was important, they said, because we had never had a woman in this seat before!

I was sucker punched. I was a woman too! And a woman of color at that, with a long history of organizing in the region. For all the doubts and insecurities that I had experienced along the way and still did, the truth was I had also built my confidence in myself over the years, bit by bit. I had learned to trust myself. Each time I did something and succeeded, I realized I could do more. I worked hard at not listening to the doubtful voices that would often arise, and I focused on giving myself my own positive reinforcement. I was also sick and tired of other people assuming I couldn't do something when everything in my career had shown that *I could, and I would.* It angered me to no end that the specific barriers and struggles of women of color in particular were often papered over. Where others had access to money, relationships to those in power, or opportunities to be in certain places at certain times that would smooth their path over, too many of us had to run the same race but at a starting point that was way behind them. And yet, still, when we reached certain heights in spite of those barriers, we were not taken seriously. I refused to be part of that equation, and I certainly was not going to let someone tell me I was not capable enough to do something or that it wasn't "my turn." "Turns" were made up by those in power to keep those they didn't know or want out. Time to "turn" the tables, baby!

I listened carefully to those white women, and then calmly retorted that I was a hell of an organizer and, if I decided to run, I would pour heart and soul into it. Whoever this other person was, she'd better be ready. (As it turned out, that woman never ended up running.)

Just a few weeks later, on January 21, I kicked off my campaign at Seattle Central College. My slogan was "Bold, Progressive, Unafraid."[3] Surrounded by a few dozen activists, both organizational and elected leaders, I declared my candidacy for the U.S. House of Representatives. It was hugely exciting. The room was packed with friends from diverse communities, again people who knew me and knew my work. The excitement about an activist woman of color running for Congress had also brought out some of the teachers of color at the college who had followed my work and decided to bring their students for a practical lesson in politics and political change.

Surrounded by cheering activists and advocates, I announced my candidacy for Congress: "I'm running for Congress because our system is rigged for corporations and the wealthy. But we can fight back. The time has come to tackle this inequality."

I was off and running for Congress. I could hardly believe it.

We had an enormous amount of work to do. Brady was ahead of all the rest of the candidates including me; he had spent months preparing for his campaign, hiring staff and readying himself. And while I and many

others had not supported his challenging Jim McDermott, the political truth is that he had earned some admiration and credibility in some
circles for taking on an incumbent. We were now all trying to catch up.

Now that I had entered the race as a strong and unapologetic progressive, Brady was repositioning himself as just as progressive but easier to
work with and more effective than me. This was seemingly centered on
the idea that I was too controversial, pushed too hard, and was unreason-
able about my progressive demands. It was a narrative that appealed to
many wealthy elites who were already angry with me for my participation
in the $15 minimum-wage fight and my opposition to my Democratic
colleagues who supported payday lending. It was also a narrative that
often follows women of color who simply are not indoctrinated into the
mainstream ways of thinking of problems or solutions, fight hard for their
communities that have long been left out of the conversations, and refuse
to go alone with the status quo bias.

The first thing we had to do was hire a campaign manager. Jeremy
helped us find Aaron Bly, a skilled organizer who had run Obama's field
campaign in Ohio and had run other Congressional campaigns. He was
moving from the East Coast for the job, so it would be some weeks before
he could join us. Once again, our dining table became our office as we
worked to put together a logo and website, hire an organizer, a photogra-
pher, a fundraiser . . . the list was never-ending!

Brady and Joe had also already started racking up endorsements. Awk-
wardly, some were friends of mine who had endorsed before they knew
I was running and some of them felt uncomfortable pulling back an
endorsement they had already promised. I had already announced that
I would take no corporate PAC contributions—mine would be a campaign powered by the people, not by lobbyists—and I had to quickly raise
enough money to make me competitive with Brady, in particular, by the
March 31 quarterly Federal Election Commission reporting deadline.

As I called everyone I knew for campaign contributions, regardless of
the amount, and began the process of asking and applying for endorsements, I was floored by the response. Just like in my state senate race, I had

the enormous advantage of my long history of work in the community and relationships I had built over many years. People knew me and had seen me work. They knew what I stood for and they knew what I would fight for. I didn't need to introduce myself; I just needed to tell them this was what I wanted to do, and they came on board.

When people ask me what they should do if they want to run for office, I tell them to do real work in the community first. People will get to know you and they will stand by you if they see that you are serious about lifting the whole community up and not just yourself. Too many people want to immediately run for office before doing the work and building the relationships. That can work, too, but building a community of support through real work gets you lots of credibility. I also felt that every experience I had, even ones I hadn't enjoyed so much, paid off now. I'd learned from each experience and I had relationships—genuine relationships, even if they were from way back—that I could build upon. Did I call my old Georgetown friends from when I was still in my teens? You bet I did. Did I call my PATH friends and my early immigrant-organizing friends? Did I call on my more recent colleagues in the state legislature?

Yes, I called on them all, and nearly universally, they understood what I was about. Though my circumstances had changed over the years, I was still that same fighter. I was relatively new in politics according to the way the game is usually played, but I can tell you there is no substitute for doing the work wherever you are.

By the end of the first quarter, I had raised an unbelievable $437,583 (in line with what Brady had raised even though he had a $233,000 head start).[4] I had also secured some very important endorsements from EMILY's List, NARAL, and the first union to support my candidacy, UFCW 21.[5] I had also won the early individual support of Representative Keith Ellison, the co-chair of the Congressional Progressive Caucus at the time, as well as Indian American congressman Ami Bera.

Still, things were tough. Some people felt that I should not have entered the race, given that Brady had already declared. Rumors were circulating that Brady was much younger than me and would be able to stay long enough to gain the kind of seniority in Congress necessary to help the region. Many corporate leaders who had fought me on the $15 minimum wage had endorsed and contributed maximum amounts to Brady or Joe, hoping for anyone but me. My own state senate majority leader, Sharon Nelson, who I had worked closely with on payday lending, had endorsed Joe McDermott, who had preceded her in the state senate. Some of my Senate colleagues who had pushed payday lending and opposed raising the minimum wage had also endorsed Brady. My opponents and some of the press were also trying to make a big deal out of the fact that I didn't live in the district—even though I had lived in that same house in that district for two decades, until I was redistricted just outside it. My public pledge to move back into the district if I won didn't seem to take that issue off the table as we thought it might.

This campaign was at an exponentially higher level than the state senate campaign. Jeremy and Aaron estimated I would need to raise about $2 million (it ended up being closer to $3 million by the end) compared to the $311,934 I had raised for my state senate campaign, which seemed like an enormous amount of money at the time. I would also need a big team, with field organizers who would help me run a real ground game.

First, I had to find a field director who knew how to really organize. This was a departure from how most folks think about field organizing in big-time politics. At the time, field organizing was largely dismissed as a waste of money and time. Better to spend on TV or mail. Of course, I planned to use TV and mail as well, but my instincts told me that field organizing and direct voter contact would be key to winning and I needed someone I could really trust on that front. I turned to my former organizing director at OneAmerica, a veteran organizer and leader named David Ayala-Zamora. David had left SEIU to come to OneAmerica and help build our statewide organizing efforts. He had been a true partner to me for five years until I left OneAmerica in 2012.

David had a powerful story about his early days of activism and organizing. In his home country, El Salvador, he was tortured for his union leadership and political activity and was exiled to the United States during what was then termed the Sanctuary Movement to support asylees from El Salvador. He was a remarkable mixture of inspiration, dedication, and organizing prowess. He understood what made people tick, and he and I both knew that to win a campaign, you had to inspire people and make them feel a part of something much bigger. He knew how to build leadership, how to develop and manage young people who were learning what it meant to organize, and he was loyal to me to the bone. David had left OneAmerica to work on the $15 minimum-wage campaign at a nonprofit called Working Washington, and when I called him to work on my campaign, he was getting ready to leave Seattle to rejoin his wife and children in Arizona. It took me about a week to convince him that he should stay in Seattle for another eight months and help me win the seat for Congress.

"Yes," he told me on the phone. "We need to elect you. The movement needs this, and you are the right person. Let's do it."

Together, we decided to divide the district up into five areas and hire a field organizer for each area. Each organizer had goals they had to reach: doors knocked, phone calls made, and volunteers recruited. In the end, our campaign (both primary and general election) knocked on 120,000 doors, made over 240,000 phone calls, and mobilized 1,200 volunteers. At the time, this was a scale relatively unheard of in a congressional campaign. Much later in 2018, the Democratic Congressional Campaign Committee and the Democratic National Committee would finally come around to the idea of deep and broad field campaigns—largely pushed by the energy of Indivisible, MoveOn, and other grassroots groups who were the power behind the resistance efforts against Donald Trump—and almost every candidate in 2018 who won a congressional race delivered on these kinds of campaigns with phenomenal numbers. At the time, however, this approach was rare, and the incredible field momentum drove our phenomenal success on so many other levels.

Elected officials are the public face of the political system, and it's true that we are the ones who take the rap for everything good and bad, and we're the ones who have our names on the ballot. But our work is only possible because of extraordinary people who stand next to us, are deeply loyal to the bigger picture of what we are trying to achieve, and also sacrifice tremendously—people whose names are not on any ballots but without whom we would not win. That's true both when we serve in office but also while we are campaigning.

Campaigns are also a powerful forum for activism: there are a range of roles for people who are considering "going into politics," and it is a real learning experience to see all the things that are required to run a campaign, in a very compressed period of time. We needed people who were good at finance, fundraising, and door knocking, but we also needed people who would inspire others to engage with the campaign. One of my all-time favorite volunteers was a young man named Andrzej who was a phenomenal baker. He often baked goodies for our canvassing days, and he made the campaign feel like a home. We had many volunteers who had never participated in a political campaign before, including some who were so nervous to go and knock on doors but learned how to do it—and then excelled! One young man who seemed so certain that he would never be able to knock on doors much less convince people to vote for me ending up being a star volunteer and even convinced some people who were planning to vote for another candidate to vote for me. No matter what skills you have, a good campaign director can find a way to put them to use. And good campaigns are as much about mobilizing and inspiring people to feel a part of them as they are about the candidate and overall strategy.

My work at OneAmerica had given me another advantage: I had access to a remarkable group of people who have been by my side for years, in some cases, who sacrificed greatly to help achieve what we achieved together. Most of them had experience working for justice and on achieving political change, but they had not been involved in electoral politics. These first-timers included Yasmin Christopher (my senate legislative aide) and another young Somali American woman named Hamdi Mohamed.

Hamdi had been a volunteer during our redistricting fights when she was a college student. She was smart and well-spoken, and she had been a great spokesperson for redistricting, stepping up powerfully when we asked her to allow a news crew to follow her around. I had stayed in touch with her and I knew she was interested in working for me, so when I ran for Congress, I reached out to her and asked her to come on as a field organizer. She did a great job and went on to work for me for several years in my congressional district office running my constituent services team and even serving in leadership on my first reelection campaign, ultimately leaving after five years of working for me to run the racial equity team at the county level.

Throughout my career, one of my goals has been to try to lift up others and create pathways for them that had not existed for me. I loved seeing so many of the women of color, in particular, who moved from working for me to holding powerful leadership positions elsewhere. It was hard to let them go sometimes, but it was almost like watching your kids spread their wings. It was good—we needed to create leadership at all levels and these women were powerhouses in their own right.

Hamdi and David were great examples of the kind of smart activists without any experience on political campaigns that helped lead my congressional campaign. I can guarantee you that until David ran my field campaign for Congress, there had never been an El Salvadorian survivor of torture/activist/leader running the field for a congressional campaign! It was game-changing for my victory, but it was also personally important as a way to ground me in this monumental challenge I had taken on. David, with Aaron's help and knowledge of the nuts and bolts of traditional campaigning, helped me implement my vision and my appreciation for his enormous role in helping me get elected is ever more bittersweet as I write this.

Shortly after I was elected, David moved to Arizona and was diagnosed with terminal stomach cancer. He died in the fall of 2018. The last time I spoke to him, he told me that he was so proud of what I was doing. David didn't use words like that lightly. He told me if I ever ran for another office, he would come back and help me again because we were really building the movement.

When I spoke at his memorial service in November 2018, before a packed church in Seattle, I recounted how David never, ever, told me my ideas were too big. Instead, he helped us all to dream bigger and build the leadership network that was the heart and soul of our campaign; with his help, we built the most powerful congressional campaign the state had ever seen, one that fought for basic rights and dignity for everyone. David knew the difference between organizing and mobilizing: mobilizing was just about turnout, but organizing was about building leadership and lasting power for the people. That is what he had done for decades. After he passed, I gave his wife a framed copy of the statement I had introduced into the Congressional Record, memorializing his life and his impact on the world.

The last text I received from David said simply this: "What kind of important journeys we have been on together." And what incredible fortune for me to have had such companions and collaborators on those journeys.

In 2004, Washington State became the first state in the country to institute a "top-two" primary system for congressional and state-level elections.[6] This means that there is no separate primary election for the Democratic Party and the Republican Party; instead the top two vote getters from the primary go on to the general election, regardless of party. Since Washington's Seventh District is extremely Democratic, this meant the top two would likely be Democrats, who would run against each other all the way through the general election.

For me, this had campaign strategy implications that would come back later as key points in the general election contest: first, I needed to keep the supporters of my opponents with me, because I would likely be competing with another Democrat for their votes if they voted for someone other than me in the primary. That, in turn, meant trying to keep things as positive as possible.

Second, I would need even more money because my race would not be over after the primary, as it could be in most Democratic districts in states across the country that operated without a top-two system. It seemed highly unlikely that a Republican would make it into the general, so the only question was who my competitor would be, assuming I made it through the primary.

Third, some political consultants in the past have put less emphasis on the primary in a top-two race, saving their money for the general election if they feel their candidate has a good chance of making it through the primary. I believed the opposite. I see primaries as critical moments to showcase momentum. A primary voter that votes for you is highly unlikely to switch candidates in the general election if you make it through the primary. The more I could do in the primary, the more loyalty and momentum I could build. If I could win big in the primary, I would also be seen as the front-runner candidate, which would help me raise the money I needed to continue organizing for November. Aaron, my campaign manager, and I wanted more than to just get through the primary, we wanted me to come out on top.

It was much harder to be directly involved and micro-managing the details of a congressional campaign than a campaign at the state level. This was bigger, and Aaron, as an experienced campaign manager, was absolutely essential to the strategy and the day-to-day operations. I desperately wanted to use the same colors and logo as for my state senate race, but Aaron and the consultants felt that we needed something new and even more bold. We hired some great national mail consultants who came

up with some drafts of potential logos. In the end (and not without some angst and disagreements), we chose a logo that was pink and purple, focused on my first name only, and had a design that looked somewhat artistically vague . . . but, if you looked closely at it, it  was a subliminal image of a bullhorn. This seemed appropriate: my campaign would amplify the voices of the people and it would do it through the megaphone of organizing.

Jeremy had also connected us to some of the most exciting and update-to-date technologies, which helped us develop a model of the most likely "Pramila voter." The technology and modeling had been used mostly in national campaigns, but this would be one of the first times to try it in a congressional district campaign. Aaron worked closely with the developers to hone the model, and it turned out to be very successful, allowing us to target our field and mail efforts carefully and also to project with incredible accuracy what the final vote count was likely to be.

We hired some excellent media consultants from the well-known firm GMMB: the *G* stood for Frank Greer, who was a Seattle native. GMMB gave our race early credibility in political circles—GMMB had worked for presidential campaigns, and Frank and his wife, Stephanie, were early and enthusiastic supporters who really believed in me and my ability to win. J. Toscano, a partner at the firm, was charged with developing my ads and we discussed how I wanted the real *me* to come out in the ads.

"I don't want to be portrayed as someone other than who I am because we think it may help me win," I remember telling Frank and J. "I don't want to run away from my immigrant story; I want to use it to win." They agreed completely and developed a set of ads that leaned into my activist background and my identity, getting across the authenticity of who I was and the bold vision I was running on. One of the ads, called "Dream," delivered a simple script that worked in my immigrant background, my activism, my boldness, my effectiveness, and the fact that this was a movement of WE—all in thirty seconds! It said:

I came to America to go to college and went to work helping others find their American dream too: stopping illegal deportations by the Bush administration, fighting for immigration reform, funding apprenticeship programs for women and people of color, and helping negotiate Seattle's $15 minimum wage. There's a lot more to do so working people have a fighting chance in this economy. Join our movement so we can get it done!

The ad felt like the real me, not some made-up me. Our campaign also put out three digital ads, all on bold issues I was running on: "Unequal" on equal pay; "Debt" on the high cost of college; and "Boys" on gender ratio/representation in Congress. They were smart, sassy, and bold ads and I loved them. The digital campaign ended up winning a silver award in the political ad awards competition called the Pollies. Our ads were second only to Bernie Sanders's campaign ad—not bad at all!

I already had a Bernie connection—albeit an unusual one—before I ever thought of running for Congress. In August 2015, in commemoration of the eightieth anniversary of Social Security and the fiftieth anniversary of Medicare, several social justice organizations, including Social Security Works and the Puget Sound Alliance for Retired Americans, were holding a huge rally. They knew it would be huge because the organizers had secured the presence of a perceived longshot candidate for president of the United States, Senator Bernie Sanders. I was in my first year at the Washington State Senate and I had not even a thought that I would be running for Congress some six months later. I was honored that they had asked me to speak at the event just before Bernie spoke.

A few days before the rally, Phil Fiermonte, one of Bernie's top advisors, called me and said the senator was going to do a rally for his presidential campaign at the University of Washington that night after the Social Security rally. Phil asked if I would be one of the people onstage who introduced him. They seemed to know of my progressive reputation and work on the $15 minimum wage and felt it matched perfectly with Bernie's message and campaign.

I was incredibly surprised and deeply honored. I told Phil that I would love to do it but also wanted to make sure they knew I had not yet endorsed him.

Phil seemed taken aback on the phone. "Really? We thought you had. But why haven't you?"

I told Phil I deeply respected everything Bernie was doing on inequality, college affordability, and so much more, but I needed to know more about his views on guns and gender and racial equity before I could endorse him.

"I understand completely if you want to ask someone else who has already endorsed him to introduce him. No hard feelings!" I said.

Phil said that made sense, but they would get me a VIP ticket to watch Bernie's speech anyway and hoped I would endorse him in the future. I agreed, and excitedly made plans with Steve and Janak to attend the rally that Saturday evening.

The day before the rally, I got another call from Phil.

"The senator would like you to introduce him," he said. "He understands that you haven't endorsed him, but would you also be willing to sit down with him for a one-on-one meeting to talk about your questions?"

"Of course," I said, and we set a time for Bernie, his wife, Jane, and I to meet after the Social Security rally and before the evening campaign event at the University of Washington.

The Saturday of the Social Security rally dawned bright and beautiful. By the time I got to Westlake Park where the rally would take place, a crowd of over five thousand people had gathered to hear Bernie speak. The coalition that had put together the rally was broad and diverse, with plenty of folks of color on the steering committee. The crowd, however, was largely white, which unfortunately was not atypical for Seattle.

I was introduced briefly to Bernie in the speakers' area next to the stage, and I thanked him for taking the time to meet with me later. I gave a rabble-rousing speech about how we needed to expand Social Security and Medicare and had everyone in the crowd fired up and ready for the main event: Bernie. As I came off the stage, Bernie gave me a big hug with a delighted smile and said, "Hey, you said everything I was going to say!"

The rest became history very quickly. Just as Bernie was thanking Seattle for being there, several Black Lives Matter activists made their way onto the stage and demanded the mic. After some minutes of discussion and argument, they were given control of the mic. They spoke for some time about Michael Brown and the many who have died at the hands of police who were supposed to be protecting them, about the racism of Seattle, and about the pain they felt. They also asked for a four-and-a-half-minute silence for Brown, to symbolize the number of hours his body was left in the street, after which they agreed that they would let Bernie resume his speech.

After waiting for a long time in the hot sun to hear Bernie speak, the crowd was up in arms about the interruption; they eventually quieted down but the quiet was punctuated by racist grumblings. When the silence ended, however, it was not clear that the activists would indeed allow Bernie to resume and, eventually and with tremendous anguish, the event organizers closed down the event and Bernie left without speaking.

When the Black Lives Matter activists first took over the event, the (mostly white) crowd turned ugly. From my vantage point near the front, it was hard to identify exactly what happened first, but it quickly turned nasty. White and black people called each other names. Black people called white people racist and vice versa. Middle fingers were raised in the air against the protestors. People booed the protestors and refused to chant Black Lives Matter with them. The rhetoric became worse, divided like two sides in a war.

In the speakers' tent, I noticed two young black girls who were the grandchildren of Gina Owens, a long-time community activist and leading voice in the fight for single-payer healthcare and ultimately for the Affordable Care Act. Gina's daughter had died from lack of access to affordable healthcare and Gina's story about her daughter's death caught the attention of our U.S. senator Patty Murray. Murray related the story on the floor of the Senate during a speech about the ACA, and when President Obama ultimately signed the bill into law, Marcie, one of Gina's granddaughters stood right by President Obama in the front as he signed the bill.

But now Gina's granddaughters were standing in the tent, weeping. When the crowd turned angry, they felt the racism and heard the shouting directed at the black activists onstage and they were terrified by the raw anger directed at black people like them. I immediately went over to comfort them and we stood there in a tight little circle with our arms around each other. It was deeply disturbing to see my supposedly progressive community being torn apart by what seemed to be an erupting form of racism as white people recoiled at the idea that even a progressive white presidential candidate had a lot more work to do to address racial injustice in America.

That night, I couldn't sleep. I finally got out of bed at four a.m. and wrote a long Facebook post in which I tried to make sense of what had happened the previous night. It felt like an important moment and why we absolutely had to talk about the institutionalized racism that continued to show itself at every turn in our communities.[7]

"It is clear to me that what happened at the rally is one small result of centuries of racism," I wrote in my post. "As a country, we still have not recognized or acknowledged what we have wrought, and what we continue to inflict, on black people. The much larger, deeply entrenched results are those that we see every day: how black kids as young as two years of age are being disciplined differently in their daycares and pre-K classes. How black people are routinely denied jobs that white people get with the same set of experiences and skills. How black people—women and men—continue to die at the hands of police, and in domestic violence, and on the streets. How black mothers must tell their children as young as seven or eight that they have to be careful about what pants or hoodies they wear, or that they should not assert their rights if stopped by police officers. How this country supports an institutionalized form of racism called the criminal justice system that makes profit—hard, cold cash—on jailing black and brown people."

I ended the piece with my belief that Bernie Sanders had a very important role to play in the movement to lift up racial injustice and fight for real solutions, and stated that we would look back on this moment as a turning point in demanding more from progressive presidential candidates on race.

The final paragraphs of the piece were a reflection of my own turning mind:

One of the questions that I have been thinking deeply about since the rally was disrupted is this: How do we call people in even as we call them out? As a brown woman, the only woman of color in the state senate, often the only person of color in many rooms, I am constantly thinking about this—even if it is often because I have to, not because I want to.

To build a movement, we have to be much wiser than those who are trying to divide us. We have to take our anger and rage and channel it into building, growing, loving, holding each other up. We need our outlets too, our places of safety where we can say what we think without worrying about how it's going to land, where we can call out even our white loved ones, friends, and allies for what they are not doing.

But in the end, if we want to win for all of us on racial, economic and social justice issues, we need multiple sets of tactics, working in tandem. Some are disruptive tactics. Some are loving tactics. Some are truth-telling tactics. Some can only be taken on by white people. Some can only be taken on by people of color. Sometimes we need someone from the other strand to step in and hold us up. Other times, we have to step out and hold them up.

This is bigger than any one presidential candidate. It's as big as all of us. Regardless of who is elected president in 2016, we all still live together. Each of us has a different role to play but we all have to hold the collective space for movement-building together. It's the only way we move forward.

Within an hour, the post had gone viral and Seattle's alternative newspaper, *The Stranger*, asked if they could reprint it as an op-ed. The intense interest in the piece and the conversation it generated showed me how people desperately need ways to think about race and be encouraged to talk about it.

My meeting after the rally was still on with Bernie, though I didn't know how he had reacted to the protests that stopped him from speaking. I took

Janak, then eighteen years old, and we met Bernie and Jane in the dark upstairs room of a Capitol Hill tavern. They were both absolutely lovely, even though Bernie was clearly still very upset about what had happened and felt that perhaps he wasn't being given the credit that he deserved for his own history of civil rights activism going all the way back to the 1960s.

We had a fantastic conversation. He answered my questions about his position on guns (that his position as a U.S. senator from Vermont, where guns were popular for use in the outdoors, was different than his position when running for president). He gave me insight into his history of supporting Jesse Jackson's campaign and working in the South during the civil rights struggle, and he told me about the work he was doing right then to put together a real racial equity platform. I told him that I felt he needed to say the words "institutionalized racism" much more often and speak directly to how it exists in so many of the systems of oppression we are still fighting. He agreed he needed to do that and said he would that very night at the rally. I was impressed at the seriousness with which he listened and paid attention. It was an excellent first meeting.

It took me another two months or so and a few conversations with his campaign team before I endorsed Bernie, but when I did, I became one of the first elected officials in the state to endorse him. Many Seattle elites tsk-tsked my decision, calling it impractical—and for some Hillary supporters, even a betrayal of Democratic values for not supporting the person who was already being promoted as the de facto nominee. I was clear when I endorsed Bernie that if Hillary won the primary, I would be fully supportive of her in the general election. But for me, the primary was about who we really wanted the president to be, and for me, that was Bernie. His greatest strengths were his rare authenticity as a different kind of leader, the consistency of his platform over the years, and his deep commitment to push for bold solutions like the $15 minimum wage, Medicare for All, and College for All. He was building a movement for bold structural change and you could feel the electricity of the crowd at the rally.

I was all in for Bernie.

At the time of the rally, I wasn't even thinking about running for Congress. Almost five months later, I declared my candidacy for Congress. A few months after that, Bernie came back to Seattle for another rally that was expected to turn out ten thousand people. I had not been asked to speak at this one, because Bernie had so far not endorsed any candidates for Congress. Instead, I was asked to stand on stage with other elected officials who had endorsed him, and I agreed. At the last minute, just as I was hanging around backstage, I got a call from Phil. "Do you want to speak at the rally?" he asked. "Bernie would like you to! But you have to go out there literally NOW!" My head spinning, I headed up onto the circular stage with no notes, speaking from my head and heart. I got the crowd up on their feet and cheering wildly!

That spring, sometime in March, my campaign manager got a call from Bernie's digital team. They said they were thinking about seeing if Bernie's enormous list that generated millions of dollars for his campaign in small-dollar donations could also help other candidates. Bernie decided he would officially endorse and send out an email to his list to raise money for three progressive women in their bids for Congress: me, Zephyr Teachout in New York State, and Lucy Flores in Nevada. "We have no idea if this will generate anything," his staffer said. "But we figure we'll try it. Don't count on anything though," he cautioned. "It might generate nothing, $10,000 or $50,000. No idea."

"Sure," Aaron said. "We won't expect anything but thanks for thinking of us!"

We heard nothing more about it for a couple of weeks and we figured perhaps Bernie had changed his mind.

From the beginning of the campaign, all the staffers in my campaign office had set a "bell alert" to ding whenever someone donated, no matter how much. One day in late April, I was at work at our campaign headquarters when I started to hear lots of bells dinging in rapid succession—ding, ding, ding, ding, ding! It was a nonstop cacophony of noise. My team was in shock—what was happening? Then someone looked at their computer and realized that Bernie had sent out that email to his supporters for all three of us.[8] Within five days, his list had raised over $180,000 for each one of us—that was over half a million dollars for all three of us! This was incredible, stunning, bewildering, even.[9] Money was such an essential part of the campaign; in my first quarter, after hundreds of hours of call time—where you sit in a dark room calling potential donor after donor to make your pitch and ask for money—we had raised over $400,000. Now, in just five days, we had raised an amount equal to almost half of that, and it was from small-dollar donors who would give again and again and again. That effort also brought us more than twenty thousand new individual contributors, and most importantly, name recognition and progressive capital in a crowded field in the district and across the country.[10]

It was a crucial moment in the campaign that gave us a nice boost and complemented the already incredible work we were doing in the field to expand the electorate and bring in lower-propensity voters. The decision I had made to endorse Bernie—with no expectation of anything in return but just because I believed he was the right candidate at the right time— had paid off mightily.

The days leading up to the primary election were nerve-racking. I felt I would make it through the primary, the question was with what percentage of the vote? Would I be first or second? And assuming I did make it through, who would be my opponent?

A month or so before the primary, our campaign had done a poll that showed Joe McDermott in first place with around 27 percent of the projected vote, me in second place with around 26 percent, and Brady far behind at around 14 percent. But with a huge percentage of voters still recorded as undecided, there was a lifetime of baseball between that poll and the primary election and everything was on the line. We simply could not leave any effort on the table. Our grassroots army of door-to-door volunteers reached out to everyone from the Somali community in West Seattle to the city's older stalwart white liberals.[11] We were determined to talk to every single voter, to reach out to communities that had been ignored, and get everyone we possibly could to vote. Diversity was our strength; our power was the grassroots organizing we had been doing for months now.

The day of the election, Aaron had me record a fun wake-up call and thank-you message to every campaign staffer. We were out knocking on doors the whole day, until I went home to change and have a nice dinner with some close friends and my sister and her family who had come in from Portland for the party. Our party was at Hale's Palladium, a brewery event space, and the energy was infectious. Although three-quarters of the district is white, the party was brimming with diversity that showcased the kind of coalition we'd built and the strength of our campaign.[12]

In Washington, election results are typically announced once, at 8 p.m. Because we have a mail-in ballot system, sometimes close elections go on for days without resolution. Late ballots often trend more progressive because they are usually cast by younger voters and voters of color. I was hoping that this was not going to be a race where we didn't know the result on election night.

When the results came out at 8 p.m., I had more than 40 percent of the vote, far beyond our wildest expectations![13] The crowd went wild with excitement and happiness. This was OUR victory—made possible because of every single person in the room. Second place was harder to call: Brady and Joe were virtually tied at around 19 percent each. The rest of the vote was divided between the other candidates in the race. It would be at least another week before Brady pulled ahead and made it into the general election.

We had done what we set out to do: snagged first place in the primaries by a wide margin to give us considerable momentum for the general election.

Brady and Joe must have had a pact for one to endorse whichever one did not make it through. Once it was clear Brady would be competing in the general election, I called Joe and asked for his endorsement of me, but within a week, he had already endorsed Brady. That led to the media predicting that Joe's followers would automatically go to Brady and that, together, their percentages meant I could still lose. I did not believe that to be true. What I know about voters is they do pay attention and they want to know they matter to whomever they are voting for. While Joe's endorsement would, of course, be helpful to Brady, I believed that every voter could still be courted. That was how I always rolled: I work hard and I never believe I've won until I've won. I always run as if I'm losing, and I always want to know that if I do lose, I can honestly say I did everything I could. No regrets—that was critically important. I just had to put it all on the table and then accept the results.

For the first time in the history of Washington State, this congressional seat would be contested by two Democrats in the general election. This had not happened before because the top-two system only was instituted in 2004, and by then, Jim McDermott had a stronghold on the district with no Democrat challenging him sufficiently to make it through to the general election. Every once in a rare while, Jim had a Democrat compete in the primary against him, but that person rarely got more votes than the Republicans, who make up barely 20 percent of the district.[14]

Competitive races boost energy, good and bad. This was a big seat that hadn't been open in a long time. The stakes were high and the gloves were off now.

As the front-runner, it made no strategic sense for me to run a negative campaign at all, nor did I want to do that. I hate nasty campaigning and I had hoped we could keep it out of this competition. That was probably naïve. I knew Brady would be a formidable opponent. He was a whip-smart Princeton graduate who had worked for the Gates Foundation and in Latin America. He had plenty of progressive bona fides and had done excellent work in the state legislature. His family had deep roots in Seattle, with grandparents and parents who were well-known in the law, arts, and activist circles. He had received the *Seattle Times* endorsement—not a surprise since the *Times* was vociferously against the $15 minimum-wage policy and saw me as a too radical lefty for their tastes.

On policy, Brady and I had a lot of common ground. We were both minority candidates, each ostensibly "change" candidates, and fresh faces. Distinguishing ourselves from each other was going to be a challenge. The media and business voices positioned Brady as the safer choice. I was *too* progressive. When asked about our differences and to defend our candidacies, Brady and his surrogates liked to point out that other state legislators from my district had endorsed him, not me. It was true: Brady had endorsements from most—though not all—of the House colleagues he served with, which was a much larger group than the Senate. I had lost some support and endorsements from a few of my colleagues: only eight of my fellow state senators (of twenty-four Democrats) endorsed me and many who knew Brady endorsed him or stayed out.[15]

This wasn't entirely a surprise to me: many of the senators who endorsed Brady were the same legislators who had opposed my position on the payday-lending bill, and I was proud of my progressive leadership on that, despite its outcome. Others didn't agree with me on raising the minimum wage and saw this as a chance to get back at me for pushing that bill. It is interesting to note that almost all the women of the state senate endorsed me, and I had mostly swept the labor union endorsements as well as all the endorsements from progressive groups like MoveOn, Democracy For America, and the Progressive Change Campaign Committee. To me, these outside endorsements would have far more pull than legislator endorsements that do not always translate to votes.

Because our primary is in August, we only had two and a half months before the general election and things got ugly quickly. Rumors had been circulated for some time that I was all talk and no results. I faced numerous attacks on my legislative record in Olympia, with my opponents citing an "effectiveness" ranking that looked at how many bills I had passed as a state senator.

These rankings are quite simply bogus. They assume it is more beneficial to sponsor any bill that passes—regardless of whether it makes a real difference. So, sponsoring bills in the state senate that lay out a bold long-term vision—for example, increasing the minimum wage, free

community-college access, and voter registration, just to name a few—
gave me a low ranking since those bills did not pass. My critics could
then write a narrative of me as an ineffective lawmaker; they apparently would have preferred me to propose no such bills at all if they didn't
stand a chance of passing a Republican-majority body.[16] The rankings
also do not account for whether your chamber is controlled by your party,
which makes an enormous difference as to whether or not you can get
bills passed. Brady served in the House, which was Democrat-controlled,
while I served in the Republican-controlled Senate.

As a gay Cuban-American, Brady also had the backing of a majority
of the national LGBTQ groups, although I was proud to have received
a stronger rating than Brady on LGBTQ issues from the Seattle Metro-
politan Elections Committee. In what felt particularly challenging for me
to accept given my record on Latinx issues including immigration, the
Latino Victory Fund and Bold PAC, the Congressional Hispanic Caucus
PAC, both endorsed him and poured substantial money into an independent expenditure against me.

In the end, almost half a million dollars—from local and national
donors to Brady's campaign as well as from the independent expenditure
campaign—were put into nasty attack ads on television against me.[17] This
campaign had quickly become one of the most expensive non-swing district races in the country.

The attacks were personal and, in my opinion, racist and sexist. They
once again relied on tropes of women of color being "ineffective," making
a lot of noise but not getting anything done. They ignored the more than
a decade of work I had done in the hardest of times after September 11,
2001, fighting for human rights, building coalitions, and helping to bring
about some of our city's and state's most progressive laws around immigrant and refugee policy as well as other progressive issues. I wish I could
say I wasn't affected by those attack ads from another Democrat, but I
would be lying.

When I saw the ads, I went to a small corridor of the campaign office
where no one could see me and sat on the floor and sobbed. Steve came to

find and comfort me, telling me that this was the nature of politics and I couldn't take it personally. He told me that people knew me, knew who I was, and would not be affected by the ads. He was trying to make me feel better, but both of us knew it was hard not to take these attacks personally. And it was also true that half a million dollars of television ads on prime-time TV in the last days of a campaign could definitely sway the still significant number of undecided voters that we needed to win.

We had to respond.

Within twenty-four hours, my campaign pulled together that response. A group of supporters called a press conference that I did not attend. We had decided it was more strategic for me not to be there and to have a fierce response come directly from my supporters, focusing on what many of them saw as the sexist and somewhat racist nature of the ads. Senator Sharon Nelson released a statement that said:

> As a woman in office, I'm really saddened to see desperate, Trump-style attacks on women and their accomplishments being used here in Washington State. Sen. Jayapal's opponent and his allies have launched demeaning personal attacks on Pramila, diminishing her accomplishments.

She and others called the attack ads "dog whistles" and demanded that the "dark money" attacks stop and we get back to a positive campaign.

At the same time, my campaign released a counterattack ad that conveyed similar messages about not needing hateful, sexist attack ads in our district and emphasized my positive message.

Everything exploded after that. Sides were drawn and fierce attacks started. Several white male columnists—including the very popular Dan Savage, founding editor of *The Stranger*—ran columns about me saying I was too sensitive and condemning my counter ads. Some of these pundits were on the radio saying that my attacks were uncalled for—completely leaving out that the opposition had put half a million dollars into attacking me. *The Seattle Times*—which had already published a nasty editorial that not only endorsed Brady but claimed that I had not really done what I had claimed I had done—chimed in as well.

In retrospect, this was probably nothing compared to the negative attacks other candidates have faced. But the difference was that these negative attacks were coming from other Democrats. Most candidates, by the general election time, are not fighting against other candidates in their own party. The general election is typically a time for everyone to come together around a candidate, but that isn't possible in a top-two primary. I understood intellectually why Brady was attacking me; he was trailing in the polls and figured this was his last option and he was willing to go there. But it didn't make it any easier to digest in the moment.

In the end, I think the ads may have backfired on his campaign. Seattle voters generally want to see positive campaigns and given my record of achievement, along with the incredible field campaign we had run, Steve was probably right. I think voters felt they knew me and I'm not sure that negative ad changed many minds. When our doorknockers went out to canvass, we tracked what—if anything—people said about the ads. The vast majority, if they had seen them, didn't like them and were quite angry about them. If they had seen Brady's ad, they had also seen our ad and they tended to agree with us that it was unwarrantedly negative.

As angry as I was with Brady and his team at the time, I understand that the stakes were high and his options were few. I would like to believe that we can all run positive campaigns, but politics is not generally guided by positivity. Media and others like controversy and play it up whenever possible. But too often attack ads seem to be based on racial or gender stereotypes: the ads try to imply things without actually saying them, and they feast on poking at deep and sometimes unconscious biases about women and people of color in particular.

Elections are a public verdict. Voters, in their supreme wisdom, give you a report card that is blasted to everyone everywhere. That's what an election is. And you, as a candidate, have to be secure enough to recognize that this is the ultimate beauty of democracy—not a personal reflection of your potential in the world, but simply the way democracy works.

Whether you win or not, you are put in that position by the voters. I had to stay positive.

November 8, 2016—it was election night. I was running for Congress and Hillary Clinton and Donald Trump were running for president.

By the time I arrived at my election night party, things were hopping. But strange things were happening, and everything felt a little topsy-turvy. An anarchist marching band had decided to pop into the same venue as our party. Since it was a public space, the venue managers could not kick out the band, so this twelve-person brass band played mind-numbingly loud music, making my head feel like it would explode. The national results were coming in like ominous clouds. It had come down to Wisconsin and Michigan, and Clinton's path to success seemed to be quickly disappearing. The local results were supposed to come out at 8 p.m., but 8 p.m. came and went without news. What was happening? A reporter came on TV and said that Brady appeared to have a lead in Snohomish County in the northern part of the district—this was a tiny part of the district, but it immediately sent fear through me. I felt like I could barely speak, and I was starting to get nauseous.

My family, my campaign leadership team, and I were sitting in an open loft-like section above the main floor where the party was taking place, so we could see what was going on but those below could not see us. Our intention was that I would make an entrance down the steps to join the party when the results were announced. But it was 8:05, 8:10, 8:15, 8:20 and still no results. By 8:40, there were still no results. The crowd downstairs was getting antsy. CNN was calling North Carolina for Trump and the stock market was plummeting.

"We have to change the speech for a Trump win," I mumbled in disbelief. I had both victory and concession speeches drafted, but both of them assumed a win by Clinton. We would now have to adjust that.

Suddenly, my campaign manager said that he had received an odd message from a political tech genius that said he had seen results on a private King County elections site that showed me way ahead of Brady. But we couldn't be sure it was right, still nothing had been announced, and no TV stations were announcing anything about the race. I was practically hyperventilating—and also feeling bad that I had not gone down to the main room to talk to my supporters. I was simply too nervous. I had thought the results would be out long before this. The mood downstairs was getting even gloomier: my supporters were realizing that Clinton was losing and they were frustrated that my results weren't out. Just as I was deciding I would have to go down without any big announcement to make, the news came from King County: the first set of results showed me with a decisive lead of 58 percent to Brady's 42 percent.

HALLELUJAH!

But at the very same time, it was now clear that the presidential election was almost certainly going to Trump. Most people around me had assumed that Trump's racist, anti-immigrant, sexist campaign would be easy to defeat. America could not elect *this* guy who bragged about grabbing women's pussies and called Mexicans rapists and murderers. No way. This was not universally true, however, particularly for those of us who are people of color and understand very deeply America's capacity to embrace racism. Witness my own household: one evening after Trump had announced he was running for president and we were watching his outrageous campaign unfold, Steve turned to me and said, "This will be good for Democrats. Americans will never elect such a horrible person." I immediately disagreed. "You're wrong," I told him. "I think he is going to win." Trump was digging into the simmering divisions of race and gender—and sadly, those dividing tactics have worked in the past and continue to work more than we would like to admit.

Eventually, though, I let go of that feeling, more and more convinced by his increasingly horrific statements and actions that Americans would never let him become our president. The truth was that I had not been a big Hillary Clinton fan—witness my endorsement of Bernie Sanders—but I knew she was a million times better than Trump and I had done everything I could after she won the Democratic nomination to support her, including holding a rally with Bernie where we endorsed her and pushed our supporters to turn out for her. I had been lured into thinking, along with other Democrats, that Trump's extremism would certainly lose and that Hillary would be our first woman president.

That election night, as the results were coming in, I had to come to terms with the fact that Donald Trump would be president, and I—one of very few naturalized citizens to serve in Congress—would be serving in the House of Representatives with him in the White House. I had no time to absorb anything, much less process it or know what to say about it but I had to go down and find a way to celebrate our incredible victory while at the same time recognizing what was happening in the country at large. Below me, the hall was erupting in screams and cheers, and people were chanting, "PRA-MI-LA! PRA-MI-LA!"

When I took the stage, I was enveloped in love, cheers, pride, joy. WE had done it! The Seventh Congressional District of Washington State had elected the first Indian American woman to the House of Representatives, the first woman to represent the district, and the first person of color that Democrats in Washington State had ever sent to Congress. It was truly historic, and I wanted to acknowledge the amazing community of supporters, volunteers, interns, and leaders who had helped make this possible.

After these words of celebration, I acknowledged the other reality that lay heavy across the room.

"It is increasingly likely that Donald Trump will win the presidency," I said, to almost pin-drop silence. "And if our worst fears are realized, we will be on the defense starting tomorrow and we will need to fight not just for our progressive ideals but to stop a disastrous rollback of mainstream progress in this country. . . . We will have to fight for justice like never before, and we will have to fight to protect our very basic rights and freedoms."

I thanked my supporters for having faith in me and for being a part of a movement that we would now need to keep mobilized. I wanted them to know the honor that they had bestowed on me was not lost—nor was the responsibility it carried with it. I wanted them to know that whatever was coming with Trump as president, we would weather it together and we would do it with the same love and generosity that had characterized the movement we had built through the campaign.

"This is not the fight that I would have chosen," I said, "but I WILL fight this and with you by my side, we WILL win."

6

The Movement Goes to Washington

THERE WAS REALLY NO OPPORTUNITY TO CELEBRATE MY WIN. MOST OF the country was in mourning and there was immediate work to do. In the next weeks and months, I appreciated more than ever my inside-outside organizing background, which came into play far more quickly than I expected.

For starters, labor and community advocates had organized a "vigil" at city hall for the day after Election Day, and I was asked to speak there. When I got to city hall, people were sobbing. It truly was a vigil: the soul of America felt like it had died with Trump's election. Black and brown people, LGBTQ, Muslims, Jews, women, and more—we all felt betrayed. More than despair, there was fear, palpable fear that seemed to fill the enormous lobby of city hall with a suffocating air. I hugged and held dozens of people, sometimes as they sobbed into my shoulder. We could not ignore the despair. My message to everyone was that they should not brush away what they were feeling; they had to feel it and acknowledge how real it was. We had to cry, shout, scream, even go and hide for a few days. But then—then, we needed to come back out, stand up, and fight back. We had to work for change because our country demanded it of us, because we didn't have the luxury of despair without action, because there were people around us who needed our advocacy and with whom we needed to band together and lift up what was good and true about America. We needed *us* to be a strong resistance.

I had started to do then what I would be called on to do over and over again over the next years of Trump's presidency. I was the hope dispenser. People needed a way to think about what was happening and why. Most of the time, I could do this—and on that November 9 right after the election, I conjured up strength when I felt shattered, when my stomach was in knots, and when I myself wanted to scream. Trump's election said something about how Americans saw immigrants, women, brown and black people. It wasn't a small number that voted for him—which meant, in a simplistic way, that they accepted what he had said or, at a minimum, were not angered enough by what he said to not vote for him. It felt like a personal rejection from my home country, a country that I would now represent on the national stage. I felt a sense of despair and fear that reminded me of how I felt after 9/11. But I was in a different position now, publicly elected to represent 750,000 people in our district. I had to pull it together and I had to listen to the words I was saying to others. I was an organizer, and organizers knew that strength can come in times of crisis if leaders are willing and ready to lead.

A month later, in December, I organized a big Hate Free Zone rally at Seattle Center, some fifteen years after that first rally post-9/11. This time I led it as a congresswoman-elect and the entire Democratic delegation and the governor attended and spoke.

We know how to do this, I kept reminding myself. My years of organizing experience in moments of crisis, of creating a resistance movement, of the relationships I'd built, and the facility with these kinds of issues were already proving to be invaluable.

In the midst of all this, I had to participate in the two-week orientation in Washington, DC, for new members of Congress, hire a full staff in DC and Seattle, and set up two offices to onboard what would eventually be a team of eighteen people.

There was no room for letting down my guard, no room really for celebrating, and certainly little room for sleep.

The days and weeks following the election continued to be scary and harrowing: how could we have elected a man to the highest office who'd campaigned on xenophobia, racism, and sexism? A man who had openly sexually assaulted and harassed women and was responsible for shady real-estate deals that enriched his family and duped marginalized people of color in his community?[1] Then again, the seeds of Trump's politics had been sown long before him; I did not believe then, nor do I believe now, that his political views were an anomaly in our country. There was much more beneath his election that we needed to understand and fix.

By now, we know that our worst fears about this president in those fragile days after the election have come true; I won't belabor the horrors of his administration or brand of political corruption here, because we know them all too well. If anything, his election only deepened my resolve to serve people who'd been forgotten and who certainly would be trampled on by this new administration.

We Democrats had lost the House, the Senate, and the White House. It was gloomy, to say the least. It seemed like people everywhere were crying. Social media was alive with posts of recriminations and finger pointing. A narrative emerged that was, in my mind, false and even dangerous, one that pitted the "working class" (read: white, working-class men) versus "identity politics." This seemed to pit white folks against black and brown, and seemed to imply that social liberalism—things like support for trans folks or people of color—was the factor that had lost us the support of white working-class people. There were so many things wrong with this analysis.

The truth was that working-class people of every color felt left behind. Hillary Clinton had not expanded the electorate the way that Obama had—young folks and people of color stayed home and too many white folks ended up voting for Trump, causing her to get 3.5 million fewer votes than Obama had in 2008. In critical swing states like Michigan, just under 100,000 people went to the polls and left their ballot blank for president, voting for every other office from Board of Education up to the U.S. Senate. Democrats ended up losing the state by just 10,704 votes. Representative Dan Kildee, who represents Flint and surrounding areas, told me that in Genesee County, where Flint is located, there were 20,000 fewer votes than in 2012—not even counting any undervote where people voted but left the presidential contest blank. The assumption here is that the majority of these voters were Democrats who simply couldn't vote for Hillary.

This is a deeply cautionary lesson about ensuring that our final Democratic candidate for president will generate enthusiasm among our base, including black and brown voters, young voters, and women. Too often, Democrats have hewed to the middle, trying to win a narrow slice of Independent or even moderate Republicans and forsaking our own base. In my opinion, this is an enormous mistake. While it is true that we need to capture a slice of Independent voters in districts across the country, we would be better off if we recognized the power of the base and did far more to address the deep concerns of our own Democratic voters so that they feel represented and inspired enough to turn out and vote. We simply must stop taking these voters for granted.

The year 2016 elevated the underlying story of deep structural problems with our economy. The election of Trump was a symptom of much broader problems, though as he governed, Trump would also become a cause of deep injustice, inequity, and dismantling of any protections for the most vulnerable. Trump captured the narrative of unfair trade agreements that had left workers behind, even though the vast majority of average Democratic voters felt trade deals did not benefit workers. It was Bill Clinton who signed NAFTA into law, after all, and Obama and Biden who had made the Trans-Pacific Partnership their lasting legacy and pushed for fast-track authority to speed up trade deals. Hillary had been for TPP before she came out against it, and no one believed her when she said she wanted fair trade not just free trade. Trump swooped into that seam between the push by Democratic leaders for these free-trade policies and the effects of those policies on working families. Despite the fact that Trump was a billionaire, voters believed that he at least understood their pain from trade inequities.

It also wasn't simply just about trade, though. Income and wealth inequality were at an all-time high (see Chapter 10). Union density across the country had gone down, and while Wall Street was bailed out, Main Street still struggled. Wages had stagnated and corporations had been hugely successful in putting in place an integrated strategy to weaken the power of labor by exporting industrial jobs to less developed countries, aggressively busting unions, and changing American labor law in corporations' favor over many years.

Most frustratingly, the outdated electoral system once again gave way too much power to certain smaller, white states so that the popular vote—and the votes of people of color and young people in big urban areas simply didn't mean what they should have. Hillary did get three million more votes than Trump, winning the popular vote but still losing the electoral college. Much later, we would find out about the ways in which Russia worked to interfere in the elections on Trump's behalf. But the truth was—and people felt it deeply—the election should not have been so close in the first place and the blame and recriminations were flying.

Had Hillary won the presidency, perhaps my personal election would not have meant so much. I would likely have become the progressive thorn in the side of a much more conservative Democratic president, not a sign of resistance. As it was, news outlets and people everywhere were looking for something good that came out of the elections. Three new women of color had been elected to the U.S. Senate: Kamala Harris from California, Tammy Duckworth from Illinois, and Catherine Cortez Masto from Nevada. In the House, I had been elected the first South Asian American woman, along with some other firsts: Lisa Blunt Rochester was the first African American woman from Delaware, and Stephanie Murphy was the first Vietnamese American woman. And Ilhan Omar was elected to the Minnesota House of Representatives, becoming the first Somali American to be elected to a state legislature anywhere. We became the symbol of

hope in an otherwise dark election, a bright spot in the doom and gloom
that was everywhere around us. One of our local papers called me the
"Anti-Trump" which summed it up well.

My party was in the minority in both chambers; I knew what being in
the minority was like from my time in the state senate, and I was gearing
up for what would end up being more of a fight than I could ever have
imagined.

Our two-week new member orientation started a week after the election,
was punctuated by Thanksgiving break, and then finished up a week after
Thanksgiving. Hiring my chief of staff was my first priority. This time, I
felt I had to have someone who knew the Hill and could guide me in what
would be a giant maze of learning. This was my first big decision and I
spent most of the week interviewing candidates, and also getting to know
the physical space that was the U.S. Congress, as well as getting to know
my fellow members of Congress.

Most folks have no idea what it means to be a U.S. congressmember and
the physical demands of the job. Many of my constituents assume I just
move to DC with my family and stay there. But the job entails something
very different. Vote schedules for the following year are established by the
majority party in December, though they can change from time to time.
Generally, the vote schedule means that we are in DC from Tuesday evening through Friday, or Monday evening through Thursday. Then, we fly
home to do in-district work for three days and see our families, and then
we fly back to DC again. Every six weeks or so, we have ten days of what
is called an in-district work period, where we are back in our districts.
Those times in the district are among the busiest: we spend our days meeting with constituents, doing tours of places in the district that we need to
see, holding press conferences, or doing in-district media, participating
in or holding rallies or events on issues we are working on, or speaking
at other people's events. The district work periods are absolutely essential
because it is your time to participate side by side with constituents and to
be visible in your district. Members of Congress who forget this and get

consumed with the desire for DC or national attention, in my opinion, will always get bitten in a challenge by any strong contender. Voters want to see you—and they should be able to do so: to connect, complain, and give you their point of view. Particularly for members of the House, we are representatives in all the meanings of that word. What that means for us personally is that there is no official time off. You squeeze it in when you can but there really is no time that is your own.

On the living front, unless our district is close enough to the Capitol to commute, most members of Congress must maintain two homes, one in our district and one in DC. Unlike the state legislature, congressional salaries are substantial, at $174,000—which sounds like, and is, an enormous amount of money compared to the incomes of most Americans. However, maintaining two full residences and all the expenses associated with that is challenging. Unlike most other jobs, which reimburse you for food and lodging expenses when you travel for work, you are not reimbursed for these expenses as a member of Congress. Nor can you write off these expenses on your taxes.

All of this means that money is often a barrier for members of Congress, some of whom at times elect to sleep in their offices—an unhealthy practice and also a problem for sexual harassment issues, among others. Congressional salaries have not been increased in the last decade and it is seen as a political hot button to even consider increases—yet we end up losing not only good people who can't afford to serve in Congress, but also top staff, whose salaries are capped because all the members' salaries are capped. The personal dynamics make it so that parents—and particularly single parents—find it a nearly impossible trade-off; how the few do it, I have no idea.

Perhaps it is no great surprise that so many members of Congress are millionaires. And, of course, Congress is a very white and very male place: out of more than eleven thousand people who have ever served in Congress over the history of our country, only seventy-nine have been women of color (seventy-three in the House, and another six in the Senate).

None of the above is to suggest that I have it hard. I am still awed by the honor of serving. These are not personal complaints; they are intended to showcase the barriers for so many people—working-class folks, women, people of color, and those who do not come from wealth—that keep our government from being truly representative.

Now that I had been elected, I needed to find a place to live in DC, and quickly. One of the members of Congress who had been extremely helpful to me in the last months of my campaign was Lois Frankel from Florida. I nicknamed her our Den Mother, because she was focused on electing women and was available night and day for anything we needed. A former mayor, she is a no-nonsense person with a heart of gold. She pitched her apartment building—which had many other women members of Congress living in it—to many of us, and within a couple of weeks, I had arranged to rent a one-bedroom apartment in the building. It was a twelve-minute walk to the office and it was furnished. With everything that was going on, I simply couldn't deal with trying to furnish an apartment, so it felt like it would be perfect for my first term until I got my bearings. In retrospect, I think I probably should have gotten my own furniture—it was hard enough to be living alone away from family, much less surrounded by someone else's stuff. But in the moment, it felt right and it allowed me to spend my time and energy on the millions of other things I had to do.

Picking our office was another big process, built around an arcane lottery system for new members. Every election, without fail, a newspaper story is written about the new member lottery. I'm not sure it is worth a story but it appears to be fascinating for others. Here's how it worked: sometime early in our orientation, we got a list of offices that would soon be vacated by retiring members or those who had lost elections. Each class of members would pick their offices according to seniority, with the newest members selecting last. By the time it got to us, we had about a day to see what offices still remained and about ten minutes to pick your office once your number was called. Of the three buildings in the Capitol for House members, Rayburn was reserved for the more senior members and would have no spaces for new members. There were a few spaces in Longworth, and then Cannon, the original House building, had the most offices. I knew right away that I wanted to be in Cannon, even though many people did not. To me, Cannon was the epitome of Congress: a gorgeous old building with dramatic stairways, and offices with high ceilings and big gracious windows. The member offices were large, with bathrooms and a small closet. But Cannon was being renovated so some of the corridors were off limits, which made it a long walk to get to the Capitol Building for votes. It didn't matter to me, my heart was set on Cannon, and as I made my list of offices by priority order, Cannon 319 was my top choice.

On the day of the new member lottery, all the members in our class filed into a big hearing room. Members of the Administrative Services Committee sit up on the dais and each member's name is called alphabetically to select a number—like the sorting hat ritual in Harry Potter. People do all manner of rituals before picking their numbers: the most energetic do cartwheels up to the front, people cross themselves, some say prayers out loud, and others run up the aisle or rub their heads or hold up lucky charms. Loud groans and big cheers erupt, depending on the number that is called. You might hope that high numbers are chosen before it's your turn to pick a number, because that means lower numbers are still available for you.

My prayer was to my grandmother, already passed on but who I still believed had a hotline to God. Somehow I felt she was there, watching me that day, and I sent her a little message that I would love her help. I walked up to the front and picked my number: it was number 4! I pulled my clenched fists with bent elbows down to my sides in a victory sign, and a photo of that moment—of me in a bright green jacket making my victory sign—found its way behind Rachel Maddow as she covered the lottery process on MSNBC that night. With such a great lottery pick, my first-choice office was available, and I was all set. Cannon 319 was mine.

The office does matter, for big and small reasons. As I would learn, distance from the Capitol mattered because you run back and forth between the buildings multiple times a day (the right shoes matter, too, something

I still haven't managed to master perfectly). The amount of space you have matters and the buildings allocate space differently. In Cannon, my office was large but the office space for staff was smaller. Our office staff grew in my second term, in part because as co-chair of the Congressional Progressive Caucus, I housed several additional staff in my office. So for my second term, I chose Longworth, where my office was much smaller, but the staff space was bigger and that was necessary. To me, light mattered too. My Cannon office was perpetually filled with light, which was wonderful but also got very hot in the summer. Still, I wanted us to work with natural light whatever office we got, given the long hours.

Once you had your office, you had to decorate it. There was a big fair-like event, with different tables where you could select your curtains, map out your office, and select any furniture you needed. I picked a setup where we could have two long couches in the office—I had a feeling that my activist background meant that we would get a lot of visitors and I wanted to be sure we could accommodate big groups of people whose voices needed to be heard.

As I reflect on all those early days, which included selecting and decorating an office, to learning about the benefits and salary of a new job, it sounds insignificant given the depth of the problems we face as a country.

But to be real about it, we all worked so hard to get me to Congress—so many volunteers, staffers, voters, cheerers on, friends and family—that those early benchmarks were meaningful because WE HAD DONE IT! Now that I am fully and completely in the role and those early memories get fainter, what arises in me is a deep and complete sense of gratitude that I am serving in Congress. Of course there are challenges, like the travel every week when my body clock doesn't adjust and then I can't sleep. But still, I get to go to DC and fight for what my constituents and I believe in on this enormously impactful national stage.

People ask me all the time whether this job is rewarding, especially in these times with *this* president?

The answer is yes. And also: I am grateful for the honor and the best way I know to express that gratitude is to work my tail off. And so I do.

I am grateful that I get to wake up every single day knowing that I am devoting my life to something that truly matters. If something were to happen to me tomorrow, I would die knowing that I did all I could to make the world a better place, no regrets. That is a very special feeling. I want to keep the expectations high—for both me and my staff. Too few people, much less women of color, ever get this chance and I don't intend to waste it.

When we got the orientation information, we were asked to bring one staff person with us to the orientation, and since I had not picked out a chief of staff yet, my pick was one of my campaign workers who I had asked to move to DC with me. Danielle Fulfs had started as my first volunteer on the campaign, initially just taking photographs. An activist herself, she had run a statewide anti–death penalty campaign and had been referred to me by a common friend. As is typical for campaigns, those early volunteers often make themselves indispensable, and she did. Within weeks, she was hired on—to do all the scheduling of endorsement interviews and campaign events and drive me everywhere. Danielle had told me she wanted to move to DC to do policy work, so I had decided she would be one of my legislative assistants in the DC office. Of course, she was brand-new like me and had to learn everything as well. She handled my office details, as well as so many of those early, frazzled decision moments with skill and grace. Perhaps most importantly, she provided me with a sense of being grounded in Seattle while we were both in the less-known-to-us Washington.

One of the most dislocating things about going to Congress is that you are operating with staff who have mostly spent their working lives on the Hill, working for various member offices. Unlike in Seattle, where I had people working for me who truly believed in me and my objectives, knew my career, and knew me and the area, DC was totally different. There were good, smart people for sure, but many had only worked in DC. They didn't know my district at all, and many DC staff are simply looking for the next place to move up. As I would later find, staff transitions in DC offices are commonplace and even understandable, because our official resources were limited and unless someone moved on, there were not as many opportunities for others to grow and be promoted. This was completely new to me from my time at OneAmerica where so many of my staff had worked with me for years and were deeply loyal.

I also hired another woman who had worked for me at OneAmerica, where she ran my New Americans citizenship program for several years. Jennifer Chan had gone off to graduate school in Chicago and then become policy director for the National Immigrant Justice Center there. We had stayed in close touch—she was the one I tapped to do the power map of Republicans in the state senate. I knew she was someone I could trust, who would understand my interest in being on the Judiciary Committee and my work on immigration, and who knew me, knew the movement, and knew the district. Thankfully, she accepted immediately. Jennifer would go on to become my legislative director in my second term, and the trust she and I had for each other was essential to my work and my sanity. In that first term, she and Danielle would be the two Seattle-based people on my DC team, providing important district perspective to the rest of the staff.

My chief of staff, Carmen Gallus Frias, was a Capitol Hill veteran. She had worked for the same Arizona Congressperson for almost eleven years until that member lost her election. She had worked her way up from the district to being chief of staff, and she was extremely efficient, had terrific relationships across the caucus with other staff, and was highly respected. I liked that she understood both perspectives from the district and DC, because of the persistent problems that cropped up between the two offices—particularly when you had to manage two offices on opposite coasts—and the tension of either office not feeling like we had attended to their needs.

Once I hired Carmen, my next priority was the district director, a position that would be absolutely critical to my success. Rachel Berkson had been the NARAL Washington director during my time in the state senate, and it was she who had taken the intersectional framework to create a novel multi-issue report card for legislators who wanted NARAL's endorsement. Rachel had also run the state community action organization, worked as state director for the many SEIU local unions as well as for the Working Families Party out of New York City. She was a strong progressive who knew how to organize, had managed large staffs before, understood race, gender, and class intersectionality, and had a keenly honed political savvy. She and I had worked together on numerous projects over the years and when she agreed to come on as my district director, I was thrilled.

The question of how resources and staff are divided between DC and district offices was a critical one and tied directly to how I thought about inside-outside organizing and voter engagement. At least for my first term, I wanted to put more people in the district. I wanted to be everywhere in the district, all the time. I wanted people to be sick of seeing me and to have unprecedented access to the office. I wanted to prioritize constituent services, so that people could see government working *for them*, one step in undermining the essential Republican talking point: government is broken. I also wanted to spend time developing relationships with the smaller cities besides Seattle that were in the district. During the campaign, I had heard over and over that the six other cities in the district often felt left out and like they didn't get attention. I intended to fix that.

Between Carmen and Rachel, we slowly made our way through the hiring processes, and within three months we had fully staffed up both offices and were on our way.

The first time I saw my name on the gold plate outside my office, tears came to my eyes. What a moment this was: the immigrant woman of color makes it to Congress! I felt the weight of the responsibility I had: to represent, to speak truth, to bring a different set of voices and tactics to this center of power, to navigate the halls of an insanely arcane body that looked nothing like the rest of the country, so that people would have better opportunities for a future of dignity and respect. All this in a moment that seemed previously unthinkable after the new president had won by cleaving the country literally in half.

I was sworn in on January 3, and I was determined to do all that I could to speak out against hateful rhetoric. I refused to normalize a leader who would use his office to fan and fuel racism and sexism and hatred.

The need to fight back began immediately. After new members of Congress are sworn in, the whole Congress must vote to certify the electoral college results of the presidential election. The Senate, in one of the rare occasions where this happens, marched over to the House to form a joint session of Congress. In much the same way that a president's inauguration comes with pomp and circumstance and tradition, this joint session is a much less well-known piece of political theater: the electoral votes are literally carried onto the House floor in a large brown crate that looks like a treasure chest. Then the votes are read out loud and "gaveled in" by the sitting vice president of the United States, who is the president of the Senate.[2] Since election night, we had been reeling with the stories of voter suppression: districts and states that had gone to Republicans because people had been blocked from voting through long voting lines and early poll closures. By then, we also had the first indications that Russian interference may have played a big role in how our elections for president ended up.

Typically, the tally and certification of the electoral college votes are pro forma, a mere formality and a highly scripted process. But in 2001, after Al Gore lost the election for president to George W. Bush, the process took a different tack. When it came time to count Florida's electoral votes, members of the Congressional Black Caucus—one of the most powerful caucuses in Congress—spoke up one at a time to object to the awarding of the state's twenty-five electors to Bush. In order to object to the electoral votes, you must have a senator sign your objection, but no senator had agreed to join in the objections then. As president of the Senate at the time, Gore was presiding over the floor and one after the other, he ruled the objections out of order.[3]

The day of our electoral college vote certification, I was approached by Congresswomen Barbara Lee and Maxine Waters. They knew of my history of progressive activism—and Barbara had been one of the most supportive members to me during my campaign. They were planning to mount a similar set of objections to the awarding of these electoral college votes—would I join them? I had no idea what this really meant, but I quickly watched the 2001 proceedings on the internet and decided I would participate. Did I fully understand what was about to occur? I cannot say that I really knew, but my instincts told me to trust the women of color congressmembers. Jamie Raskin of Maryland and I were the only two new members who participated, and many others thought we were crazy to do so. But to us, it seemed that we had to lodge our protest: perhaps in my mind, it was the beginning of bringing the resistance right into Congress. We owed it to those who, across the country, felt that this president was illegitimate to raise our voices. So, raise them we did.

Five of the members who objected were people of color, plus Jamie and Congressman Jim McGovern of Massachusetts, who is a longtime human rights champion and progressive stalwart. Joe Biden, president of the Senate, was presiding. As in 2001, we did not have a single senator who had agreed to sign our objections, so we knew we would be ruled out of order. Biden and congressional leader Nancy Pelosi knew our plans ahead of time—it's a typical courtesy to allow people to know what is going to happen, so they were prepared. McGovern went first and was allowed to finish his sentence before being ruled out of order. Each of us gave a reason for why we were challenging the tally, from voter suppression and state measures that effectively disenfranchised voters to Russian interference in our elections.

I was third.

"For what purpose does the gentlewoman rise?" asked Biden.

"Mr. President, I object to the certification from the state of Georgia on the grounds that the electoral votes were not—"

Biden cut me off, slamming his gavel. "There is no debate," he said. But I wasn't done, relying in part on how I had seen Gore allow members to finish their point.

"Mr. President, even as people waited hours in Georgia—"

Biden was not having any of it. He slammed the gavel down again. "There is no debate," he said testily. "It's over!"[4]

The Republican side of the House, newly emboldened by the Republican trifecta of winning the presidency, the Senate, and the House, erupted in laughter and applause, as GOP legislators rose to give Biden a standing ovation for cutting me off so abruptly. If you witnessed it on TV, you saw the cameras zooming in on Speaker Paul Ryan laughing out loud.

It was a grueling debut moment, for sure. I was a brand-new member of Congress and I had just been cut off by the Democratic vice president and booed by my Republican colleagues who stood clapping. Biden continued to cut off the members who went after me, ordering the mics to be turned off as they were speaking.

Later, I told reporters that our objections were important, and Biden should have allowed us to state them without cutting us off. "The American people need to know we understand the issues with the way this election happened," I said. And turning it into a light-hearted moment, I said, "And it's wonderful that my Republican colleagues gave me a standing ovation in my first week!"

The presidential election may have been over, but the hard fights were just beginning. I was not about to let Joe Biden and a bunch of jeering House members laughing at me stop my colleagues and me. Taking to the floor was one last attempt to challenge Trump's legitimacy. I knew that it would not succeed, but it felt critical that the American people saw our resistance and knew that we would fight for them and refuse to compromise.

One of my greatest worries about a Trump presidency was numbness. I worried that the American people were being constantly bombarded with shocking, racist, sexist remarks and tweets—and that all the hatred that Trump spewed would slowly become the "new normal." I had no idea yet just how much Trump would bombard us on a practically daily basis. None of this was normal. We were not going to stop being shocked. We were not going to be complacent. And we were never going to give up. I knew how important it was for my constituents to see what that looked like coming from an immigrant woman of color.

I refused to attend Trump's inauguration. Instead, the day after, I marched with more than five hundred thousand people in the 2017 Women's March. If you attended the Washington, DC, Women's March or any of the hundreds of other Women's Marches across the country that weekend, you know how powerful and hopeful it felt to have a visual, visceral reminder that the majority of the American people did not choose our current reality. Millions of people came together in a spirit of love and generosity and determination, wearing pink hats, all to say: we see women, we see people of color, we see LGBTQ people, we see immigrants. This man does not stand for us, and we will not stand down.

On January 27, it became clear that whatever shred of hope we may have had that this administration would be less hateful and divisive than the campaign we had just endured was misplaced. President Trump, at the behest of the white nationalists he'd chosen as his advisors, signed an order banning all immigrants, including lawful residents and visa holders, from seven Muslim-majority countries (Iran, Iraq, Libya, Somalia, Sudan, Syria, and Yemen) from coming to the United States for ninety days. Refugees from those same countries were banned for one hundred twenty days. This patently xenophobic order sowed chaos, confusion, and fear. Within just a few days of taking the oath of office, this president had confirmed that our worst fears about his leadership were coming true.

I was alerted immediately about what was happening by Port Commissioner Courtney Gregoire and I became one of the first members of Congress across the country—along with Representative Jerry Nadler from New York City—to race to our airports in defense of immigrants who were being turned away. When I got to SeaTac International Airport, I demanded to speak with the Customs and Border Patrol officials. Airport officials were balking at letting me through to speak to the CBP officials in charge, so I threatened to just go through myself.

"You can't, Congresswoman," one official said with trepidation. "It will trigger the alarms and shut down the airport."

"Well, then, get me through to the CBP officials I need to speak with or bring them to me," I said firmly. The airport officials weren't the problem, but they were not used to challenging power. When I made it clear I wasn't backing down, they found a way to shuttle me and other elected officials out to the depths of the airport where the CBP office was located.

Meanwhile, I called my organizer friends and told them we needed a giant protest at the airport. They immediately went to work and within hours, over three thousand people had showed up to protest the deportations of Muslims who were being refused entry into the country. In the chaos of a great protest, I took to the bullhorn to speak with the protestors, who had crammed into the airport hall with beautiful signs saying, "We love our immigrant neighbors" and "Trump doesn't represent us. Welcome, immigrants."

Pro bono attorneys from the ACLU, Northwest Immigrant Rights Project, and an excellent local firm, had already put together an emergency legal challenge, and one of them with whom I had worked after 9/11 asked if I—now a congresswoman—would sign the amicus brief. Unlike my colleagues who were more cautious about saying yes, I immediately agreed because I understood precisely the urgency of amicus briefs and the nature of emergency challenges like this from my experience with the Somali deportations case after 9/11. Within hours, a federal judge had granted a stay of deportation to a Somali family who was already on a plane that was sitting on the tarmac, ready to leave. In a dramatic moment, we were able to stop the plane from leaving and deplane the family. The crowd went wild when they heard the news.

Across the country, similar things were happening. People shut down airports in protest, residents were left stranded overseas, families waited anxiously at airports, unsure whether their relatives who had lawfully lived here for years would be detained or make their way to baggage claim to greet them.[5]

I co-wrote a letter with my colleagues to then-Department of Homeland Security secretary John Kelly condemning the order and demanding an emergency briefing on the policy. Administration officials were only meeting with select committee chairs about the policy, but this administration needed to understand that such a sweeping policy change required a briefing for *all* members—not just the ones likely to be sympathetic to their policy. We needed to know how many people were being lawfully turned away, and whether Immigrations and Customs Enforcement (ICE) and Customs and Border Protection were complying with temporary court orders. We suspected that the administration did not want to place an undue burden on anyone coming to the United States who was white and Christian, so we needed to hear them to spell out their dog whistle—"religious minorities" in these countries would be granted exceptions to the order—so that this administration's motives would be made plain to the American people who deserved better.

Over a hundred of my fellow Democrats signed on to this letter.[6] It gave me quick credibility in the caucus on immigration issues. After all, I *was* an immigrant and a naturalized American citizen. Although I was a "freshman" congresswoman, all this put me in a position to be a counterpoint to Trump, particularly on issues related to immigration. In those first Trump years, people were looking to me and a small handful of other elected officials, along with outside groups like Indivisible and the Women's March that had formed to embody the resistance, to keep progressives engaged, to lead us into fighting *for* what we believed in *and* against the administration all at the same time. Along with more established outside groups like MoveOn, the resistance was born. I was in on the resistance, but the difference was this time I was on the inside.

As one of the members of Congress with the most recent grassroots connections and organizing experience, I started putting my inside-outside strategy into effect, coordinating closely with the outside groups as we put together our plan of opposition and resistance. Those groups played such a crucial role in the early days after Trump took the oath and the nation watched a news cycle dominated by his racist, incoherent tweets and the swirl of chaos around his staff and the entire executive branch. Yet people who opposed him—both progressives and members of the Democratic Party at large—were feeling hopeless and helpless. I found myself over and over again trying to rally the troops and dispense hope to crying faces to not retreat and instead to fight back. We had to trust our strength as a movement, and we had to do all we could to build that movement of resistance. Unlike 2018, when there was a group of progressives elected into a House majority, we were a small but determined group that was still very much in the minority. We were fighting still with one hand tied behind our backs.

A few publications—looking for hopefulness in a time of despair—were writing some flattering profiles of me. What I cared about was that they emphasized the importance of inside-outside organizing, and the need to stand up and fight. In July 2017, *Mother Jones* published an article called "She Didn't Pick the Resistance. The Resistance Picked Her. Now She's One of Trump's Most Fearless Opponents." The piece highlighted that I was not afraid to challenge the electoral college vote, the Muslim ban, or individual members of Congress who tried to diminish me. When a Republican House member told me to "learn how to read" in Judiciary Committee because he objected to my description of Trump's travel ban as a "Muslim ban," I took to Twitter to take him on.[7]

My constituents desperately wanted this from me. My town halls back in district were always packed—at the very first one, a thousand people showed up—most of whom had never engaged with a congressmember before! People were on fire, they wanted to take their hopelessness and anger and turn it into action. Our job was to find the way to channel that hopelessness and anger into productive forces and to keep people in the field, not wringing their hands with despair and hiding their heads in the sand. The only way we would win again was if people stayed engaged and recognized that they still had power.

Many things in Congress are opaque, and one of the most obvious examples of this process cloudiness is the committee selection process. With a few exceptions, new members never get assigned seats on the most powerful "money" committees, also known as the "A" committees: Ways and Means, Appropriations, Energy and Commerce, and Financial Services. These committees largely control decisions on major issues around healthcare, tax policy, and climate, as well as controlling how the federal government spends its money. They also are plum committees where, if you take PAC contributions, which I did not, you would likely raise a lot of money, for yourself and—more important to the maintenance of the status quo— for the party. The number of seats allocated to the minority party for each committee is assigned by the majority party. That meant that Democrats, as the minority party, would end up getting relatively few seats on major committees. During transition years when Democrats went from the majority to the minority (or if the minority shrunk further), it could also mean that the most junior members of a committee would get kicked off if we were assigned a smaller number of seats on that committee.

Almost immediately upon election, we began to get asked what committees we wanted to serve on. Knowing I would likely not get an "A" committee, I had my eye on the Judiciary Committee as my top priority. This would not be easy to get either. Judiciary is also considered a very prestigious committee, since it deals with issues from voting rights and immigration to criminal justice and the courts, all the issues that I had spent my life working on. To get your committee of choice, you had to work every member of the Steering and Policy Committee, which nominally made those decisions, to advocate for you, and also the regional representatives to your own delegation. The decider-in-chief, no matter what anyone told you, was House leader Nancy Pelosi, who nominated the Steering and Policy Committee and largely determined who she wanted on each committee. But having members know you and advocate for you was still helpful, and I found that calling members to introduce myself and ask for their support was a great way to get to know the key players in the caucus.

One extreme example of lobbying my peers came during a late-night pizza delivery. Steve was with me in our new DC apartment and we had ordered from the local pizzeria called "We the Pizza" (EVERYTHING in DC is about the government!). The doorbell rang and we opened the door. The pizza delivery guy had his arms outstretched, a pizza in each hand, delivering to both us and our neighbor across the hall who had also ordered pizza and had just opened her door. We all laughed, and that was how I met my new colleague, Representative Terri Sewell from Alabama, who also happened to sit on the Steering and Policy Committee. When she saw me and recognized me as a new member, she said over the out-stretched hands of the pizza guy, "Hey Pramila, which committee are you looking for?"

"Judiciary!" I yelled back. "Can I have your support?"

"Absolutely! I'll see what I can do," she replied merrily as we both took our pizzas and went back to our lives. Did it help? It sure didn't hurt.

When I led a congressional delegation on a visit to the southern border around the issue of family separations, Terri came with me, diving into immigration for really one of the first times, she said. And a year later, we got to see Terri in action in her own district when Steve and I participated in Representative John Lewis's annual Civil Rights Pilgrimage to Alabama. It's not often you get to see your colleague at home in their district, but when you do, it is a powerful window into why they were elected, their knowledge, and their leadership style. Terri fights for her district and her constituents, many of whom are in poor, forgotten towns and rural areas. Of course, Terri and I don't agree on everything, but the personal connections with colleagues make up some of the glue that makes Congress work. Relationships matter, and forging relationships can occur on a Civil Rights Pilgrimage or over the head of a smiling and ambidextrous pizza delivery guy.

In the end I was one of only two freshmen to get placed on the Judiciary Committee from the beginning (later in the term, two additional freshmen members were added). That placement would end up being of supreme importance in my second term, when Democrats regained the majority, thus adding many new seats to the committee, giving me the opportunity to become the vice chair on the Subcommittee on Immigration and Citizenship. In the majority, we were able to bring forward and question the numerous administration officials who presided over the horrendous family separation events and mass detentions of immigrants. I questioned tech executives and CEOs and listened to heart-breaking testimony from gun violence survivors and LGBTQ members fighting for equality. Importantly, after 2018, a seat on the powerful House Judiciary Committee meant that we would be in the lead on the critical questions of violations of our Constitution, including questioning Special Counsel Robert Mueller about his investigation into Trump's ties with Russia and ultimately presiding over impeachment hearings in December 2019.[8]

Before getting to Congress, I heard that as a new member, I would have no power or authority to do anything, that everything depended on seniority and that the "turf elbows" were sharp. That proved both true and not true. Seniority is paramount in Congress, no question about that— demonstrated by everything from the office lottery to which committees you could get on. At the same time, Trump's election may have begun to upend things: there were so many opportunities for resistance, and my connections to organizing and outside groups helped tremendously. So did my real expertise on issues like the Muslim ban or immigration, more broadly. The fact that I had worked on so many issues before coming to Congress was somewhat unique: I had been on the committee that helped develop Washington State's $15 minimum-wage agreement. I was heavily involved in the movement to get money out of politics (in fact, at the time, I was one of the few members who did not take corporate PAC money), and I had helped pushed for public financing of our local elections in Seattle. I had worked on passing paid sick and safe days policy in Seattle and later in Washington. I had also worked for a decade in global health and development and human rights, and been heavily involved in advocating for women's rights and reproductive choice domestically and internationally. And I was deeply involved with and understood the nuances and the challenges of the labor movement in fighting for collective bargaining rights.

This wide and varied experience was a blessing and a curse. Unlike many members who come to Congress with one signature issue, I wanted to work on everything, and I had been elected by a coalition that *expected* me to work on everything. This taxed my office and staff, and it meant that we were running one hundred miles a minute. At the same time, it gave me tremendous opportunities. I understood the politics of turf, having negotiated that for years as an organizer. I focused on figuring out who the people were who were leading on something, offered my help, and also carved out space to do my own thing and invited them along so that they also got exposure and benefits. I had learned from my days of organizing that generosity and humility were key in these situations—there was plenty of room for everyone to be a champion, and sharing space was critically important to building the broader movement. At the same time, I fought for the appropriate recognition of what I was doing. I learned that you had to stand your ground and even toot your own horn if others wouldn't. It isn't so much about my own ego—if you run for Congress, you definitely have an ego and that's not necessarily a bad thing—but it's also about making sure the woman of color is fully recognized. My constant struggle is making sure that as a woman of color I am not publicly dismissed, while at the same time being careful not to make it about me personally. It's a delicate balance I'm aware of all the time, sometimes erring this way or that.

In those early days, as both an organizer and an "inside" member of the resistance, I sometimes felt challenged—both politically and psychologically—to define what we were *for*. In the minority, we were an opposition party. So much of what we did was about resistance and, in many ways, it held us all together. It was painful, but also more uniting to be against Trump. For the first time, I saw Democratic members pull together to oppose the Muslim ban, immigration actions, or on stripping healthcare away. But as a minority party, we could not simply be an opposition party, we also had to be a *proposition* party—introduce legislation that would help define who we were as a party and call people into a vision of the future that was hopeful and positive. I had been an organizer for far too long to not know that people need hope. They need a positive vision to be excited about. We had two years and then there would be another election—for our party to win, we had to know what we stood for.

I decided that I needed my own proposition agenda, and I worked to create it through the bills I signed onto and led on. I immediately signed onto HR 676, the existing version of the universal healthcare bill, then sponsored by Representative John Conyers. I spoke with Bernie and together, we introduced the College for All Act that provided free tuition to all students at public colleges and universities and cut interest rates in half for those with existing debt. I was one of the four lead sponsors of the 100 by '50 Act, to transition the country to 100 percent clean energy by 2050. I signed on right away to the $15 minimum-wage bill. And I wrote my own transformational bill on reforming the for-profit immigration detention system and providing access to counsel for immigrants.

The Democratic caucus more broadly, however, did not necessarily want to focus on the proposition agenda because it would highlight the differences within the caucus. This constant back-and-forth would only get worse when we took the majority, because then the opposition agenda would not be enough—we would have to propose solutions, and those would create fights in the caucus on what was bold enough or was a true solution.

People often asked me what the difference was between being an organizer on the outside and being an elected official in U.S. Congress. Both roles were important and necessary, but there was a real difference that came in part from the power I held as a member of Congress to gain access to places that regular people could not, see for myself what was happening, and use the power of the office to get information or question people directly around injustices I saw taking place.

Take the Muslim ban and airport rally situation. Had I been an organizer at OneAmerica during the early, harried days of the Trump administration and the Muslim ban, I would have been on the outside, organizing the rally and challenging power—a critically important role. As a member of Congress, however, I was able to demand entry into the airport to speak to the top Customs and Border Protection officials, albeit with a threat to shut it down!

Later during the family separations, because I was a member of Congress, I was able to get into the federal prison where 126 mothers and fathers were being held and speak directly to them, instead of being the person that organized the rally outside the detention center. We could get information that advocates did not have access to, and we could use our platforms in a different way to draw attention to abuses through letters, shadow hearings (later hearings, in the majority), and floor speeches.

I also used our platform on the unofficial, campaign side. We were members of Congress but we could still organize rallies and protests on the campaign side, as long as we did not use official resources. In the very first month of my first year in Congress, when Trump and the Republicans were pushing to pass TrumpCare—a healthcare bill that would effectively undo all the most protective and important provisions we had gained in the Affordable Care Act—Pelosi, Bernie, and Chuck Schumer called for a coordinated day of rallies across the country, and the one we organized in Seattle was one of the largest in the country. The platform of Congress conveyed a certain legitimacy that the press responds to, and often drew a different and often larger crowd by virtue of the office.

The other big difference between being a member of Congress and an outside organizer was that I had to take a vote—many times a day, each day, each month, each year. As activists, we could be as pure as we wanted. We could push for the best. But as legislators, I had to vote on issues every single day and make a decision on whether something was good enough to vote for. In the minority, this was a little bit easier because so many of the Republican bills were so terrible, so all Democrats were united. I often joked that in the minority our voting job boiled down to "No, no, a thousand times NO!" Once we were in the majority, this decision on how to improve something to the point where you could vote for it, versus simply voting against something, became a bigger issue, as did how to build and leverage the power of progressives in Congress when the power often came down to the moderates or conservative Democrats who could tank something easily by voting with Republicans. This would only become even harder to navigate with later leadership roles.

Hearings were another important place to make an impact. There were viral moments of resistance, aided by the new digital platforms like Now

This and Credo, like the time I questioned then-head of the Office of Refugee Resettlement, E. Scott Lloyd—a lifelong antiabortion activist who tried to stop an immigrant refugee teenager in Texas from getting an abortion. Lloyd, who had no medical experience and very little experience with refugees—but a long career's worth of experience trying to assert control over women's bodies—sleepily hemmed and hawed, refusing to look me in the eye, as I asked him a series of straightforward, yes or no questions that he could not answer.[9]

He looked completely inept, and the video went viral within minutes. A year later, when the administration announced its family separation policy and I became the first member of Congress to enter a federal prison and talk to parents separated from their children, Republicans refused to hold hearings. But on several occasions, I turned the hearings we had into moments to broadcast the atrocities that were happening.

The truth was, I unfortunately had a few too many instances of turning gender and race prejudices into moments of resistance and opportunities to stand up for a different vision of leadership that was inclusive of women and minorities. It wasn't always popular, but it was necessary.

The number one question that women and people of color ask me when I do candidate trainings is: how do you put up with the racism and sexism you face every day? And, most importantly, how do we train ourselves to be seen as effective, still stand up to both the well-intentioned and the bullies, and not exhaust ourselves doing it every day?

Being the only woman of color and the only immigrant in the room has just been a fact of life for me, and through time, I've learned—mostly—how to pick my battles. It requires knowing when to hold emotions in check and when to unleash them for a purpose. I critique myself often, on everything so that I can get better at what I do. Steve has often remarked that I always review video or audio of speeches, interactions, testimony, TV appearances over and over. I study myself, I modify, and I always search for new and better ways to communicate clearly and concisely. This is a specific tactic that works for me, but the broader lesson is about preparation. I prepare for everything I do so that even when opportunities arise all of a sudden, I am not taken unaware. Preparation can be a great equalizer, and for those of us accustomed to being dismissed, we know we must prepare and stay aware.

As women and people of color, it's all too familiar to have to work harder than everyone else to prove you can do the job. When I was campaigning for Congress, my consultants told me that I had to tout my accomplishments hard—and repeatedly. "The research shows that people literally don't hear the accomplishments of women and people of color, even when they are stated; and if they do, they don't believe it," they told me.

It's hard to pinpoint and it is not always easy to know when to say something in defense of our abilities. If we do, we are seen as overly sensitive, too focused on racism and sexism, or too shrill and angry. If we don't, we have to contend with our own frustration at consistently being portrayed in a way that minimizes our accomplishments. Intuitively, we steel ourselves for this all the time even if it's unconscious. I had to deal with this early and often in my first months in Congress.

One example was a late night in a week of late nights. The night before, I had been on the floor late at night offering an amendment to the Appropriations bills, and then had a very early morning appearance on C-SPAN's *Washington Journal* show where a Republican caller had called in to complain loudly about immigrants and I had listened carefully, empathized, and then pushed back in a way that would ultimately generate 10 million views on the video clip and several complimentary articles including from the *Washington Post*.

I was tired but my legislative aide, Danielle, asked me if I wanted to speak in opposition to an amendment being offered by my Republican colleague, Representative Don Young from Alaska, that would have allowed for predatory hunting on federal parks lands in Alaska. I said yes, because environmental issues are critically important to me and in my district. In my first year in Congress, I had developed a clear plan to work on a number of different environmental issues. I started the United for Climate and Environmental Justice Task Force, with my colleagues Nanette Barragan and Don McEachin. I was one of the original co-sponsors of the 100 by '50 bill in the House, to get to 100 percent renewable energy by 2050. And I had continued my work—started in the state senate, where I was ranking member on Parks and Natural Resources—to protect our public lands and habitats and all our species from continuing attacks.

Representative Young was positioning his amendment as a state's rights issue, but I firmly believed it was not, given that we were talking about federal lands, lands that were to be enjoyed and visited by people from across the country not just those from Alaska. Danielle had quickly drafted, and I had approved, the speech I would give on the floor.

It was close to 11 p.m. when I rose to claim my five minutes of time in opposition to his amendment on the House floor. I focused my comments on legitimate disagreements between us: "These national lands are intended to be enjoyed by all Americans, including those who visit and hope to have the rare opportunity to see bears and wolves in their natural habitats," I said. "These are reasonable regulations that prevent cruel hunting practices."[10]

What happened next was completely unexpected. Instead of challenging me on policy points, Representative Young turned personal and nasty.

"You know," he said, "I rarely do this but I'm deeply disappointed in my good lady from Washington . . . she doesn't know a damn thing what she's talking about." He accused me of not having written my own comments and having a staff member write them who was affiliated with "an interest group . . . like the Humane Society." He continued with his "disappointment," saying "You may not know me, young lady . . ." at which point I had had enough.

As Young was speaking, I was starting to boil. Why wasn't the House speaker stopping him from insulting me, as during my time in the state senate where the chair had the authority to call out and halt insulting comments? Somewhere in the recesses of my mind, I remembered that in Congress, no one polices disrespect except the member that experiences it. I remembered too that our Democratic whip, Steny Hoyer, had told us during an orientation session about floor procedures that when someone disrespects you on the floor, you can demand that the person "take down his words." I vaguely remembered that this was the procedural move to tell a member who is out of line to take back what they said. But the truth was I had no real idea what would happen when I made the demand. Still, I knew I had to do it.

I calmly (on the outside, shaking on the inside) interrupted Representative Young, and demanded of the presiding speaker that the "gentleman from Alaska take down his words." Young tried to speak over me, saying, "I am still talking," but I refused to be silenced and kept going.

"Mr. Chairman, the gentleman has already impugned my motives by saying that I don't know a damn thing about what I'm talking about . . ."

Young was now interrupting me saying he never said "damn." But I knew what I had heard and I wasn't going to be thrown off, so I continued, "He has now called me 'young lady,' and Mr. Chairman, I ask that he take down his words."[11]

The minute I made my demand, a hush came over the floor. The presiding Speaker, advised by the parliamentarians who are on the floor at all times, immediately told Young to suspend and asked the clerk (who takes down everything that is being said) to "report the words."

I saw the parliamentarian come rushing out from his office, and Speaker Ryan's floor director from his. Apparently, behind me, a number of staff from both parties came out to observe the proceedings. I stood still, conscious that I was being observed and that I had begun a process that I was not entirely sure how it would play out.

My colleague, Betty McCollum, who was presiding over our side's time, said she would try to get Representative Young's eye to get him to come over and apologize. In the meantime, the Republican House speaker's floor director came rushing over to me. "I'm sorry that happened," he said. "Would you accept a motion for unanimous consent to strike those remarks from the record?"

I recognized dimly that if he was asking me to accept the consent motion, then perhaps I actually had some leverage still, even if I wasn't sure exactly what it was! I decided to push the point.

"Only with a public apology," I said.

He looked at me as if I was crazy. I didn't know it at the time, but Don Young was somewhat legendary for his past public statements, slurs, and even physical violence against a reporter.[12] The parliamentarian later told me that he had never heard Young be challenged on the floor for anything, or apologize. He had been in Congress longer than any other current member except John Conyers at the time, and he had a reputation.

"Well, I can try, but I can't guarantee an apology," he said. "After all, it's Don Young."

By this time, I was mad and I wasn't going to back down.

"Well, I'm Pramila Jayapal," I said. "And I want a public apology."

It seemed absurd to me that someone would be able to say those things in 2017 and get away with it. And it felt disrespectful not only to me, but to the 750,000 people I represented.

In the meantime, McCollum had caught Young's eye and motioned for him to come over. He came over, took my hand, and said, "I'm sorry, I just care so much about my district, I couldn't help myself."

"Well, I care about my district too," I responded. "And I represent 750,000 people just like you do." (Later, Whip Hoyer reminded me that the Alaska representative—there is only one—is elected by fewer than 750,000, because the State of Alaska has fewer than 750,000 residents.)

"Would you let me off the hook?" Young asked. "I'll make a motion for unanimous consent to strike the words from the record."

"I would accept that," I responded. "But I want a public apology as well."

Surprisingly, Young agreed. It turned out that the leverage I had was strong! Later, the parliamentarian told me that if I had not agreed to accept his unanimous consent motion, the House floor would have been shut down for a few hours, likely well after midnight, as the parliamentarians reviewed what had happened. They likely would have ruled in my favor, which would have then meant we could have a roll call vote of all members to censure Young by not allowing him to speak for the rest of the evening, even about his own amendment.

I accepted Young's apology as graciously as I could, saying that we should get to know each other and work together on something. I don't think Young had ever been challenged that way before, and I'm not sure he knew what to do. I wanted to take the high road: I had challenged him, gotten my public apology, and he had apologized—all apparently unheard of from him. Most importantly, I had made my point and hopefully, other women—and men—had benefited from the exchange.

In moments like this, I often find I manage to hold myself together, but then feel the rush of emotion after. I went to the Democratic cloakroom to collect myself. I was just starting to let myself feel fully what had happened and I was furious. Furious that we have to still deal with things like this, furious that this was the second time in just seven months that something like this had happened. I dashed off a quick tweet—without referencing what had happened directly—saying, "To all the women of color out there: refuse to be patronized or minimized. Let all those small guys out there be intimidated by you."[13]

That tweet went viral within moments. Unbeknownst to me, my friend Ilyse Hogue—the President of NARAL—had been watching and immediately tweeted out a clip of the incident with praise for how I had handled it and not backed down. Reporters began tweeting about it. Prominent women—including Chelsea Clinton—joined the chorus. Now This and Credo made short videos with the incident to spread. Seeing all of that helped me to pull myself together. My legislative aide, Danielle, who had been sitting behind me the whole time and whose stunned eyes in the moment are captured on video as everything was happening, gave me a big hug and told me how much what I had done meant to young women like her.

In the moment, I didn't think about anything except that I had to take on this arrogant, sexist man who was disrespecting me on the floor of the House of Representatives. I had every right to be there and he had no right to do what he did. That's all I thought about. The rest of it was years of training to stand up for myself and for women in general that allowed me to trust myself and my intuition, some false bravado, and a prayer that it would all go okay.

And it did.

Not all acts of standing up to sexism and racism are easy calls to make. But in the fall of 2017, we saw hundreds and thousands of women make some of the bravest, toughest calls of their lives when they decided to come forward and tell the stories of their sexual assaults—regardless of how much power the men accused wielded. It began with women speaking up against producer Harvey Weinstein and brought light to the #MeToo movement, started by a powerful black woman named Tarana Burke as early as 2006. Then the #MeToo movement came into the political arena, too, which should have come as no surprise, since no field—politics included—is free of sexual harassment and assault; after all, President Trump has, to date, been credibly accused by at least seventeen women.[14] That fall, an Alabama senate candidate, Roy Moore, was credibly accused of sexual assault and having relationships with women as young as fourteen (under the state's age of consent) when he was in his thirties. And not long after that, unfortunately, a longtime civil rights hero of mine was accused too.

Congressman John Conyers was the chairman of the House Judiciary Committee, on which I served, and a lion among progressives as well as one of the founding members of the Congressional Black Caucus. I'd looked up to him for decades. But it came out that fall that several of his former staff members said he had sexually harassed them, and then paid out settlements to prevent past accusations from coming to light. I saw the difficulty within my party to come to terms with this when it happened to one or our own, but I also knew we would lose all credibility if we had double standards. If we were going to be a party that champions women, we had to be the party of zero tolerance. I had been vocal and loud on Roy Moore, and I had spent many years working to stop violence against women on multiple fronts.

After a very difficult period of reflection and assessment, and as reports of Conyers's actions from multiple women continued to come out, I felt I had to call for Conyers to resign. I was the only member of the Judiciary Committee to do so and I felt the sting of that from my own colleagues. I was also one of only two female members of Congress who called for Conyers's resignation before Nancy Pelosi, then the minority leader, did so. Conyers did in fact retire, and it was painful to see a civil rights hero have to step aside in that way. But what I knew was this: we had to be able to hold two truths together: that as a civil rights leader, he had done many incredible things, *and* that in a position of power, he had badly violated women in his path. We could not paste over the wrongs that had been done simply because he had done so many "rights."

#MeToo taught us—and continues to teach us—that it doesn't matter if the transgressor is a famous television anchor, movie star, congressman, or client in a restaurant: the abuse of power by the men who have had it must be taken on by all of us, including when the transgressor is someone we might love or want to believe. Sexual harassment hurts women, yes—but it also undermines democracy. In Congress, like elsewhere, these men had to relinquish power. It was the only way.[15]

Soon after that, Brett Kavanaugh would be nominated to serve on the highest court of the land, the United States Supreme Court. I was among millions of women across the country who watched Christine Blasey Ford testify to a Republican-controlled Senate Judiciary Committee and the world about the worst night of her life, when she was sexually assaulted by Kavanaugh. I imagine many of us were weeping and furious at the spectacle of a hearing conducted by an all-male Republican majority that made a mockery out of Blasey Ford and any women who dared to come forward to testify. Kavanaugh's outrageous behavior and disrespect for the senators should have been enough to disqualify him from the highest court of the land, but the stakes for conservative, antiabortion Republican senators and the movement behind them were too high to have any respect for what this meant for women across the country and for the trust in our judicial system.

When the Senate Judiciary Committee voted to move Kavanaugh's nomination to the full Senate, I joined a handful of other House Democratic women in a march over to the Senate and stood in silent, furious protest as man after man on the Republican side voted to move the nomination forward. After the vote, I went down to the lobby of the Senate building where hundreds of women activists and advocates were gathered, many weeping and retraumatized by this event after their own experiences of sexual assault. The pain was palpable, but what I said to them— through my own tears—is that this was exactly why we *could not give up*. We women needed to take back our power, we needed to demand change from the bottom up, because the institution we served in did not serve us.

As it was, that was exactly what happened. In 2018, women powered the elections across the country. The rage, frustration, and resolute demand to change the status quo of male domination ended up in the biggest rout of Republican, mostly male, congressmembers, who were replaced by the most diverse, most female, and most progressive Congress in the history of our country. Change may happen slowly, but it *can* happen if we refuse to be silent or silenced, refuse to give up our power, and refuse to be defeated.

I had used my first term in Congress to add new skills to those I had already honed as an activist. I now knew how to question a witness and how to use the time I had in a hearing. I prepared like crazy for everything and I worked eighteen hours a day to make sure that I would be ready for whatever was coming. I pushed the boundaries of the platform as much as I could, and I learned what it meant to organize inside the building, not just outside. It was not easy being in the minority party, but in a way, it prepared me for the next chapter when I would be part of the Democratic majority and pushing for a bold, progressive agenda.

7

Building, Pushing, Surging: The Squad, Pelosi, and Me

WE REALLY DID MAKE HISTORY IN 2018. THE RESISTANCE WENT FROM AN idea of opposition to the declaration of propositions. I was thrilled to win reelection myself, running against a ferocious anti-immigrant opponent and winning with more votes than any member of Congress anywhere in the country, thanks to a wonderfully supportive and tuned-in district and a fantastic turnout operation on our part. Now, I was also part of a wave of exciting progressive energy that swept in a record number of women and people of color, including the first two Muslim women, the first two Native American women, numerous African American women who were elected as firsts in their states, and the youngest woman ever elected. Among them were the brilliant, social-media savvy, and courageous women who later self-titled themselves "the Squad": Representatives Rashida Tlaib, Ilhan Omar, Alexandria Ocasio-Cortez, and Ayanna Pressley.

I had known Rashida for over a decade and had met Ilhan when she was elected to the state legislature, the same year I was elected to Congress. I had been the first member of Congress to endorse both of them in their campaigns for Congress, and I had followed Ayanna's and Alexandria's races with great interest. I simply did not agree with many of my colleagues who felt it was wrong for these women to challenge sitting Democratic members of Congress.

First, I don't feel any of us are entitled to our congressional seats. If we are elected, we should work hard all the time to make sure we are representing our districts, and we have to respect the very Democratic process of people running against us and the voters making their selection. Our job is to make it hard for someone to beat us by running great campaigns and actually connecting with and appropriately representing voters. Too many times, there is a notion that once you are elected, you have the right to stay. I disagree. Nobody owns a seat in Congress. I know that I work my tail off to make sure I win—not just during the election, but in actually doing the work to listen to and represent the people who elect me.

Second, the truth of the matter is that the majority of people of color in Congress win in Democratic districts because those are the districts that most often give them a shot at winning. The existing seniority system in Congress motivates some members to stay for interminably long times. Even if members are excellent—as was the member of Congress I replaced—the truth is that change is important. If we want to build a leadership pipeline, we have to actually agree to step out of the way at some point so others can rise. This has always been important to me: it's why I decided to step aside as executive director at OneAmerica after founding the organization and serving as the leader for almost twelve years. People thought I was crazy to step aside when I had grown it to the size and power it had, and to give up that platform. But for me, I had seen too many people hold power for too long, and it bothered me. We needed the new energy to come in—and I needed to leave to grow in other ways, too. Someone once said there are three ways to leave elected office: die, be voted out, or step aside. Unfortunately, the latter is exceedingly rare. That meant that if you wanted to see a real change in the composition of elected bodies, with more women and more people of color, you have to be willing to respect the challenges made to incumbents.

I also found that the entrenched network of established connections made it difficult for people of color to break through or get necessary assistance or validation. Challenging incumbents also seemed more acceptable when the challenger was male and white, or had a set of relationships to wealth and power, than if the challenger was an "upstart" woman of color. Herein lay the same racism and sexism that we have all known and felt. The Progressive Caucus had felt bound to endorse Representative Mike Capuano, whom Ayanna was challenging: Capuano had been a strong and stalwart progressive member. However, when the caucus was discussing investing in a separate independent expenditure *against* Ayanna, I was instrumental in killing the idea. To me, it was one thing to endorse Capuano; it was another thing to work to defeat a strong, progressive woman of color running against him.

As a side note, Republicans experienced many more retirements and changes in leadership, in part, I believe, because they had instituted a system of limits on chairs. A Republican chair could go on to become a chair of a different committee, but the reality of stepping down from being chair of a powerful committee to become a mere member of that same committee made Republican chairs weigh the pros and cons of staying more carefully than Democrats.

For Democrats, keeping seniority and not having term limits had become equated with respecting the rights of Black Caucus members who had finally won seniority among a very white caucus. I had tremendous respect for this view, but in my book, we now were in a different place where we had more and more members of color being elected that could rise to levels of power if given a chance with some sensible term limits, at least term limits for committee chairs if not term limits for members. As it was, the conventional wisdom was that you had to stay in Congress for at least two decades in order to gain the seniority required to have real power.

It wasn't just the members of the Squad that I was excited about, though. Equally important were progressive women and men who had won in previously Republican districts on strong progressive platforms that belied the myth that progressive ideas couldn't win in swing districts.

Because of my year-round organizing campaign, which I had kept going strong during my first term, I had turned out many of my campaign staff and volunteers to work on knocking on doors and making phone calls for other competitive districts across the country. I had also financially supported many campaigns and gone to campaign for several progressive candidates, including Katie Porter, Katie Hill, and Mike Levin in California's Orange County area; Andy Kim in New Jersey; and Jahana Hayes in Connecticut, among others. These were progressives in swing districts who wanted to do what was right for their districts and even stand up for ideas that mainstream Democratic consultants advised them against. And they won. It was exciting to watch and to be a part of it.

I had also supported and endorsed some inspiring progressive candidates who got extremely close, sometimes without the help of the mainstream Democratic establishment: people like Andrew Gillum in Florida, Stacey Abrams in Georgia, or House candidates like Sri Kulkarni and Gina Ortiz-Jones in Texas. Many of them tossed the old formula of appealing simply to the middle to the winds and instead worked to expand the electorate, to bring in and inspire new voters who would get them closer to being elected than ever before. Often, they did not receive early help from the Democratic establishment, where many feared that their progressive platforms (which included in some cases Medicare for All) were "too progressive." Does this sound familiar?

These candidates, however, ran inspiring campaigns and won their primaries, boosting turnout in their states during the general elections often to higher levels than ever before. They also had to combat racism and voter suppressing that—in the case of Stacey Abrams—even stole the election from the rightful winner. They didn't win, but they proved themselves so they could be first in line to challenge the incumbents in 2020 with good chances of success.

For the first time in 2018, we also saw a new phenomenon of down-ballot races driving votes for the top of the ticket. Conventional wisdom had it that the races at the top of the ticket—like for governor or congress—would drive turnout for state representatives, local judges, and the like. In 2018, we saw something different. Trans people, women, and people of color running in local and state races were actually driving turnout for the top of the ticket. In Virginia, for example, trans and Latina candidates for state legislature helped drive energy for the governor's race—which was far less inspiring for many people.

Unlike most congressional campaigns that stashed away money for their own election, I wanted to operate differently. Just as I did when running for the state senate, I wanted to have a year-round campaign, but this time I had more campaign resources, more volunteers, and a bigger platform to engage. I also had the anger of voters who were against Trump, and their deep desire to do something that would make a difference.

I had always had a real problem with the way elections typically are conducted: candidates would ignore voters until just before the election and then suddenly work to court them. It was infuriating, both because the interactions were episodic and late, and also because it wasted the power of the platform to organize year-round. During my first-term in Congress, using my campaign funds that most candidates kept only for themselves and their campaigns, I ran a year-round organizing operation to work on other competitive swing districts and on issues that pushed against the status quo, like our positions on healthcare and immigration. I hired staff and put more than a thousand volunteers to work, training them to learn the skills they'd need and putting them to work on door knocking and phone banks for other swing district candidates in the state and across the country. It was exhilarating, and a different way to utilize my campaign infrastructure as a sitting member of Congress.

Of course, it also meant that I spent a lot of my campaign cash organizing for others, something other members did not do, which would put me at a disadvantage in terms of stocking my campaign account for any future runs. I didn't care much about that. I cared about using my platform and my power in the best way possible for NOW. My advice to others who wanted to run was always to think about what you want to do, not what you want to be. I was not going to stop listening to my own advice.

On my side, I was now—oddly, after just two years—considered a more "senior" member of Congress, at least relative to the new members elected in 2018. Recognizing my activist background but also that I was not a new member, a local reporter named Essex Porter went on our local NPR station and called me the "Godmother of the Squad." I wasn't so sure about that, but I had made it a point to reach out to the new women and particularly the people of color who had been elected. I visited all of them in their offices in the first weeks of the new Congress, sent Seattle chocolates to each of the newly elected members as congratulations gifts, and did what I could to be helpful. As soon as they were elected, several of them asked me for help in how to set up their offices. As a member who had recently gone through everything they were going through, I was able to talk them through the decisions I had made and what to look for. I asked my staff to give them all our documents—from budgets to office processes—and help in any way we could.

I knew how hard it was to be a newcomer to Congress and how little mentorship there really was, and I wanted it to be different for these newly elected congresswomen. My training as an organizer is also all about building relationships and supporting the collective, and I knew these early moments of assistance would be crucial as we built our team of progressives. Later, these relationships would get even closer. My apartment became a place for many of the women of color to come and vent or strategize. Word got around that I liked to cook and that I made comfort food dishes, like hot vegetarian soups or Indian favorites like a chickpea dish called chana masala. Sometimes, a member would call me up and say, "Can I come over for homemade soup and wine?" I couldn't always deliver on homemade soup, but the answer was always, "Of course. There'll be wine and boxed soup, if necessary!"

Those have been some of my favorite moments, when members drop their guard and share their problems and support each other. That was much more prevalent in the activist world. Here in Congress, there was more competition and less time. Even to each other, we were supposed to pretend that we had it all under control, when the truth was we were all struggling in different ways. All of us struggled with the demands of the job—from staff management and transitions, to competitiveness with other members, to trying to make our mark on the issues that mattered to us the most when there were many other members who cared about those issues too.

Beyond the issues, it was the conversation, the camaraderie and the sense of community that helped. With the women of color, in particular, we needed our own spaces to talk things through, to vent and to share experiences that were unique to us. Sharing food, drink, and time helped rejuvenate our souls and spirits, and these get-togethers gave us that space that felt so desperately necessary.

One of the other things I am always asked is, how do you take care of yourself and bring balance into your life? These are important questions, and particularly for people of color who don't always have the same support networks in the bodies in which we serve. As a woman of color, I tell other women in Congress that you cannot take on *all* the things that come at you that are racist, sexist, xenophobic, anti-Muslim, or dog whistles for any of those things—you name it. You've got to preserve yourself for the work you have to get done. Be strategic about what you take on, and where and when you bring your personal experience into the picture to illuminate an issue.

But one reframe that I have recently come to is that sometimes for us women of color, the urgency of the work is so much greater. *Doing the work* actually becomes the balance for us, the hope of what might be and the way in which we steel ourselves to face what is. That's true for me, certainly. I am driven when it comes to change. It takes its toll on me and on my staff because there is always more to do and I feel so damn *responsible*. But it is also what I know I *must* do, because the injustice is so great and we do not have the luxury of time. Each of us gets only one life, and my goal is to make every moment count for something much bigger than myself.

For me, finding ways to calm myself and take on my insecurities in the moment has been paramount. I know that familiar flush of indignation, or even misplaced shame, when I feel disrespected. I know the dangers of self-flagellation because I suddenly feel like I'm not good enough or perhaps I just don't belong here. Those feelings have lessened as I have gotten higher in power and platform, but they certainly haven't gone away. I work hard to be more prepared, more articulate, more armed with facts than anyone else; but sometimes, I still flounder or fear I will flounder.

In those moments, I breathe. Literally. I have perfected some deep-breathing techniques, where I take whatever moments I have and I focus on my breath. I have mantras that come to me in the moment, for example, where I breathe in power or confidence and breathe out insecurity or fear. I focus on my center, right there around my belly, and I try to feel my feet grounded in the earth and imagine my arms reaching to the sky. I bring forth the voices of those who came before me, and the responsibility of those who will come after me. Often, if I am in a hearing room and about to speak, I bring the faces and the voices of people who are directly affected into the room with me, people that I have worked with and know. They help me to feel less alone and to know that our power is vast; sometimes we just have to recognize that this is so by conjuring it up.

This book would not be authentic if I were not honest that there are many times when I feel completely defeated, as if I don't know how I will continue. But, fortunately or unfortunately, I have had lots of training. I've been threatened with lynching, I've been denied a room because of the color of my skin, I've been told countless times to "go back" to my own country, and I've had horrible, hateful words directed at me personally. I'm not saying it doesn't take a toll—it does. But you have to find ways to replenish yourself and surround yourself with love instead of hate.

In those moments, my greatest source of grounding is my family and close friends. Steve has been with me, at my side, since the beginning, and when I come home exhausted and fall into his arms after a long week away, he knows to just hold me and even let me weep. Janak, as they have grown older and faced the challenges of their own explorations of gender, race, and identity, has become an advisor, confidant, and friend—even as I strongly hold onto my own role and responsibility as mother and protector of them, too. Janak's political sensibilities, born of an acutely aware and even threatened millennial generation that does not even know if they will still have a planet for their kids, have been like crystal clear bells of responsibility for me. But more than that, their recognition of what I am fighting for and their protectiveness gives me a shield of love, an armor of strength from which to do what I do. Coming home after a long hard week in DC and going for a walk along the Puget Sound with Steve and our dog, Otis, have become a regular ritual to bring air, beauty, and spaciousness back into a world that sometimes feels too dark and overwhelming.

I suppose in the end, we just have to learn to trust ourselves and to build a small but strong circle of love around us. It is the nature of a highly public job such as this, where being on television all the time and taking on some of our biggest and most controversial challenges, means that there is not much private space even to go out for a quiet dinner with Steve and Janak or to walk in an airport without being recognized. I learned to receive the gratitude of people at airports, in restaurants, or on the streets who came up and told me that watching me stand up for our country gave them hope. So far, most of those who approach me do so to say thank you—but I know that may change. This public nature of my work has also meant that I have had to become increasingly protective of my time, and so my close circle of friends who I can truly trust and be myself with is small but fierce. Their deep understanding and support are part and parcel of any success I might have, and I work hard to make sure I am being a good friend back to them because I know how mutual friendships must be to be real.

In a world increasingly dominated by stories that prop us up and celebrate successes without talking about the real loneliness, insecurity, or fear that almost always accompanies any successes—particularly for members of minority communities—I work to remember that fears, insecurities, and emotions are part of what make us human. And humanness is something desperately missing in our political arena today. Being human is a courageous act and I try never to forget that.

Perhaps that is why I also have taken the unusual step of using my own personal narrative on the House floor. It's not common, nor is it easy or comfortable, to use "I" or speak about your own experience publicly. However, the use of personal narrative and story are among the most basic of organizing strategies and I believe they need to play a greater role in policymaking and politics too.

Donald Trump's election and the fact that I was one of very few naturalized citizens in the United States Congress made immigration personal for me, and I knew I had to call forth that personal experience even as I recognized that the issues around immigration were far worse for so many others. Telling my personal story as an immigrant grounded the discussion and gave me a perch from which to speak.

Too many people think that as elected officials we are supposed to be unemotional, intellectual, above it all, in order to be seen as fair and unbiased. To my mind, that view is as unrealistic as the idea that the British colonialists who wrote about India were unbiased simply because they did not express "raw emotion" when, in fact, their analysis was loaded with false assumptions and personal biases.

When I spoke about the family separations that were occurring at our southern border, I was noticeably moved and emotional. Those videos went viral within minutes, and I believe it was because when we show our own emotion, that emotion allows others to tap into that deep emotion in themselves. When emotion is authentic, it opens up paths to power and it allows a connection that simply isn't possible with a mere analytical argument.

For women of color in particular, tapping into this emotion can be dangerous. Everything in society teaches us to move away from emotion, intuition, and the heart, and toward an "intellectual," mind-centered focus. If we stray, we are deemed "too emotional" or "not rational," fulfilling somehow the stereotypes that we are different and ought not be fully seen. And yet: the sharing of human emotions is perhaps the most basic way to connect with people we don't know.

There's also this vague expectation that we ought not share what is personal to us because it will be undermine our political careers, or because
our platforms are so broadly encompassing that the public sharing of some
of our most personal experiences leaves us feeling naked and exposed. Yet
again, the platform we have *is* the very reason we should use our personal
experiences to full effect.

That's why in April 2019, during a House Judiciary Committee hearing on the Equality Act, which would provide critical nondiscrimination
protections to LGBTQ individuals, I decided to share Janak's personal
story with the world. I had no intention of doing so when I walked into
the hearing. Janak had told me the summer before that they were gender nonconforming. To those that don't know, this means that someone's
behavior or appearance does not conform to prevailing cultural and social
expectations of what is "appropriate" for their outwardly appearing gender.

Janak had come downstairs in our house one day wearing a dress and
lipstick, and shared that they had been exploring the fluidity of both
gender and sexual orientation. Janak asked us to use the "they" pronoun
instead of he or she, to reflect their identity better. I listened closely and
learned tremendously. As progressive as I was, this was new for me as a
mother. And yet, what I knew is that I would do everything I could do
to support my child in understanding who they really were. What I saw
unfold was a new freedom for Janak to be who they fully were, a newly
released creativity and resilience, a happiness in not having to hide parts of
themselves or conform to society's expectations. I saw beauty, even in all
the challenges and judgments that taking a different path brings.

Janak and I had discussed whether or not I should publicly speak about
their identity, and we had decided that I should not to do so just yet. As
a musician, they had just released a new album on an independent label,
and the album picture (taken by Steve) was of Janak and their musician
collaborator, Gabe, where Janak was in a beautiful dress and wore lipstick.
They wanted to own their own identity fully before I started speaking
about it, and I respected that.

During the hearing, however, I became more and more irate at my

Republican colleagues who were mocking, undermining, and berating the concept of gender nonconforming, nonbinary, and trans people in particular (perhaps it was a sign of relative progress that lesbians and gays were not as much under attack as these other identities). As the mother of a gender nonconforming child, I was furious and the attacks felt directed at Janak. I began to feel that I wanted to say something about Janak, even though my stomach was in knots about making such a personal statement. No members themselves had come out as trans or gender nonconforming, nor had any member revealed a close relative as such. This would be a first and it was sure to make news. I knew that I would never say something if Janak did not want me to, so in the middle of the hearing, I texted them.

"Babe, we are doing a hearing today on the Equality Act. I don't have your story written in to my comments, but how do you feel about my referring to you and what it makes me feel like to hear my child talked about in these horrible ways? If it feels like you are not ready yet, I won't do it."

Almost immediately after I sent the text, I felt it was unfair to spring this on them as I had, and I texted again that perhaps we should just wait and do a video where Janak could approve the script. I didn't want them to feel pressured in any way.

But within minutes, Janak had responded to say that if I felt moved to say something and I thought it would help others, I should say something, that they would prefer to have it come up situationally, rather than as an official "announcement" video, an idea that they didn't feel drawn to personally.

With Janak's permission, I decided to speak about them right then and there. I was nervous about getting it right, so I wrote down what I wanted to say on my notepad. When I told the story, I got emotional and had to stop, but what I said was from the heart and true. Again, within minutes, the video of my speech was all over the place and articles were being written about it. But most importantly for me and for Janak, tweets, texts, and emails began flowing in from across the country, things like the following:

This hit me right in my queer brown girl feelings. Excuse me, I need to take the rest of the day off.

@RepJayapal, today you became the honorary mom to a LOT of trans, gender nonconforming and nonbinary folks out there. Thank you—for your leadership in Congress and for being an incredible mom.

It shouldn't be so revolutionary, but I can't get over how amazing it is to hear a congresswoman using they/them pronouns for their kid, on the floor of Congress.

There were negative things too that came at me, but they washed off me in the sea of positive impact that came from opening up. To this day, I hear about what that speech meant and about how it made so many people across the country feel seen, in some cases for the first time. And to this day, I am so grateful to Janak for teaching me about their identity, and then for allowing me to share their story. It mattered to so many who deserve to be seen and respected for who they are. It also reemphasized how important it is that we take on public displays of disrespect coming from Republicans. Sometimes we are ready, and often we are not, but our courage to do so resonates with millions who are counting on us to speak up.

In the wake of Brett Kavanaugh's appointment to the Supreme Court, I had another opportunity to use my platform to share a personal story. At the time, conservative activists had been moving a strategy of passing state bills to ban abortion, hoping that the legal challenges to those bans would make their way to the Supreme Court and allow a chance to reverse *Roe v. Wade*.

In the first five months of 2019, nine states had already passed laws to limit or ban abortion. Louisiana had passed a law to ban abortion after the fetal heartbeat is detected, limiting abortion to a ridiculously early stage of around six weeks of pregnancy. This law was similar to the bills passed in Georgia, Kentucky, Missouri, Mississippi, and Ohio. Alabama had banned abortion in almost all cases. The proliferation of abortion bans was terrifying to women across the country. After all, the overwhelming majority of Americans believed abortion should be legal. Kavanaugh's appointment had made it crystal clear that the fight we thought we had already won in *Roe* would have to be fought all over again, and that the health and well-being of women and families across the country were urgently at stake.

I had had an abortion shortly after meeting Steve back in the mid-2000s, during the years following Janak's traumatic premature birth and all the attendant complications of not knowing if they would live or die. I had not even shared this with my mother, much less publicly. I had considered talking about it publicly several years before when the "Shout Your Abortion" movement had just begun, but I didn't feel ready and I knew with certainty that I had to be ready if I was going to talk about what happened.

In watching the abortion bans, I suddenly felt I might be ready. As often happens, the idea of writing an essay or op-ed rattled around in my brain for days. One morning, on a flight from Seattle back to DC, I took out my computer and just wrote. The op-ed came out whole and complete. It started with Janak's traumatic birth and detailed the challenges of that birth and my own state of mind as I dealt with my own depression and what was later diagnosed as post-traumatic stress disorder. It went on to describe my knowledge that, as much as I wanted to, I was not ready to have another child, given the risks associated with any future pregnancies. It described my ultimate decision to have an abortion. I was clear that it was the pregnant person's right to choose that was important, whatever that choice was, and there was no judgement for whatever that choice was. I was also clear that while my abortion was traumatic, every abortion wasn't and didn't need to be. We needed stories of all kinds to show the diversity of the experience. The right to an abortion is a constitutional protection and that right should never rely on whether there is a medical necessity or whether a woman feels badly about having an abortion.

I sent the draft to Steve, Janak, my sister, my niece who I am close to, and to Rachel who knew the abortion issue well from her time at NARAL. I also sent it to my close friend, Ilyse Hogue, the national NARAL president. Each one gave me valuable comments, including Janak who asked me to use the "they" pronoun instead of their name. I had shied away from using "they," constructing the sentences to use Janak's name instead, because I thought it would confuse the reader who did not know Janak's gender nonconforming identity. Janak pointed out to me that readers could just google me and quickly find out about their identity, but also that it was important to them that I used the correct pronoun to help "popularize" it, in a way. Tara, my niece, also provided me with important feedback that I should use "pregnant people" instead of "women" throughout the piece to give acknowledgment to trans and nonbinary people who might not identify with the term "women" but could still be pregnant. What a gift to learn from young people!

I took all their suggestions, which were relatively minor fixes, and sent the op-ed to my communications director with a directive to try to place it in the *New York Times* or the *Washington Post*. The piece was 1,500 words—long for an op-ed—but it felt worth a try. Within twenty-four hours, we had a positive response from the *New York Times*. They made only a few edits for space, cutting it down to about 1,200 words, still long for an op-ed. It was now ready for publication—first online and then in the print version of the newspaper a few days later.

My stomach was completely in knots. I had a tremendous amount of anxiety once it was clear this was really going public. And yet, I still knew it was what I wanted to do.

On June 13, 2019, my piece was published under the title: "Rep. Pramila Jayapal: The Story of My Abortion" with a subtitle of "What it taught me about the deeply personal nature of reproductive choice."

Like the speech about Janak, the op-ed was reposted and tweeted everywhere, eliciting enormous response from across the country. Perhaps my favorite response was a letter I received from a constituent who wrote this:

> I'll start by saying that we likely disagree on a lot of issues. I'm a rare bird as a pro-life, lifelong Democrat . . . as a Christian (some say Evangelical although that term is now fraught with misunderstanding based on the President), [but] I've made the point that the faith community and progressives have so much more in common than we have differences. No issue is more divisive than abortion. . . . When your NYT feature came across my newsfeed, I thought, "Oh my, another shout my abortion story." Boy, was I wrong. And it showed me a side of you that honestly I had not considered before. Your bravery in sharing you and your husband's personal story plus the empathy you show for those that may have chosen other paths is exactly the kind of conversation we need to have . . . When the conversations go to who is the real deal and who speaks for the movement, I always mention my district and my congresswoman as being the gold standard. While we won't always agree, you have my great respect.

So, you see, our stories have tremendous power. We just have to be unafraid to use them and to use the platform we are given to humanize ourselves and the things we fight for. We've got to be willing to be transparent; and to do this, we've got to be willing to get a little personal. Sound scary?

Maybe. But consider that it is part of the connection we need to make between a government that seems too far removed and too remote from the everyday realities of life for millions of people.

People wonder why Alexandria Ocasio-Cortez has used her social media platform the way she has, particularly given the negative coverage and death threats she receives. She would likely tell you that for many of her constituents in the Bronx and Queens, her Instagram is their first glimpse inside the halls of power, or into the life of a congresswoman. She wants to demystify the process, to be approachable to constituents. Perhaps if they see a real human in the halls of power, they'll be able to see the power in themselves, too.

I've seen Barbara Lee do this effectively, too, using her own experiences as a single mom on welfare to demystify poverty and to connect her to the experiences of millions of low-income people across the country. Before I spoke out about my abortion, I had watched a clip of Congresswoman Jackie Speier do something similar on the floor of the House and it gave me strength.

Our vulnerabilities are part of our power, and they give us opportunities to model a different form of courage. If we can do this as congressmembers, we give permission (that should not be necessary) for others to have the courage to share their stories, too. In this way, we show that we have so much in common and we know, understand, and see people fully.

When I got to Congress, I had a big realization: we needed a new strategy and infrastructure if we were really going to be serious about building progressive power.

In my first term, I had been elected the first vice chair of the Congressional Progressive Caucus (CPC), where Representatives Mark Pocan and Raul Grijalva served as co-chairs. When Raul said he was ready to step down at the end of 2018, I decided to run for the co-chair position and was elected unanimously in January 2019.

This was a big deal in our new Congress. Because of the number of progressives who were elected, the CPC had grown by over twenty members to ninety-eight members total, or about 40 percent of the total Democratic caucus. I would serve as co-chair with Mark, who quickly became one of my closest colleagues in Congress.

Mark was born and raised in Kenosha, Wisconsin, and had been politically active for most of his life since college, eventually serving as the only openly gay member at the time in the Wisconsin State Assembly and then in Congress. His beginnings in political activism came in part due to an incident soon after he graduated college, when two men followed him after he left a gay bar and beat him with a baseball bat, calling him a "faggot" and other slurs. As a college journalism major, he was smart about communications and about political strategy. In the Wisconsin State Assembly, he was widely credited with moving the state's political debate to the left, and was known as one of the most outspoken progressive members in the assembly and later in Congress. It truly was a joy to be elected to serve as co-chair with Mark.

A caucus in Congress (or "congressional member organizations," as they are formally known) is simply a group of lawmakers organizing themselves around issues and identities. They meet to share information, strategize on legislative tactics, and determine common goals and platforms. As boring as this may sound, it seemed to me an important tool for organizing from within the halls of power, a place to flex the same muscles I used while organizing hunger strikes and holding Justice for All town halls with OneAmerica.

Congressional caucuses are all over the place in terms of what they do or don't do. Some are issue oriented and serve simply as a place to show shared interest in that issue to constituents. Some are identity based—like the Hispanic Caucus and the Black Caucus—and highly organized. Within the broader Democratic Caucus, the "values-based caucuses," as we referred to them, constitute views along the spectrum from progressive to conservative: there's the Progressive Caucus, the New Democrats Coalition, and the Blue Dogs Coalition. These ideological caucuses or coalitions have been more or less powerful and more or less organized, depending on the size and the leadership.

Right now, these groups can't take any outside money or have their own office spaces, and staff must be paid for through dues paid from each member's congressional budget, not from a central, assigned pot of money. But this wasn't always the case.

For many decades, there existed something called the Democratic Study Group. Formally called a Legislative Service Organization, the DSG's principal activity was to disseminate detailed written materials to congressmembers about upcoming legislation and policy issues—in other words, an inside research and policy force that could keep pace with the needs of legislators both in terms of rapid response as well as strategic vision and guidance. Formed in 1959 with a big budget and staff, the DSG was initially started in part to make sure Southern Dixiecrats did not stymie the passage of the 1964 Civil Rights Act and later worked to curb the excesses of Reagan-era austerity measures like cutting Social Security. Crucially, the DSG also helped push for procedural reforms that make the House a more democratic governing body today: these included weakening the authority of committee chairs, and making information and activities of lawmakers that leadership wanted to keep under wraps more open and accessible (this was before the internet—we take much of this information for granted today.).[1]

The group was so successful that in 1994, then-Republican House speaker Newt Gingrich shut it down and took away all the budget and staff. This left legislators much more reliant on outside groups and lobbyists, particularly when legislation would appear suddenly and lawmakers had to decide quickly how to vote. The ensuing armies of lobbyists made it easy to open your office door and hear from the closest lobbyist instead of having quick internal research available to see what the consequences of proposed legislation would be. In the years since the disbanding of DSG, Republicans and more conservative Democratic organizations worked to build their organizing power by creating outside organizations whose primary purpose was to do policy and research work that educated lawmakers, and their funding came primarily from corporations who were pushing their perspectives and values.

The CPC, as it emerged under my colleagues Maxine Waters and Bernie Sanders in the early 1990s, initially formed more as a relatively informal social group where progressive congressmembers could come together and discuss ideas. But without much staff or resources, like the DSG had, it had little ability to really leverage power. When Representative Keith Ellison, along with Raul Grijalva, had taken over as co-chair some years before, they had begun the process of bringing the CPC back to life and shaping it into a bigger coordinating force for progressive ideas, building the idea that the CPC could be a substantial player in helping negotiate the politics within Congress and beyond, laying important groundwork.

However, when I arrived in Congress in 2017, I was surprised to see how little power was really leveraged among progressives. Nothing had replaced the DSG, and there was no flow of information back and forth between the inside and the outside on key policy ideas and platforms, much less information to address the rapid response needs to fight the bad legislation that would suddenly appear. CPC members did not get the data-driven information they needed to either support progressive positions on important issues like Medicare for All or the $15 minimum wage, or to fight some of the ever-present attempts to cut funds for programs like Social Security or restructure the tax system to benefit corporations.

A big part of the problem was a lack of infrastructure to support real leveraging of progressive power. CPC staff was comprised of one full-time executive director, as well as a policy fellow placed at the CPC by an outside fellowship program. The executive director, Mike Darner, was a super-smart guy with in-depth knowledge of the progressive movement and politics including specific progressive issues as well as legislative procedures. But for him to try to try to fully staff our caucus was simply absurd. There was no way that he and the CPC fellow could adequately staff a caucus of what was at the time seventy-eight people, much less a larger CPC when we elected more progressives. I like to look at things from an infrastructure and capacity perspective, and it seemed to me that we needed a lot more infrastructure on multiple levels if we were going to have the capacity to move significant progressive priorities.

Mark and I decided that we would raise the dues—they hadn't been raised in years and were significantly lower than the dues for all the other ideological caucuses; this would allow us to hire additional permanent staff. But that still wasn't enough for us to replicate or expand on the DSG's former power in terms of policy and research, and in today's world, there were new opportunities for leveraging the power of organizing and movement groups, on the ground as well as in terms of communications strategies. We clearly needed a real organization—and I knew how to build organizations!

Together with the other members of the board, Mark and I set out to rebuild a newly envisioned and powerful organization, a 501(c)(3) non-profit that we called the Congressional Progressive Caucus Center. This was a new and much more robust iteration of an organization that had previously existed at a low level, with the primary activity of putting on a conference once a year.

Sitting at the intersection of policy makers, movement groups, and progressive think tanks, the board envisioned a center that would help drive a more strategic and aligned progressive movement. Within six months, we had raised $1.5 million for the first year of operation, and obtained multiyear funding commitments from a number of donors, including labor unions and groups like MoveOn and End Citizens United that were excited about having more direct ability to harness progressive power to move key priorities forward, as well as foundations that saw this as an opportunity to coordinate existing resources on both the policy, research, and movement organization fronts.

The board envisioned the CPC Center as an organization that would coordinate, convene, and align a more powerful progressive coalition and movement. Today, the center has a full-time staff of fifteen, including six legislative fellows who are placed in congressional offices to build a more diverse talent pipeline on the Hill. It coordinates a policy and research council and a movement table consisting of the major organizing groups. And it still puts on a yearly conference that now brings together grassroots organizations from all across the country to be in direct conversation with elected leaders and Washington policy types.

In many ways, the CPC Center embodies the philosophy and theory of change I developed when I first decided to run for office in 2014. To be effective, the progressive movement needs a strong infrastructure—on the inside and the outside. And to be an effective progressive legislator, one must truly appreciate the power of organizing and advocacy movements. Today, we have a caucus nearly one hundred members strong committed to fighting for change alongside a progressive movement that is stronger and more powerful than ever.

The one final piece of necessary infrastructure was on the political side.

Before I had arrived, Mark had already been working on growing the CPC Political Action Committee. It had gone from raising only half a million dollars per cycle to raising over $2 million per cycle, which we could use to support progressive candidates across the country.

These three pieces—the internal CPC expanded staffing, the new CPC Center, and the CPC PAC—formed the bones of the progressive movement's infrastructure and capacity to leverage inside and outside organization that supported our bold vision for progressive change.

Now, we had to learn how to flex our Progressive Caucus muscle as it related to the larger Democratic Caucus. The only model for this that we had was the Republican's Freedom Caucus. Mark and I knew we did not want to be compared to the Freedom Caucus, which was in our mind a caucus of "NO" while we were a caucus of "YES." But the challenges of figuring out how to flex our progressive power while not shutting down our own Democratic majority was complicated and required organizing, training ourselves, and strategy. It also required backbone and being comfortable with making some of our broader House Democratic Caucus leadership unhappy. It was made both particularly necessary in the era of Trump but also particularly challenging to take on our own Democratic majority at a tenuous time in history, with so much at stake and a desire from most Democrats to stay united against Trump and minimize divisions among ourselves.

Now in the majority, Democrats had real opportunities to pass legislation in the House that could set the party's agenda going into the 2020 presidential elections. As the majority party, we were charged with this new responsibility and a greater sense that perhaps brighter days were ahead, but our Democratic Caucus was still very diverse. While progressives made up 40 percent of the Caucus, the ideologically centrist New Democrats Caucus and the conservative Democratic Blue Dogs caucus had also grown, and they believed in a very different path forward than many progressives.

Our first big fight would be the fight for speaker of the House. Many

House Democrats were challenging Nancy Pelosi for the job of House speaker. She had held the position before from 2007 to 2011 and she assumed she would get the role. But the Republicans had succeeded in making her into a somewhat divisive figure for some of the new members, who had—in some cases—made a 2018 campaign promise that they would not support her for speaker. Some existing members had also decided to mount a fight against her candidacy—the only problem being that they didn't seem to have another alternative and certainly not one as progressive as she is.

Mark and I discussed what kind of support we should request from some of our members and outside allies. This could be an important moment to leverage the vote for speaker into some early progressive wins. We came up with three key asks that we would put to Pelosi in return for supporting her candidacy as progressives.

First, we realized that one of our problems was that progressives simply were never put on the four "A" or "money" committees—largely because, as horrible as it is, committee assignments were partly defined by who could raise the most money for the Democratic Caucus by sitting on those powerful committees. Progressives tended to want to hold corporations' feet to the fire, which meant they would not likely raise much money for the caucus through those prestigious assignments. As a result, progressives were woefully underrepresented on all these exclusive committees. But these committees were important beyond the money-raising opportunities they provided; they were committees where real power was built and exercised that would help us to advance—or stop—much of our progressive agenda.

Our ask of Pelosi was that progressives would have representation that was proportional to our percentage of the caucus. In other words, we wanted 40 percent of all the Democratic committee members on these four exclusive committees to be members of the CPC. This was a clear and crisp ask with a sensible rationale. We also wanted to include freshmen in at least some of the "A" committees. While it was unlikely that Ways and Means, Appropriations, or Energy and Commerce would take first-term members, there was significant precedent for including first-term members on Financial Services, where Maxine Waters would be chairwoman and wanted new and expanded progressive energy.

Second, we wanted more leadership spots that progressives could run for. Leadership roles in the previous Democratic caucus were limited in number and relatively closed. Other than Pelosi herself, there were no progressives in the top leadership. This made it hard to push a progressive agenda on numerous fronts. We wanted to expand the leadership spots and then run more progressives for those spots. We also wanted to have budget and staff for some entities like the Democratic Policy and Communications Committee, which would help give those entities more responsibility and capacity.

Third, we were concerned about the reinstitution of a set of rules requiring bills to be paid for through budget cuts or tax increases before even being considered. For progressives in my caucus, these requirements were troubling because they make the kinds of bold, structural changes our voters had asked for difficult to propose because they do not account for the long-term fiscal savings these policy proposals would net—not to mention the moral imperative of proposals like Medicare for All or the Green New Deal. These rules requiring that the short-term funding be identified in order to be considered, known as PAYGO, have historically been political footballs; both parties implement them on and off when it is convenient. And no one ever seemed to ask Republicans to offset the cost of their multiple rounds of tax cuts over the last decade.[2] Similarly, increased Pentagon spending was never subjected to fiscal scrutiny of any kind, by Democratic or Republican majorities. It seemed important to register our concerns and ask for PAYGO to be excluded from the rules package.

Once we had our asks in hand, we talked to MoveOn and Indivisible who were thrilled at the idea of leveraging our support for Pelosi as speaker to get some real wins that would help us structurally leverage our power. They also knew that the lack of an option for a more progressive choice was a real limitation. They had been getting numerous calls from Pelosi's office asking them to support her for speaker, but they agreed to withhold their support until we could present our asks to Pelosi and see if we could get her commitment. We also asked our CPC members to hold their support until we talked with her. While some had committed early and others were certain to commit, we were able to get a substantial number to agree to hold off on their support until we knew the results of our conversation with Pelosi.

Mark and I set up a meeting with Pelosi for one night a few weeks after the 2018 election. As we walked in, her longtime senior aide said, "I'm hearing from the groups that they want to see how this meeting goes before they will give their support. I see you're playing hard ball here!" Our power plays were being noticed.

It was an excellent discussion. Pelosi agreed to our first two requests. Regarding PAYGO, while she would not commit to our request, she agreed to discuss the issue further with us before reinstituting those rules. Still, the agreement to both proportional representation on the money committees, as well as expanded leadership posts that we could run progressives for were huge wins. After the meeting, we sent a quick text to MoveOn and Indivisible with the news. They were ecstatic that we had flexed some muscle and won!

Within minutes, they had tweeted their support for Pelosi as the next speaker: "We strongly support and call on all members of the Democratic caucus to support @NancyPelosi for Speaker," MoveOn tweeted. "Were it not for her skilled and effective leadership, the ACA would not be law today. Dems must reject attempts to defeat her and move the caucus to the right."

Later fights did not go nearly as well. They also showed the tremendous difference between being in CPC leadership while trying to govern, versus being in the minority or not in leadership of the caucus. My responsibilities were different now: I could not just speak for myself, I had to both coordinate with Mark, so we were on the same page, and we collectively had to represent the views of our very large and diverse caucus.

Two occasions stand out to me as examples of the challenges and the opportunities for progressives when navigating power.

First, the budget caps deal. Democratic budget chairman John Yarmuth (of Kentucky) had come to a number of us progressives on the budget committee to propose a budget caps deal that would set defense spending at a ridiculously high $733 billion, and nondefense discretionary spending (that's most of the domestic priorities you care about, like education, transportation, and housing), at almost $100 billion less than defense spending. Decades of austerity spending had put us in a place where we were desperately underfunding these domestic priorities, and money was increasingly going to military funding without even questioning whether it was necessary and without even a full audit of the Pentagon, despite rampant waste, fraud, and abuse. We wanted to reverse that trend. We wanted to go back to the days prior to 9/11 when nondefense discretionary spending had actually been *higher* than defense spending. At a minimum, we wanted to get to the point where they would be equal.

Democrats, however, who were constantly in the minority, had stuck to an outdated idea of "parity," which was defined as increasing both by the same dollar-for-dollar amount. That would do nothing to reverse the decades of austerity spending, it would simply increase nondefense discretionary spending while also increasing military spending. It was better than no increase in spending on those domestic priorities (which is largely what conservative Republicans wanted), but it would not fix the long-standing problems of austerity spending on our critical priorities, nor would it address the outrageous amounts of money we were spending largely on military contractors rather than on our troops.

The progressives on the committee banded together to demand a better deal. In what was deemed publicly as a "divisive, intraparty fight," Democratic leaders had to pull down the budget caps vote on the floor because there simply weren't enough progressive votes in favor to pass it. This win of holding our power in order to kill a vote was an important muscle that needed to be flexed, and it showed that progressives would be willing to withhold votes and kill a Democratic leadership priority if we weren't taken into account. This was the role we needed to get more used to playing if we were going to move progressive priorities. It was not comfortable for many people, and it still isn't.

We did allow another vote to go forward, however, that essentially set a total amount of spending, without allocating it between defense and nondefense, and still allowed the committees to continue their work. At the time, we didn't fully understand the consequences of letting that vote go through and it may well have been a mistake in retrospect.

Still, the win of withholding our power in order to kill a vote was critical to showing what this could look like, and we were able to get other significant concessions—including helping Ayanna Pressley get an important and wide-reaching bill on backpay for federal contractors during the Republican shutdown of government to the floor for passage.

Most importantly, we were able to negotiate for a critical cost assessment study on limiting nuclear weapons as part of the National Defense Authorization Act, as well as move forward the idea of some sort of advisory body of experts that could lay the groundwork for substantial cuts to bring down our military budget in the future, and the choices those would require. Not all of these were easy wins to explain to the broader movement, but they absolutely were significant for the longer-term movement and, had we not flexed our muscle on the budget fight, we would not have gotten these concessions.

The second example was equally complicated and with equally mixed results. It concerned a controversial bill to provide additional money to the Department of Homeland Security, Immigration and Customs Enforcement, and Customs and Border Protection (the trifecta of regulators for our immigration system and our borders). This was a highly charged time, filled with severe anti-immigrant rhetoric from Trump and a growing crisis at the border that was created by the Trump administration's policies and the increasing violence in Latin America. Pressure was high to reduce funding for the Department of Homeland Security, given its abusive actions. The country had watched the crisis of children in cages and immigration enforcement abuses unfold with what felt like very little accountability. At the same time, pressure was also high from leadership and from some progressives who represented border states to "do something" to address the terrible videos and stories that were coming out about children without food, water, or medical care.

The "Squad" (Alexandria Ocasio-Cortez, Ayanna Pressley, Ilhan Omar, and Rashida Tlaib) had announced early on that they would not vote for any bill that gave more money to DHS, period. This was a legitimate position to take, and probably one I would have joined with had I not been co-chair of the CPC. This bill would send $4.5 billion to the border, at a time when both the number of migrants being detained, separated from their families, and held in squalid conditions there, and the president's hateful rhetoric, were at a fever pitch. And all this on top of dealing with a president whose very campaign was launched by calling Latinx immigrants rapists and criminals.

In my co-chair role, however, I had to assess, with Mark, the amount of power we had. Which members of our caucus would vote against the funding bill? We held an emergency telephone call with our members two days before the vote was to take place. It was clear that we would not have enough votes to fully defeat the bill, given all the pressures of the moment to do something and the divided sentiment among some of the progressives. That meant our strategy needed to be pushing for a series of changes that we and the Hispanic Caucus, which was also concerned about the bill, felt would be essential if we were to vote for the bill. We asked members to not say how they would vote on the bill, which would give us more power to push hard for the inclusion of these priorities and at least attach some important accountability to the bill to make sure that the money was spent as we intended it to be spent, not on a presidential vanity wall.

Over a tense forty-eight-hour period, Mark and I—along with Barbara Lee, who was a member of leadership and extremely helpful—negotiated hard with some of the other leadership. Our top priorities ranged from not giving additional money to ICE, to not detaining children for more than ninety days, to creating real accountability by cutting off funding if certain standards of care for detainees were not met.

The last was critical to me: for years as an activist and later as a member of Congress, I had been pushing for Congress to use the power of the purse to get accountability from the agencies. The largely private, for-profit detention contractors simply refused to comply with the standards we set, even though they were the law. It was a big problem, and when Republicans controlled the presidency (and, therefore, the agencies) and Congress, there was little recourse. It seemed to me that the only way to fix that was to have real consequences like cutting off funding if our conditions weren't met. We had never before been able to achieve this because Congress (including Democrats) had been loath to use this power. It was infuriating. If we were able to get this agreement into the bill, it would not only be a great victory for the moment but I hoped it could help us negotiate similar provisions into future bills.

On the other side, though, some of the Blue Dog Democrats didn't like the changes to the original border bill, fearing they would personally be blamed for the border crisis if funds were not sent immediately, and some feeling that these changes made Democrats look "soft" on immigration enforcement and would cause problems for their reelection. It was a ridiculous argument in my mind but one that has been used over and over to divide us over immigration.

Even when it seemed that some members of House leadership were not going to agree to this important accountability provision, Mark and I kept pushing. I even went to Pelosi, who told me she thought it was an excellent idea and that she was willing to support it. In the end, we improved the bill significantly and Mark and I gave the green light to the rest of the caucus to support the bill. It was disappointing that we did not have the votes to kill the bill, but given that it would have passed anyway, we were able to make it significantly better in some truly revolutionary ways. All of the CPC members followed our lead, held our noses, and voted for the bill, with the exception of the Squad who we already knew would not vote for the bill. This was really not a problem to me. In organizing, it helps to have a left that is further out because it can bring about a better end result, as long as everyone is coordinated and do not undermine each other, which none of we progressives did.

Some news media tried to drive a wedge between the Squad and the CPC leadership on the first vote. But I didn't feel that at all. I had spoken to the Squad and I knew they would vote against the bill even with the changes we had negotiated. I deeply respected their resistance on this. In this instance, it was my job to play the longer game, and their job to resist what was happening. That's part of making a movement, and in fact, is much how policymaking works when you're on the outside: You have to have people in multiple places on an issue or strategy. You need the ones who want to blow up the whole system because it actually gives leverage to those who are negotiating the best we can get. You also have to look at what power you realistically have in these leverage situations. If you can hold enough people to a no so that you can kill a bill, as we did with the budget caps deal, you have more leverage and you can powerfully exercise it. If you don't, you can try to fake it and ask people to hold out as long as they can in stating their position, but in the end, you don't have the same kind of leverage. That was this situation. Too many people were feeling the pressure of doing something at the border, even though I firmly believed it was not going to mitigate the crisis. The emotional nature of the situation also made it much harder to keep people poised to vote no, as outrageous as it was that we were giving more money to these rogue agencies and rogue administration.

If only that had been the end of the story, but it was not. Many Senate Democrats unfortunately joined Senate Republicans in voting for a much worse bill without any of our changes and sent it back over to us. A big bipartisan vote in the Senate takes away our leverage in the House, particularly when our more conservative Democrats were already unhappy with our changes. Pelosi was ready to amend the Senate bill to include most of our changes and send it back to the Senate, but the Blue Dog Democrats saw an opportunity in the bipartisan Senate bill and refused to support the amended version at the last minute. It was an unprecedented move to leverage their power and it worked. Without them, we could not pass the amended bill with the protections, and instead leadership put forward the Senate bill. It passed. Most of the progressives in the House voted against it, so it had barely more Democratic votes than Republican votes.

The worst part of all of it was that, because of electoral fears and cow-towing to Republican majority wishes, I feared that nothing we had done would really make a difference. The horrific conditions at the border, in my mind, had little to do with lack of money. It had to do with the cru-elty that Trump and his administration intended to inflict, all to try to illegally deter legitimate asylees and other immigrants from coming to our country to seek refuge. I was certain that we would continue to hear sto-ries from the border about malnourished children and jail-like conditions; and still, there would be no real accountability.

It was a huge, huge loss and the caucus erupted in massive fights and finger-pointing. I blamed the Senate Democrats for taking away our lever-age and I was not shy to say it publicly. When a reporter asked me what I would do to stop Senate Dems from doing this again, I said I was looking for a new pharmaceutical drug that would help grow spines. That com-ment was immediately relayed all over the news. Within days, however, I received a call from Senate Minority leader Chuck Schumer, and we had a long and productive conversation about what had happened and how we needed to coordinate more closely to ensure we leveraged our power across the House and the Senate as well.

I care about the strategy, short- and long-term, and the role of co-chair requires that we think carefully about how to hold our caucus togeth-er and also how to play a constructive role in the broader caucus. That doesn't mean we always have to win every fight; sometimes, just standing up even if we lose is the strategy that makes the most sense. Whenever I can, I find I am trying to bridge whatever divides do exist in our progres-sive movement, and to always remind people that we are strongest when we are unified. I've also never been afraid to fight my own party, going back to the days when I fought Democrats because they had not embraced immigration reform, or the days when I called Obama the Deporter-in-Chief because of his deportation policies.

We've got a lot of tools in our organizing toolbox and we have to be willing to use all of them at the right times. Sometimes that is negotiation, sometimes it is confrontation. Sometimes, it's getting arrested in the streets (as I have now done multiple times in acts of civil disobedience in and out of Congress) and, other times, it's working to make the policy in front of us better. We are still learning exactly how to leverage our power best, and we have to openly analyze what we did right and wrong so we can get better in the future.

I've been in the movement long enough to understand that while it's true we can't let the perfect be the enemy of the good (often what leadership tells us), we also can't let the good be the enemy of the much better or what's right. We settle too easily, in my experience, and we need to learn to flex more, even as we are always strategic and thoughtful. I also believe in determination and discipline, and I never give up easily. The deeper lesson is to organize your base—outside of Congress and within it—so that when that leverage opportunity arises, you are as fully unified and prepared to pounce. If you haven't done the organizing beforehand, lamenting powerlessness is of no use.

Another very important tool that I bring from my experiences as an English literature major to my outside activist days is a focus on a "communications infrastructure" to bring along the people we need to convince. In my own congressional office, I devote three staffers to the task of communications—far more than most offices. At the Progressive Caucus, where Mark also drew on his own background in journalism, we added a communications person to help elevate our work and make the broader case for progressive policies.

There are particular benefits that a successful communications infrastructure can help provide to those who we are trying to help move in the right direction. First is simple and clear talking points and public messaging. Unity, clarity, and simplicity of message do wonders for moving along an issue; and lack of these things can be the death of a successful campaign. Second, elevating personal stories of those most affected takes an issue from being dry legislation or words on a page to being something real, that people across the country can connect with and understand the importance of. Third, combining policy and communications, we will be most successful if we can find ways to help articulate the underlying analysis built on data and sound logic. This is easier said than done. Elected leaders can be just as susceptible to the messaging of the opposition, and with all the issues in front of them, they often don't take the time to understand the basic premise of a policy idea such that they can fight back against the lies. If we can help people to do just that, providing the clearest analysis and points to make our case, we are more likely to win. Fourth, sharing the best tactics to push back on regressive, oppositional talking points is critical. Knowing what those opposition points are and preparing our own allies for them so they are never caught off-guard is important work. So is finding external validators that provide particular expertise or speak to a particular constituency that we need to bring along. Finally, always trying to remind people of the moral grounding that anchors our policy proposals is absolutely critical in all the communications we do, internal and external.

By providing a communications infrastructure that can deliver on these points, I am saying to those that I am trying to shift leftward that I've got their back. I'm committing that they won't be out there on a limb: I'll do all I can to assist them in the shift so that *they* succeed. That strategy builds our base and the leadership of those that step out to take even more perceived risks in the future.

The work that I am doing at the helm of the Progressive Caucus is the work that has felt most challenging but also most important to me. We have important work to do to build the core of the caucus, progressives who are willing to use their power by holding their votes, even when it's tough. I believe we are laying the essential foundation for a Democratic presidency in January 2021 (if all the stars are aligned) and teaching the entire progressive caucus how to be brave and fight for what we believe in. Even if we sometimes lose and even if it makes people uncomfortable, that willingness to stand up and fight is a necessary precondition for taking on the big legislative policy fights that will truly change the lives of millions of people across the country. Courage is a muscle, too, and like all other muscles, it gets stronger every time we use it.

Part II

MORAL VISIONS

8

Moral Vision — Immigration

TURKISH WRITER ELIF SHAFAK ONCE SHARED HOW HER GRANDMOTH-
er, a healer of sorts, used to get rid of people's warts by drawing circles
around them. When she asked her grandmother what it was that made
the warts go away, her grandmother told her to "beware of the circle."
The power of the circle, Shafak said, is that if you surround something
completely, cut if off from everything else, it will dry up and die. "If you
want to destroy something in its life, all you need to do is surround it with
thick walls. It will dry up inside."

I heard Shafak's words in her 2004 TED talk and I have never forgotten
them. They seem entirely appropriate to the issue of immigration today.
If we keep building thicker and thicker walls around us that prevent the
flow of ideas and people, America will dry up and die.

In June 2018, in the wake of early reports that massive numbers of children were being systematically separated from their parents as a result of
the Trump administration's "zero-tolerance" policy, Senator Jeff Merkley
attempted to enter the Casa Padre facility in Brownsville, Texas, where
children were being detained. He was not permitted to enter and eventually the police were called and he was asked to leave the facility. He filmed

the whole set of incidents, drawing the first attention to what was happening and putting the severity of what was happening center stage.

At almost exactly the same time, I got a call from my friends at the Northwest Immigrant Rights Project (NWIRP) in Seattle. NWIRP provides legal services to immigrants who are being detained, and they suspected that over two hundred mothers and fathers separated from their children might be at a federal prison just south of my district. NWIRP was eager to help but had no way to contact people in the facility. On the same day, it was announced that ICE had temporarily contracted with federal prison facilities across the country, including this one in my district, to detain more people. Apparently, the detention center was full—or perhaps ICE did not want to alert anyone to the presence of these mothers and fathers in the detention center.

I was flying home two days later, so I asked Jennifer Chan in my office to immediately call the Federal Bureau of Prisons where they were being held to get permission for me to enter the prison and meet with the people detained there—I knew we had to get the truth about who was there and hear their stories. Permission was granted within twenty-four hours, which was a surprise to us. ICE typically makes it extremely difficult for even members of Congress to visit, often delayed the granting of permissions and routinely turning away congresspeople who show up without notice to conduct unannounced inspections. It is an ongoing outrage, given that we fund these entities and we have oversight responsibilities for what happens there. The difference here was that this was a bureau of prisons facility not an ICE facility, and it was government-owned and operated using union employees. They seemed to actually respect Congress's oversight, unlike the privately owned ICE facilities, and they didn't have anything to hide.

I arrived at the prison at 9 a.m. the day after I got home. Understand the context, please: this is a federal *prison* with top-level security clearance that holds the worst offenders, such as murderers and convicted terrorists. This was the place our government had decided to hold asylum seekers, including parents who had just been traumatically separated from their children. We left all our things in small lockers, went through metal detectors, and then the prison warden took us through numerous heavy secured doors to the wards. We learned from the warden that ICE had transferred 220 people from the border. I met with 174 women who were being held in three different pods (the 50-plus men were being held in a different ward and I would go back to see them two weeks later; they had very similar stories to the women).

I met with each pod of fifty or so women in the central area of their ward, with small prison cells all around the central area. Initially, they eyed me with some fear and suspicion, but that changed the minute I told them that I had fought for immigrant rights for a long time and I wanted to apologize to them for the fact that our government had separated them from their children. Then, they started talking, pouring out their stories through their tears. What I heard that day will haunt me forever.

They took my son away.
I asked if we could say goodbye, and they said no.
My child kept asking for me.
They were the ones who took away my children.
The [Border Patrol] would yell and scream at you, like you
   weren't a person.
I could hear my child screaming in the next room, but I couldn't
   go to him.

The majority were asylum seekers, and about 30 to 40 percent of them had come with children, some as young as just six months old, who were forcibly taken away from them. They came from sixteen countries, as far as Eritrea and China, but the vast majority were from El Salvador, Honduras, Guatemala, and Cuba. They talked of fleeing rape, murder, and persecution.

None of them had even had a chance to say goodbye to their children. In many cases, the women described being deceived by CBP officers who told them they could go to the bathroom or to go get their pictures taken, and when they came back their children were gone.

One mother told me through her tears that DHS officers threatened to take away her six-year-old daughter, right in front of them, and her daughter started screaming. She was separated from her daughter on the second day of custody and hadn't had contact in over a week.

Another woman came from Guatemala with her children, ages eight and twelve. Her husband was in prison back home for raping a twelve-year-old child, but he was getting out. She was afraid her children would be raped either by him or some of his fellow gang members, so she left for America. She had been separated from her two children, and she didn't know where they were.

Another woman came fleeing gang violence. She had a fourteen-year-old child who was killed nine months ago by gangs. Her second child was in a wheelchair, shot and paralyzed by gangs. She had taken her third child and made the journey to America, just to get one of her children to safety.

Another woman came with her two sons, eleven and sixteen years old— for whatever reason, her older son was going to be reunited with his father in Virginia, but the younger son was still in custody, which made no sense.

What I simply could not fathom was this: *the majority of the moms did not even know where their children were and had been separated from them for more than three weeks by this point.*

Just the day before, many had been given a slip by ICE agents that had their names, the names of their children, and the facility their children were held in. But one mom stabbed at the paper in front of me saying, also through tears, "These are not my children!" Somehow, she had been given a slip that identified the wrong children as hers. This was my first clue that the ICE and CBP officials were not tracking which kids belonged to which parents with care, as we would find out much later. We collected all the slips we could so we could start to find out where these children were and have lawyers help their parents get in touch with them.

The women also spoke of being demeaned and humiliated by Immigrations and Customs Enforcement and Border Patrol agents. They were called "filthy" and "disgusting" and were told they would never see their children again. They called the places they were detained by the nick-names "dog pound," because they were kept in cages, and "icebox" because of the frigid temperatures. They had no blankets or mats in the icebox, and some women reported being without clean drinking water for days. Their treatment was made all the more clear when they said that the first time they were treated as human beings was here, in a federal prison, in a government-controlled unionized facility where there was more account-ability than privately contracted, for-profit facilities with no accountabil-ity. Imagine what ICE and CBP custody must have been like if a federal prison was the first place where they were treated as human beings.

I spent three hours with the women, and when I was leaving, we hugged and cried as mothers, as women, as immigrants. I was heartbroken but also furious that our government was doing this to people who were sim-ply seeking refuge, seeking to escape terrible conditions and to find safety for their children. I told the women that I would tell their stories, over and over and over, until people started to hear them.

When I came out, my staff recorded a video of me in front of the pris-on talking about what I had heard. We contacted every media outlet we could think of, and when I didn't get responses from some, I started tag-ging prominent TV hosts like Chris Cuomo, Chris Hayes, Rachel Mad-dow, and others. "Cover this," I kept saying. "America deserves to know how shamefully we are treating people seeking refuge."

When I got back to Congress, we were having a hearing on an unre-lated issue in the Judiciary Committee and I used my five minutes to talk about the horrors of what I had seen and to demand hearings on family separation. The room was pin-drop silent as I spoke and it set a sleepy committee meeting on fire, spurring other members to also make remarks on the issue, all of which were shared widely by Democrats on the com-mittee. It took a few days, but soon the stories were everywhere. I was tireless, seized by the injustice and trauma of family separation that I had witnessed—I appeared on any news channel that asked, no matter how small or large. I went on radio shows, I called up reporters, many of whom covered what I had seen. I also asked for time in our Democratic Caucus meeting, and there I told my colleagues what I had seen and that they had to visit the detention centers in their districts to see what was going on and demanding answers. Sen. Merkley was just as tireless in his efforts to communicate what was going on, even though he had been unable to get into a detention center.

As the stories began to get out and Americans realized what was happening, they were horrified. I began getting calls from people across the country asking what they could do. A former state senate colleague of mine wrote me a long text saying all her constituents (and she was not in the most liberal district) were so angry, how could they help? What could she tell them? People were beginning to understand what America was doing in their name and they desperately wanted to channel their rage and anger into something, but what?

Two Saturdays later, after another sleepless night and as the pressure was building, I sat up early in the morning and felt like I knew what needed to happen. We needed a huge mass protest of family separation in the streets in every state, a place for people to channel their anger and horror, and to demand that Trump end his zero-humanity policy (my new name for his "zero-tolerance" policy).

I called my friend and executive director of MoveOn, Anna Galland. It was 7 a.m. but this could not wait.

"We have to do something," I said. "We need a half a million people in the streets for a massive rally. We have to show our outrage."

Anna responded immediately. MoveOn had been hearing from their members and they too wanted to do something that would leverage the anger on the ground and build momentum to stop the policy.

"When?" she said.

"In a week," I responded, to her gasps. (We joke now that she may never take another call at 7 a.m. from me again!) We didn't know if this was possible, but we called some of our other friends that MoveOn works closely with on immigration and that I had organized with and been friends with for a long time: Cristina Jiménez from United We Dream; Ai-jen Poo from National Domestic Workers Alliance; and Vanita Gupta, formerly the U.S. attorney for civil rights under Attorney General Eric Holder and now the new president of the Leadership Conference on Civil Rights. It was a matter of particular pride for us that this effort would be spearheaded by five powerful women.

The rallies ended up being organized in two weeks. In a record amount of time, MoveOn swept into action, calling for rallies everywhere across the country, in every state and including a big one in Washington, DC. Our goal was to shoot for 300,000 to 500,000 people, but time was short and we had absolutely no idea what would happen. But, as organizers (which all of us were), we could feel the energy. We felt the moment and we knew that as difficult as it was to pull everything together, *we had to respond to the moment.* That is the organizer's battle cry: you can never tell when a tipping point may come, but when it does, you have to be attentive to it, notice it, and then jump into action.

Two days before the rallies were to take place, the Women's March had decided to organize a civil disobedience protest in the Senate building in Capitol Hill. Linda Sarsour, Ana Maria Archila of the Center for Popular Democracy, actress and playwright Eve Ensler, and many others came to Washington, DC, to lead the protests and get arrested. Over five hundred women showed up and took over the lobby of the Senate Hart Building. Armed with the tinfoil blankets that were being given to the migrants on the border, these women staged a sit-in right there, refusing to get up and leave, while singing a haunting song that echoed through the halls of the Capitol. Capitol staff and visitors lined the galleries and stairwells that looked down onto the hall, as speakers including Senators Merkley came to speak. I had been asked to speak as well, and when I arrived, I stood next to Senator Kristen Gillibrand as we breathed in the tremendous power of five hundred women filling the Senate lobby. The Capitol Police came up to us and told us that they would shortly be starting the arrests since the women had refused to move from the lobby. If we didn't want to be arrested, they told us, we better speak and then leave.

I hadn't actually planned on getting arrested, but I knew then that I needed to do just that. To support these women but most of all, to support the women and men who had been separated from their children and jailed. I turned to my staff and said, "I think I'm going to stay and get arrested."

They were slack-jawed but immediately supportive, taking my purse and phone so I would not have anything on me when I was arrested. I knew that my staying—the image of a sitting congresswoman being handcuffed—would draw further attention to the crisis. And my years as an activist, as a leader on this issue had prepared me mentally. I had organized massive civil disobedience protests before—at the Capitol and in Seattle. While at OneAmerica, I remember measuring the lobby of the Seattle skyscraper where the state has its immigration court, heel-to-toe, trying to figure out how many of my fellow advocates and I could fit in a sit-in to protest the Obama administration's deportations.[1] I understood the tactics and the solidarity of putting your body on the line. I knew, too, that I would come under tremendous criticism, that there would be some in Congress who would be outraged that a member of Congress was arrested. I also knew others like John Lewis had continued to use civil disobedience as a critical tool to draw attention to moral outrages that had to be addressed. My adrenaline was high at what I was about to do, but I was not afraid. I knew this tactic, and I felt the beauty of the crowd around me.

I spoke to the chanting, singing crowd and when I sat down in the middle of them and linked arms with the women around me, the entire crowd started cheering that I had joined them. The Capitol Police—who are incredibly skilled at handling massive protests and do so regularly— were beginning to lead women off to the tables they had set up outside to process the arrests. One of them who knew I was a member of Congress came over to me and whispered, "Ma'am, are you sure you want me to arrest you? You can leave right now, you know!"

I smiled at him. "Yes, Officer, you can go ahead and arrest me. I'll be fine."

I thought I saw a glow of pride in his eyes as he took my arm to lead me off. I punched my fist high in the sky as people cheered—and to this day, that picture of me being led off by two officers, with a gloriously loving crowd of women who had staged this courageous protest, makes me so proud to be a small part of the massive resistance that had formed.

In the end, more than five hundred women were arrested. Later, a Capitol Police officer told me that that was the largest protest they had ever seen, and the most orderly. "Thank you, Congresswoman," he said. "We need people to say what is necessary. I'm a father, too, and I can't stand watching this."

By then, CBP officials had officially acknowledged that more than 2,400 children were separated from their families from October 2016 to February 2018, a stunning number that would only continue to balloon as the ACLU and others took the administration to court and demanded answers and documents. The tide had definitely turned and we felt we had Trump on his heels as we demanded an end to the policy.

Significantly, this was one time when it was not just Democrats but also prominent Republicans, in a rare move, speaking out against Trump. Evangelist Franklin Graham slammed the policy, calling it "disgraceful . . . it's terrible to see families ripped apart and I don't support that one bit."[2] Four days later, the former first lady Laura Bush wrote a powerful op-ed that was published in the *Washington Post*, saying, "this zero-tolerance policy is cruel. It is immoral. And it breaks my heart."[3]

On June 20, Trump was forced to retreat—though not much. With great fanfare, he signed an Executive Order meant to quell outrage over the separation of families, saying that families would now be housed together—but indefinitely, in ad hoc detention centers. However, the order also made it clear that U.S. authorities would still continue to criminally prosecute adults who crossed illegally. Trump's advisors and allies used this to declare that "family separation was over," but it was far from true, as court proceedings continued to show.

On June 30, two weeks after my call to Anna, half a million people swept into the streets in almost every state across the country. They knew America was better than this and they wanted to do something that would meaningfully show their outrage. In Washington, DC, a giant wave of people crowded through the streets around the Capitol—I was at the front right behind the banner, with Anna, Ai-jen, Vanita, and some celebrities like Lin-Manuel Miranda, the playwright and an actor in the musical *Hamilton*. The enormity of what we had been able to do reminded me again that our inside-outside strategy mattered. We had put forward a bold vision and then used our skills as organizers and the grassroots infrastructure that was just looking for leadership to pull together the rallies. We had paid attention to our anger and channeled it into purpose, together.

There probably could not have been a better time for me to serve in Congress. As a long-time immigrant rights activist and an immigrant myself, I had a unique role to play at a time when the president had campaigned on and governed with xenophobia, fear, and cruelty; where immigrant bashing was the tried-and-true mechanism that he resorted to every time he wanted to fire up his increasingly shrinking base and distract from the very real rigging of the economy he was doing to favor the wealthiest among us.

We should be very clear, however, that anti-immigrant fervor didn't start with Trump. We are a nation of immigrants, yes, but America's history on immigration is complex and contradictory, one of tolerance and intolerance. We are a country built by immigrants—unwilling and willing: some were forcibly brought over on slave ships while others sought to escape drought, war, or persecution. Some labored as contract workers, others on plantations or the early railroads of America. We are a country that excluded Chinese immigrants in 1882, and in 1923, our Supreme Court deemed immigrants from India not "white" in the common understanding and therefore barred them from naturalization, laws that did not change until 1952.

Racism is the original sin of America starting with the genocide of Native Americans and enslavement of black Americans and it has continued into the present, covering vast territory with great cruelty—from hate crimes against Muslims and anti-Semitism against Jews to locking up children in cages on our southern border.

We cannot ignore the fact that part of the reason this all continues is because it benefits those in power to keep the rest of us divided. This is an age-old strategy and it is used because it can work. The question for America, then, is not *just* can we move from intolerance to tolerance of religion and of race, but how we can regard all of us, brown, black, or white, Muslim, Jew, Christian, straight or queer, man or woman, rich and poor . . . with love and generosity? How can we refuse to be divided, even as we celebrate our differences, and recognize that we have core human values in common that have always defined America's greatness?

This question becomes even more important as we recognize the global context for migration today and the causes, benefits and challenges of it. Of the 258 million people who live in a country other than the one in which they were born, 68 million were forcibly displaced, due to persecution, conflict, violence, or war, and two-thirds of all of those are women and children. Nineteen million are environmental migrants, displaced by sudden onset disasters. At least 20 percent of all these migrants are estimated to be irregular migrants, or what we in America call undocumented immigrants. But also importantly, migrants contributed about $6.7 trillion to global gross domestic product (GDP), about 10 percent of the total global GDP.[4,5]

We have embraced easier travel across oceans and borders, conjoined our economies so that a financial crash in America or China affects the whole world, signed treaties that willingly shuttle goods and services under the control of multinational corporations freely across national boundaries, and popularized technology that allows for the widespread posting of videos and pictures that can focus world attention on an otherwise far-away military coup.

Many of these developments have not led to better living conditions for the vast majority of people, particular as public assets have been privatized and utilized for the few rather than the many. Still, these trends have occurred, leading to a world that is far more interdependent—in every way except the flow of people. Here, countries reassert their nationalism and their authority over boundaries. Even as the idea of country borders has given way to the concept of regional identity in the European Union, the debate over what is truly French or Dutch or Swedish has flared when it comes to the influx of Muslim migrants.

In the United States, our embrace of a global economy has led to a natural flow of not only goods and services but labor across our borders, but we remain stuck about how to have a sane discussion—much less policy—about immigration in America. Without a policy solution that fixes our current broken system, we have let immigrants become the scapegoats of every recent decade. We allow anti-immigrant attitudes to latch on to the deep fears that exist in most of us, fears of the "other." As long as humans have been alive, we have feared those who are seen as different from us. And while race and skin color factor in to this more and more in our present-day debates, the reality is that the early American settlers did not like those with the same skin color either—the Irish, Polish, Germans, Italians. All immigrants to this country over the course of our history have been required to prove themselves as real, patriotic Americans in ways that were meaningful to the existing population, even if the barriers for those who were immediately identified as "different" made it that many times more difficult.

At the core of this fear are two basic concepts.

The first is the "What About Me?" concept. This is not new. Historically, times of economic downturn have engendered fear about my share, my children's share. A mentality of scarcity can push people to feel there isn't enough and they have to protect what they have. When people are having trouble putting food on their table, keeping a roof over their head, or sending their kids to school, it is easier for them to be manipulated. And it is always easier to blame someone else for the problems that you are experiencing.

I remember a moment from my first term, the same day when I took on Don Young on the House floor. I started my morning off early by appearing on a live C-SPAN program, where you take calls from Republicans, Democrats, and Independents on a variety of topics. A caller named John called in on the Republican line to rant about "these illegal aliens," and to call for children of undocumented immigrants to be "deported just like their parents." As John described how his son couldn't get a job, I could hear the pain he was feeling and responded from that place.

"John, it sounds like you are in a lot of economic pain and that is true across the country," I said. "There is no question we as a country need to deal with economic inequality and make sure we have good paying jobs for everyone. I am committed to that and I'll tell you that right here looking into . . . I can't see your face, but looking into your eyes, I'll tell you to blame immigrants is completely wrong and here's why."

I went on to explain to John that most undocumented immigrants don't even qualify for the majority of public benefits, and I urged him to focus his blame on corporations that don't pay their fair share and don't allow workers to have dignity, respect, and a fair wage on the job—not on immigrants. I don't know if John could really hear me, but I hope he did. I hope he understands that the underlying pain is what we have to deal with—and neither he nor I can afford to give in to those who want to use his pain and then his anger to divide us. After John hung up, I told the C-SPAN host that throughout my years, I've heard a lot of hurtful things, I have dealt with lynching threats and death threats, and that, yes, they hurt. And yet, still, it has never deterred me from believing the best about Americans.

That's truly how I feel, though I will admit that the extreme cruelty we see from this president, and the lack of Republicans pushing back on it, makes me question this more and more. Still, I think it must be rare for people to just acknowledge the pain that underlies the hurtful things that sometimes get said, and the fact that I did just that was noticed immediately. NowThis Politics turned the exchange it into a video that, as I write this book, has over 10 million views.

The second concept that is at the core of this fear is the idea of "the other"—and what it means for *my* culture and way of life. Central to this is what it calls forward of racism. I sometimes think of this as the "I Am Not Changing, and You Can't Make Me" concept.

Any massive wave of immigration has always and will always require change. We see the social upheaval in America taking place as we speak. The influx of tens of millions of Latinos has meant new ways of doing business in all realms, from marketing products to winning elections to going about daily work. Movies like *A Day Without a Mexican* illustrate how interwoven Latinos have become in our everyday worlds, how necessary their contributions are, and how American culture is changing to reflect all the new influences. That is always how it has been, but today's white majority is soon to be a minority and I believe this exhibits almost an existential threat, a sense of a loss of one culture and language to a new culture and language that people feel they will no longer be a part of. This existential fear is easily tapped into by malevolent politicians and their acolytes whose only goal is to keep us divided so they can keep more power.

The odd thing about the most anti-immigrant president in recent history is that he may have actually pushed Americans to reaffirm their tremendous support for immigration. Today, public polling shows that the vast majority of Americans believe immigration is good for America and they don't want to limit it. A 2019 Gallup poll found that a record 75 percent of Americans consider immigration "a good thing."[6] A 2017 poll found that the percentage of Americans saying immigrants "mostly help" the economy reached its highest point since Gallup began asking the question in 1993.[7] Simultaneously, fears that immigrants bring crime, take jobs from American-born workers, or damage the budget and overall economy are at an all-time low.[8] The share of Americans calling for lower levels of immigration has fallen from a high of 63 percent in the mid-1990s to an all-time low of just 29 percent, as of June 2018.[9]

Perhaps it is not surprising, then, that even as Trump pushed forward his most cruel policy to date—separating children from their moms and dads—Americans of every stripe rose up to oppose it. In perhaps one of my proudest moments in Congress, I was there to help lead the inside-outside resistance to these zero-humanity policies.

———

A few weeks after my reelection in late 2018, Donald Trump barreled down with his fearmongering about what he called the "migrant caravan invasion" at the southern border. He had spent months characterizing the flow of migrants from Latin American countries as a lawless and never-ending stream of immigrants who were coming to America take your jobs and rape your children. The truth was that the vast majority of these people were seeking refuge and asylum from gang violence, poverty, political repression, and the effects of climate change, often trying to escape what they saw as certain death in their own home countries. These dire situations and their reasons for migration would always carry more weight than any deterrent policies that the U.S. administration implemented. Over and over again, when one migration route closed off, another one opened. It was Janet Reno, then governor of Arizona, who famously said, "Give me a 100-foot fence and I'll show you a 101-foot ladder." Such is the truth of desperation.

Trump had been ranting for months about asylum seekers who entered the country illegally. Asylum is the legal protection granted to people who come to the United States and are afraid to return to their home country because of persecution or a well-founded fear of persecution based on race, religion, nationality, political opinion, or membership in a political group. Unlike refugees, who are approved for refugee status from *outside* the United States, asylees make their claim once they are *in* the United States. Seeking asylum is legal, both within our own domestic laws and in the human rights treaties that the United States is signatory to.

Trump's goal—as documented in a memo from his white nationalist immigration adviser, Stephen Miller—was to "persistently . . . present aliens with multiple unsolvable dilemmas to impact their calculus for choosing to make the arduous journey to begin with."[10] Historically, most asylum seekers apprehended at the southern border of the United States would have been released into the country while waiting for the decision on their case to be made. Instead, the Trump administration began quietly making a series of changes that makes seeking asylum all but impossible. These included criminally prosecuting everyone who crossed the border between legal points of entry, while at the same time, shutting down the legal ports of entry to those seeking asylum in a policy called "metering"; sending migrants back to the dangerous countries they were fleeing and forcing them to apply for asylum from those countries or other "third-party" countries that posed just as much danger; making Mexico a bottleneck for asylum seekers through the "Remain in Mexico" policy that forces asylum seekers to wait in Mexico as their applications are being processed; massively expanding the detention of asylum seekers and separating them from their children; undermining the ability of asylum seekers to get any due process or a fair day in court; and, most recently, instituting a fee—for the first time in history—for asylum applications.

Trump has essentially succeeding in closing the border to asylum seekers who are, in the words of one of the mothers we met with in Mexico, "trying to do it the right way." The metering policy forced asylum seekers to remain in Mexico, with no official way to hold a spot in line, secure an appointment, or even seek legal representation from an attorney. A random "line" was created by people with no legal or official authority but with the unfortunate tacit approval of both the Mexican and U.S. governments. Accounts surfaced of women being forced to give sexual favors in return for a place in this line, while the vast majority were forced to wait with no way to hold a spot in the so-called line, secure an appointment with U.S. officials to seek asylum, or access legal representation in the United States.

Equally important, these policies did nothing to address the real issues of how to quickly process the flow of migrants, which was not unprecedented in number and could have been addressed through more humane methods. In a report from the Office of the Inspector General, one Customs and Border Protection official said that metering likely resulted in more unauthorized border crossings not fewer, as some of the most desperate migrants seeking to escape violence and persecution in Mexico began trying to cross between the legal points of entry that were now closed to them, even if that meant terrible consequences like dying as they tried to cross the river.[11]

As asylum seekers waited for months on the streets or in over-crowded shelters, prey to the very violence they were trying to escape, the desperation grew to a breaking point. In November 2018, Trump's new policies led to huge clashes in Tijuana, in which Border Patrol officials fired tear gas at migrants who were desperate to come into the country, an action that many of us believed was a violation of both domestic and international law.[12] In the wake of horrible pictures of women and children fleeing tear gas, U.S. Customs and Border Protection officials defended the use of these "nonlethal" forces. Mexico, however, presented a diplomatic note to the U.S. Embassy asking for an "exhaustive investigation" of the use of nonlethal force such as tear gas.

I was horrified when I saw the pictures and videos of the clashes. I decided to visit Tijuana to see for myself what was happening, and to talk to the asylum seekers directly. The first member of Congress to do so, I arranged travel to Tijuana. I was joined by Jennifer Chan, my senior legislative aide on immigration issues who later became my legislative director. Because I was traveling in my official capacity, we were met at the border by the U.S. consul general in Tijuana and accompanied by her and her security detail for the time we were there, though we got them to agree that the security staff would keep their distance from me so that I could make sure people did not feel uncomfortable talking with me. The consul general was a thoughtful career officer; she and her team were easy to work with and seemed to understand the need to give me space to do what I wanted while still protecting my safety. I also had arranged for an interpreter who worked for a human rights organization to accompany me throughout the visit, and we arranged to have lunch with a human rights nonprofit organization without the consul general and her team in attendance.

In Tijuana, we spoke with migrants staying right at the border, sleeping in tents, subservient to the illegal process of the unofficial "line," waiting and hoping their numbers would be called to be allowed to even approach the legal point of entry. We visited youth shelters and women's shelters run by religious organizations, toured a large compound that only had covered shelter for two thousand but was designated to hold up to eight thousand people. We also met with human rights organizations who were challenging and protesting both the U.S. and Mexican governments' treatment of migrants.

At the unaccompanied youth shelter, I met a seventeen-year old boy, who I will call Ramon.[13] Ramon had fled Honduras with his fifteen-year-old brother, in fear of being shot by gang members. He told me his story haltingly, his head down the whole time. One day as he was taking his siblings to school, a gang member had come up behind him and held a gun to the back of his head, demanding his watch. When Ramon resisted, the gang member shot him in both knees, then tied him up and left him there all day until someone found him and took him home. Ramon had already watched gangs kill his father when he was three years old, and he and his mother knew that he could not stay in Honduras. His mother told him he had to go to America for his own safety and find his aunt. It had been almost three months since Ramon left Honduras and he had been in the shelter for two weeks.

In that quiet back room in the youth shelter, Ramon finally looked up at me, tears brimming from his eyes. He was a child in a man's body, weeping as he played me a message on his phone from his mother that he had saved: "You cannot come home," she said. "You will be killed if you do. Get to America, go to safety. I love you and I will always be with you."

This boy was so brave, but as I spoke to him we both wept. I thought about my own child. I thought about what any parent would do, what any humanitarian would do, in that situation, or simply if they were to hear his story as I was: they would keep fighting for a young adult like him to have a better future, for him just to be safe.

We then visited a women's shelter run by Catholic nuns. It was over-flowing, with a hundred people in a space meant for forty. We talked to many of the women, including a Honduran woman who had previously lived in the United States for four years and had two children who were U.S. citizens, ages eight and nine. She had gone back to Honduras with her children to take care of her sick parents, but while there, a gang leader with MS-13 had killed her brother and threatened her whole family. They all scattered to protect themselves, and she moved three times within Honduras. The first time the gang members found her, they threatened her. She decided she could no longer keep her children safe so she sent them back to the United States to live with a friend. She could not leave because she needed to look after her parents. But when the MS-13 gang members kept coming back for her, she knew her life was in grave danger and she needed to leave and rejoin her children in the United States.

There were so many more of these heartbreaking stories: Veronica from Michoacan, who had already lost her cousin and brother to the cartels and was now trying to keep her daughters from the same fate. Elena from Honduras who had three young children, the youngest of whom had watched her father being killed by narco-traffickers. Another woman from Honduras, who was seven months pregnant, was fleeing from her former partner who was a soldier and had threatened to kill her.[14]

At the border, when I asked one woman what she wanted Americans to know, she said, "Please just tell them who we are and how afraid we are for our lives—this is a life and death situation. And I hope that God will touch the hearts of the American people."

It was so clear to me that Trump's "crisis at the border" was, indeed, a crisis but one that was completely manufactured by him and his new policies, which piled up asylum seekers in Mexico instead of quickly processing them as had been done by previous administrations—a fact that Mexican officials were quick to point out to me. These policies were in service only to Trump's political instinct of riling up his base by dehumanizing vulnerable immigrants.

At lunchtime, we left the consul general and the security detail and climbed a long set of stairs above a bustling restaurant to a set of rooms at the top of the building where we met with the staff of Al Otro Lado, a nonprofit human rights organization. Al Otro Lado had been helping migrants connect with legal services and challenging the Trump administration's use of metering and the blocking of asylum seekers. We enjoyed a delicious home-cooked lunch, and I met the impressive staff, including

Nicole Ramos, the border programs director who had previously been a federal public defender in Montgomery, Alabama, where she defended death row inmates.

"Would you be willing to accompany some of our most vulnerable asylum seekers across the border into the U.S.?" Nicole asked me. "All of the asylum seekers we take are being denied, but with you there observing, perhaps they have a chance of getting across."

I thought about this carefully. Nicole had told me that Al Otro Lado had worked with these individuals for a while to vet their stories and their asylum claims, and Jennifer and they believed their claims were legitimate. I had also spent the last hour at lunch talking with these migrants and getting to know them a little bit. Their stories were heartbreaking.

Raul, a twenty-seven-year-old Nicaraguan, had fled his country after being threatened by the Sandinistas for his participation in protests against the government, which had engaged in gross human rights violations against large sectors of civil society.* In September 2018, Raul was severely beaten by the Sandinistas. Afraid to seek treatment because he feared it would lead to more persecution, he simply stayed home instead of treating his serious injuries. Several days after the beating, the police and Sandinista officials went to Raul's mother's house and threatened her, asking her to turn over her son. When she refused, the Sandinistas killed his mother and Raul's whole family. Terrified and with no other choice, Raul fled Nicaragua and made his way to Mexico where he connected with Al Otro Lado.

Veronica was twenty-seven years old, with a nine-year-old daughter named Alejandra. They had also fled gang violence in Honduras, after gang members murdered Victoria's partner, then threatened to kill Alejandra. Victoria hoped to reach America, where Alejandra's grandmother—a U.S. citizen—lived.

David, a seventeen-year-old unaccompanied minor, was fleeing gang violence, parental abuse, and child labor as a farmworker in Honduras. He had worked in the fields since he was four years old, and recently, his

---

* Names have been changed throughout this section.

parents had abandoned him and his siblings, leaving him in his grand-mother's care. Miserable and afraid, David had fled and made his way to Tijuana alone.

Then there was Auriel, the only one of the five not from Honduras. Auriel was a fifteen-year-old from El Salvador traveling by himself to join his mother, who had fled gang persecution in a great rush and had some-how been separated from her son. His mother had made it to the United States and was in the asylum process. The same gang members who forced his mom to flee persecuted Auriel as well. He had fled, too, hoping desper-ately to join his mother, who was living in California.

Their stories moved me deeply. I knew what the risks were, but I also felt I needed to take on the challenge of accompanying the asylum seek-ers across the border. CBP continued to tell us that they were not turning back unaccompanied minors who were seeking asylum; and yet we heard very different stories from advocates and the migrants themselves. I want-ed to observe exactly what was happening at the border, without revealing to U.S. agents that I was a congressmember. After careful thought, I told Nicole I would accompany the five and try to make sure they were able to request protection.

We spent some more time discussing the details. The Al Otro Lado activists had procured nice clothes and a couple of nice backpacks for each of the individuals to make sure Mexican officials wouldn't stop them from approaching the border: "You need to look nice, then maybe you won't get stopped." We determined that we would try to cross at a smaller border crossing rather than the main one, which I was likely to be returned to by CBP. That meant that I would somehow need to ditch the consul general and the security detail, because they would immediately alert the CBP officials about what I was doing, and it was important to me to observe what happens at the border to asylum seekers every day. It also meant that I could not be fully transparent with the consul general about what I was going to do, and I felt bad about that because she was a career officer, spoke fluent Spanish, and clearly seemed to be concerned about and in touch with the migrants on the ground. I knew, however, that I would not lie to her. I would just have to figure out a way to orchestrate the trip.

When I left the lunch to meet the consul general again, it turned out that some newspaper reports had just come out implying that I was planning to begin crossing the bridge and do a protest right on the bridge. She looked at me worriedly and gently said, "I hope you're not planning to do anything that gets us all in trouble!" I assured her that I certainly would not be doing a protest on the bridge, but I also did not tell her that I was planning to accompany some asylum seekers across the border.

When the consul general dropped me off at the main border crossing, I noticed she left the security detail with me. I also noticed that the border checkpoint had been extended even further out than when we came in. Now, agents were stationed substantially further away from the actual crossing than before, checking papers only to allow people to get in line. This was a tactic that was being used at all the border crossings: asylum seekers had the legal right to ask for asylum once on U.S. soil, so the Trump administration's strategy—with Mexico's complicity—was to never allow them to reach U.S. soil and to push the checkpoints further and further into Mexican territory.

We had made a plan with Nicole that she would pick us up at the main crossing and take us to the smaller crossing some fifteen minutes away by car. I would need to leave without catching the attention of the security detail that had stayed with me, though unobtrusively stationed further away. After some picture taking at the bridge, acting like regular tourists, Jennifer and I managed to steal away in the midst of a big crowd to Nicole's small car without being followed. We immediately drove to the other crossing, parked in a parking lot some distance away, and began walking to the bridge.

It was dark now and I had no security. I started to sweat, imagining what would happen if I was attacked and it came out that a U.S. congresswoman had ditched her security team and was wandering alone in the dark of night in the somewhat dangerous streets of Tijuana. I kept my head down and continued walking toward the bright light of the border crossing. There, we met a group of half a dozen volunteers and Al Otro Lado staff, who had come with the five migrant asylum seekers who I would try to accompany across the border.

We got into a relatively short line and waited our turn. I initially stood behind the group as they presented themselves with their attorney. I did not display my congressional pin or identify myself as a member of Congress. I wanted to see what happened without anyone knowing who I was. Sure enough, when the asylum seekers presented themselves to the Border Patrol agents, they were turned away. When the attorney began to argue with the agents, saying that they were legally presenting at the border to ask for asylum, the Border Patrol agents got impatient and curt and cut them off, refusing to listen. At that point, I stepped forward and said, "This is a legal process. These are unaccompanied children and it is dark. They are on American soil and they can seek asylum."

The agents turned to me and rudely interrupted. "We're not yet on American soil," one of them said, pointing to the actual gates some ten feet away. "And besides, we have absolutely no room to keep these people inside. Our Border Patrol station space is small and it's full."

"I'd like to see the space," I said, undeterred.

Now they were really not happy. "Who the hell do you think you are?" one of them said, angrily.

It was time to tell them. "I'm a U.S. congresswoman," I responded calmly. "And I am telling you that we need to allow these people through to seek asylum."

He turned to me in shock and started to register what was happening. He asked me for proof of identity, and then said again that they simply couldn't accept more people, there was no space and the orders were that people had to wait in this "metering" process for their names to be called. I responded that we had been told children would not be turned away, and these asylum seekers needed to be let in.

After a wait, the officer came back and said they would allow the two unaccompanied children in but not the others. That wasn't enough for me. We still had Victoria and her daughter, Alejandra; as well as Raul, who had a serious medical condition.

"I'd like to speak with the chief of the station," I said. He said that wouldn't be possible as they didn't know where the chief was. I said we were all happy to wait and we settled ourselves on the concrete pathway outside the border entrance. It was clear we were not leaving, so the agents conferred with each other and then said they would try to get the chief. We waited. . . . for a few hours. When the agent finally came back, he told me that I could come with him and he would take me to the border chief. This meant I had to leave the group of asylum seekers, and I wasn't sure that I would be allowed to return to them. But there was no other way to talk to the chief, so I decided to go inside to meet her. More waiting ensued before the chief finally came out. She was empathetic but also firm that she couldn't do anything.

"Do you have children?" I asked her. Her eyes softened. "I do," she said.

"Then, please," I said. "Please help them. We cannot send these people back out into the dark. We have a legal responsibility to take them. They are seeking asylum, and this is our history and our responsibility."

She looked at me for a moment, then I saw her shoulders drop and she was silent. "Okay," she said finally. "I can't promise anything because I have to get permission. I'll call up the chain and see what I can do."

That was good enough for me. I texted the attorney who was still waiting with the group and gave her the somewhat optimistic news, cautioning her that nothing may come of it. One of the hardest things in these situations is how to be honest with the people who will be directly affected but also not get their hopes up. There is no telling what ends up happening and the roller-coaster ride for the people involved takes so much out of them. And yet, that little glimmer of hope helped them to continue to sit on the cold hard pavement and wait.

The chief finally returned. "We got it!" she said, and her excitement came through as much as she tried not to let it show.

"Oh my God!" I said, delightedly. "You're amazing! May I give you a hug?"

She nodded and we hugged briefly. It reminded me again that there were many good Border Patrol people who were just carrying out orders. They were often in untenable positions, and despite all the money we had given to the border, instead of putting it into facilities to process people humanely and hire more immigration officers, that money had gone to all the wrong things. I just could not believe that most of these agents wanted to be tear-gassing mothers and children, but Trump administration policies and the culture within the agency was bringing out the worst in people instead of the best. By looking for the goodness in this chief, we had touched something in her and it had brought us to this moment where five people would have a future instead of facing death and violence. That was what we were trying to achieve. Humanity, generosity—and yes, adherence to the laws and our responsibilities under domestic and international human rights conventions.

"I want to stay here until they come in and say goodbye to them," I told her. She was in too deep to tell me to go, even though we were not supposed to be there, and she nodded with a somewhat resigned smile.

It was an amazing moment when the asylum seekers I had accompanied walked through and presented their documents for asylum. It was the kind of moment that sustains us as organizers, a moment I will remember for a long time as if it happened yesterday. Once again, I saw the difference a position and platform made. As an activist, I simply would not have been able to accomplish what I did as a congresswoman. But as a congresswoman, without the work of Al Otro Lado, I also would not have been connected to the asylum seekers, have their trust or the wherewithal to plan the strategy that allowed us to succeed.

Nine-year-old Alejandra was weeping but she and all of them looked as if the sun had just come out. Raul was hugging me as if he would never let go. Everyone gathered around, beaming. Five lives that had a whole new set of hopes because I wasn't afraid to speak up and step in. I knew

nothing was guaranteed—all that had happened was that they had started the asylum process and the majority of them would not be detained
for too long. Beyond that, it would be a long series of steps before we'd
actually see if they would be granted asylum.

Over the ensuing weeks and months, Jennifer kept track of each of
them, notifying me each time one of them was released from detention,
reunited with their families, or moving through the asylum process. Victoria and Alejandra were living with family in Connecticut as they pursued
their asylum case. David was eventually released and was living with his
mom as they both waited for their asylum process. We never were able to
find out what happened to Auriel. Raul's nightmare, however, continued.

After requesting asylum at the border, ICE detained Raul at the Theo
Lacey Detention Center in California, a facility whose conditions have
been criticized by the DHS inspector general for "slimy, foul-smelling
lunch meat that appears to be spoiled;" "moldy and mildewed shower
stalls, refuse in cells and inoperable phones."[15]

During Raul's first month in detention, he experienced difficulty gain-
ing access to a medically appropriate diet, and consequently lost weight.
In addition, he was sexually assaulted while in detention and placed in solitary confinement as a "protective measure" after he reported the assault.
Although this is standard practice, solitary was difficult for Raul, who
was already struggling under so much. My office advocated on his behalf
to ensure Raul's access to a medically appropriate diet and release from
solitary confinement. In February of 2019, ICE finally released Raul on
parole as he continues to pursue asylum.

It was an amazing result. However, it simply should not have taken the
intervention of a member of the U.S. Congress and a single, compassionate Border Patrol chief to enable people to exercise their rights. Just like
Article 2 of the United Nations Charter, otherwise known as the Universal Declaration of Human Rights, states: "Everyone has the right to seek
and enjoy in other countries asylum from persecution."[16]

When I got home and put out a series of tweets about successfully
accompanying the five asylum seekers into the country, I faced plenty of

blowback and ridicule from Republicans. One of my Republican Judiciary Committee colleagues, who is one of the fiercest anti-immigrant pro-Trumpians, even called me the "caravan coyote" congressmember and suggested that I should be arrested for breaking the law.[17]

For me, I knew I had helped people get a shot at safety and a new life. It was one of the proudest moments of my life.

In the summer of 2018, my colleague Congresswoman Lucille Roybal-Allard and I co-led a delegation of eight members of congress on a trip to the border. We visited a processing center in McAllen, Texas, only to find the stories unchanged. Family separation was still occurring. We saw children held in cages. Mothers told me they were only allowed to see their children for an hour each day. We went to courtrooms where seventy people were prosecuted at once—a kind of assembly line justice that has no place in our democracy, and no place in how we treat those seeking asylum.[18]

Once Democrats were in the majority, the Judiciary Committee dragged countless administration officials who led various agencies to testify before us, only to hear them tell us they knew about the irreversible damage these actions would cause to children and families and yet they still went forward. The few that tried to speak out were ignored.

Trump had continued to roll back policies and change laws, including those that forbid indefinite detention of children. He denied flu vaccines to those being held and, for the first time in history, put forward a new rule to charge asylum seekers a fee for seeking asylum. As I write this, reports have emerged that Trump wanted desperately to have a moat built along the southern border, filled with alligators and crocodiles, and even suggested shooting migrants in the legs to "slow them down."[19] The cruelty is mind-blowing, and willfully inflicted with a clear political motive. What is so disgusting is that no Republicans even speak out against any of these injustices anymore. It also came to light that Border Agents—people who work for and are supposed to represent the people of the United States—demeaned and mocked migrants and my fellow women of color in Congress in a "secret" Facebook group, where they posted racist comments, lewd images, and memes. They joked about migrant deaths, calling the migrants "subhuman" and worse.[20]

All this is happening here in the home of the Statue of Liberty—an iconic American symbol that has been denigrated by the current head of Customs and Immigration Services, Ken Cucinelli, who rewrote the famous Emma Lazarus poem about the Statue, saying it should be "Give me your tired and your poor who can stand on their own two feet and who will not become a public charge."

The tragedy of it all is that there *are* other ways to deal with the increase in migrant families at our southern border. An extremely successful federally funded program, called the Family Case Management Program, offered a cost-effective and human alternative to detention. The program provided social workers for the families who were released from detention, so that the social worker could explain the process, refer families to services, including legal counsel, and ensure migrants met their court dates. The program had a 99 percent success rate of participants attending court appearances and check-ins, countering the false narrative of the Trump administration that migrants simply flee and don't show up. According to staffers, the families in the program also thrived, and those who were not granted asylum left the country once their case was clear. However, instead of utilizing these program alternatives to detention, in 2017, the administration shuttered the program. Apparently it wasn't cruel enough.[21] Later in 2018, our Democratic House majority was able to reinstate funding for the program, but six months later, we were told that it still hadn't restarted.

The complexity of migration increases with the recognition that, in many cases, the United States has been complicit in propping up foreign leaders that become dictators, or in fostering economic conditions that lead to devastation. Whether unstated or tacitly recognized, this contributes to the idea that we also need to take responsibility for the migration that ensues from war or economic devastation. The logical, cost-effective way to address the root causes of migration is to focus our efforts on building equitable economies and rights in countries that send the biggest flows of people to America. This means ensuring that our trade agreements do not result in massive worker displacement and that U.S. military intervention, economic sanctions, and security policies do not fuel human rights crises abroad. We also have to address climate change, which has increased droughts, floods, and other natural disasters, forcing people to move. And we must stop providing assistance to governments that brutally suppress human rights.

Investing in development and diplomatic solutions must be part of the answer and would do more to stem the flow of migrants to our southern border than any vanity wall. Yet, Trump's administration—in the midst of the flow of migrants and just as I was on a congressional delegation to these countries—suspended nearly $4 million in foreign aid to El Salvador, Guatemala, and Honduras—countries the United States has long assisted, in part to help reduce the poverty and violent conditions that spur those families to migrate to the United States in the first place.[22]

Finally, the slashing of asylum processing and refugee admissions is exactly the wrong approach during times of violent crises like what's happening in Latin America. In the past, we have opened up America for those fleeing violence, and those programs continue to exist in the form of the Lautenberg Amendment. The Lautenberg Amendment, first enacted in 1990 as part of the U.S. foreign operations budget, allowed for tens of thousands of Jews from the former Soviet Union to be safely resettled in America. As the worldwide refugee situation changed, the Lautenberg Amendment was expanded to include persecuted religious minorities in other countries, such as Jews, Christians, and Baha'is from Iran. Creating a similar program that would include the ability for people from Latin American countries in crisis to apply and be resettled in America is the humane and smart approach to addressing the issues of a part of the world that is so close to us geographically and facing serious issues.

Research shows us that militarizing and "hardening" the border with a wall or more troops doesn't reduce illegal immigration, but rather produces exactly the opposite effect. In fact, this "crackdown" strategy paradoxically led to enormous surges in the numbers of undocumented immigrants who set down roots in the United States.[23] In the past, a "circular flow" of migration meant workers moved back and forth across the border more easily, which encouraged them to stay in the homes they loved while supplying our economic need for temporary labor. Those programs needed to be ended because they had weak worker protections, but the idea of a nimble system that relied on smart policy, not a hardened border, is a road map forward.

The truth is that there are plenty of ways to deal with surges of immigrants on the border, both temporary and longer term. But Trump's administration has no interest in solving any immigration issues—it simply wants to create a perception of massive waves of "criminal" immigrants coming across the border to harm Americans, so it can scare Americans into giving more attention to otherwise untenable restrictive immigration policies. These changes are ones that conservative, anti-immigrant citizens have long wanted—both on the border and inside the country: things like vastly expanding the ability to detain and deport individuals without any due process, decimating the asylum and refugee systems for legal entry, undercutting the right to obtain automatic citizenship for those born in the United States, and drastically slashing legal migration of anyone who is not white and wealthy.

I do not believe that America will tolerate this in the end, but this is a fight for the soul of our country. In the end, immigration has never been a question of policy, it has always been a question of who we are as a nation and what we are willing to stand up for.

What troubles me most in the current discussions of immigration is the widening divide between the inherent complexity of immigration laws and the simplistic, generally punitive rhetoric that aims to criminalize migration. Our system of immigration laws is one of the most complex and few people in America today understand it or the way in which it has evolved. Few people know of the tremendous battles that have been fought to revamp these laws and how policy has rarely been the problem, but rather politics. We no longer trade in facts, but instead allow myths and lies to permeate our discourse, blocking progress to real solutions.

Consider, for example, the false anti-immigrant rhetoric that immigrants take more from our economy than they contribute. Economists from both parties are well aware of the economic benefits of immigration. Back in 2005, they were extensively summarized by President George W. Bush's *Economic Report of the President*, which found "a comprehensive accounting of the benefits and costs of immigration that shows the benefits of immigration exceed the costs."[24] The report noted, among other things, that Social Security payroll taxes paid by undocumented workers, who can never claim those benefits, led to a $463 billion funding surplus.[25] In other words, undocumented immigrants are paying for the retirement of this country's aging, mostly Caucasian, population. The following year, the conservative Heritage Foundation wrote in a 2006 report stating that "the argument that immigrants harm the American economy should be dismissed out of hand."[26] Economic projections from a 2013 White House report showed that passing comprehensive immigration reform would contribute an additional $1.4 trillion to GDP by 2033.[27]

This is just one of many myths—from "immigrants commit crimes" to "immigrants are stealing benefits they don't pay for." These myths allow the current system to stay in place, benefiting only the few who take profit from it politically and economically, even when that profit comes at the price of our nation's soul. They also confuse the issue—it is as if we are working from two entirely different sets of facts, making it impossible to get to a shared solution.

This was displayed clearly in a hearing on immigration detention that I chaired in September 2019 in the House Immigration Subcommittee. In my first term, I spent over six months working with a broad coalition of groups and my colleague Congressman Adam Smith to craft and introduce a comprehensive bill that would transform immigration detention in our country. The Dignity for Detained Immigrants Act took on the basic construction of an immigrant detention system that had dramatically expanded and now was detaining over 52,000 immigrants a day, and nearly 500,000 people per year,[28] largely in private for-profit prisons and county jails that had been emptied out by our successful (even bipartisan) efforts to reform the criminal justice system. The bill would get rid of the for-profit prison system, transitioning from for-profit prisons to government-owned and -operated detention centers; eliminate mandatory detention, a policy that takes away any judicial discretion for those who do not pose a public safety risk; and increase oversight, accountability, and transparency. The bill would also eliminate family detention and prohibit shackling of pregnant women and the detention of children.

I had been organizing hard on the inside, and with allies on the outside, to get 136 co-sponsors on the bill and to tee it up for a hearing in the House on detention. When we finally had the hearing, we invited three compelling individuals who had been detained in horrific circumstances to attend. Two of the three had been detained despite having had legal papers to be in the United States. I had also invited Northwest Immigrant Rights Project's executive director from Seattle as well as two excellent experts on immigration detention and alternatives to detention. The main purpose of the hearing was to bring forward the terribly negative human consequences of detention and to show that the vast majority of people who are being detained have never committed a crime much less been charged with one. Even those with criminal charges were largely charged for minor crimes. With the changes I was proposing in Dignity for Detained Immigrants, we could release the vast majority of people in detention with the utilization of alternatives to detention, save the American taxpayers enormous amounts of money (the cost of alternatives to detention is a fraction of the hundreds of dollars we spend per person per day in these private, for-profit detention facilities), and return to a more humane and effective system of only prioritizing those who really needed to be detained because they posed a flight risk or a public safety risk.

Unfortunately, one of the Republican witnesses was Thomas Homan, the former acting director of the Immigration and Customs Enforcement agency. Homan launched into his opening statement with an angry and rude tirade against Democrats who weren't in the room, painting a picture of all the "illegal immigrants" who were murderers and rapists (propped up by a family sitting in the front row whose loved one had been murdered by an undocumented immigrant) and extolling Trump's harsh immigration policies. Throughout the hearing, he continued in this way, even refusing to respect my authority as chair when his time had expired and, in accordance with committee rules, we needed to move to the next questioner.

At one point during the hearing, the ranking Republican member leaned over to me and indicated that he had not wanted Homan to be a witness and that it was unfortunate that we couldn't have a reasonable conversation about areas that we would agree on. In one hopeful sign, he told me that he would be interested in working with me on a more targeted bill that would ensure that immigrants like those I had invited to testify before us were not put into detention.

That was hopeful. But the larger problem was exactly this: Trump and his anti-immigrant allies didn't want to talk about the truth of what was happening. They simply wanted to paint all these immigrants as murderers and rapists, instead of telling the truth about a system designed only to benefit for-profit private prison corporations and the political ambitions of a divisive president.

The most important point here is that our failure to address our broken immigration system has never been due to a lack of understanding of how to fix it. We know exactly what the solutions are and what needs to be done.

As recently as 2013, the United States Senate passed—with a remarkable sixty-eight bipartisan votes—a comprehensive immigration reform bill that would have fixed many of the most outdated parts of immigration law. The bill was a major compromise for both the left and right, setting aside $40 billion over ten years to pay for more border security while creating a roadmap to citizenship for the 11 million undocumented immigrants—including Dreamers—and fixing the outdated family visa caps, processing the immigration backlogs, and addressing the critical workforce needs of employers. Had that bill been allowed to come to the floor of the House for a vote, everyone acknowledges that it would have passed. Instead, since then we've spent over $20 billion on border security, but with no underlying solutions to our immigration policy. Worse, we have besmirched America's reputation and betrayed our values with the inhumane separation of families and detention of children (many of whom will likely never see their parents again). Americans know this, feel it, and abhor it.[29]

While at OneAmerica and then later as the co-chair of the We Belong Together campaign, I had worked on the provisions of that 2013 bill. We were able to incorporate some of our most important provisions into that bill to make it better, even as we continued to detest some of the enforcement provisions that were still a part of that bill. It was a compromise, but one that would have had enormously positive consequences for millions and millions of immigrants across the country and would have provided essential reforms to a system that simply has not been reformed in decades.

I must be honest and say that Democrats have had as much to do with the lack of reform as Republicans. If we are to fix the system once and for all, it will require deep education and real courage from Democrats to counter the myths and lies that permeate our environment. Today's Republicans have been successful at pulling dialogue so far to the right on immigration that it will likely take a giant and perhaps uncomfortable (for some) push toward policies like transforming our detention system, instituting Lautenberg-type provisions for Latin American countries, and giving permanent status to DACA recipients, to return America to some semblance of humanity and sanity on immigration policy and the values that undergird it.

Leadership means leading, not just following polls. Leadership means helping our constituents to understand what is happening and then following a set of core moral principles, finding real solutions, and refusing to give in to convenient, simplistic but false stereotypes that leave us no further in solving the issues before us. Never is this more important than when we have dictators and demagogues wielding power. History shows us that the road to fascism is littered with moments when people could have said or done something but did not. Let us never make those same mistakes again.

One of the big challenges we have in addressing our broken immigration system is that most Americans have no idea of the history and the under-pinnings of our system that have led us to where we are. Immigration policy in America is both complex and deeply institutionally racist in how it was built. For all the outrage over "illegal immigration," the fact is that undocumented immigration and the tension of the need of immigrant labor have been the norm—not the exception—for most of our country's history.

During the nineteenth century and into the twentieth, the demand for labor in this new, growing nation meant that almost anyone who arrived here was allowed into the country with just a physical exam—unless they fell into a few deeply exclusionary categories. Before 1921, the only immi-gration laws that existed were ones that restricted Chinese people from immigrating (repealed only in 1943), as well as excluding most other Asians and certain categories of people such as sex workers, those with "dangerous and loathsome contagious disease," or "the insane."

Later, in 1921 and 1924, quotas were established based on race and nationality, heavily favoring immigrants from Western Europe. Because there were few laws and little bureaucratic control over who came and stayed, undocumented immigration was the norm for generations. As much as "amnesty" has become a dirty word today, amnesties were applied to waves of European immigrants who were here without proper authori-zation. The 1929 Registry Act, for example, granted "law-abiding aliens" to register as permanent residents if they simply proved they were "of good moral character" and had lived in the U.S. for several years.[30]

It wasn't until 1965 that the national-origin quota system was abolished and replaced with a system whereby immigrants were admitted on the basis of relationships to immediate family members or employers. The last major overhaul of the immigration system to increase legal admissions caps, in 1990, focused largely on employment-based visas.

As America grows and baby boomers age, our economy needs immigrants to replenish America's workforce. In the fast-growing industries of domestic care, home health aides, nursing assistants, and personal care aides, immigrants make up the vast majority of workers. The Bureau of Labor Statistics projects that in those industries alone, from 2016 to 2026, the U.S. will need workers to fill 1.2 million jobs.[31] Yet our legal immigration system is groaning under the weight of outdated category caps that simply don't meet the needs of our economy or our people. The number of visas for nonagricultural workers (such as construction workers, housekeepers, or forest workers) is stuck at the 1990 level of 66,000 visas—even though our economy requires millions.[32] In 2018 alone, more than 3.9 million U.S. citizens and permanent residents who had applied legally for their closest family members—parents, spouses, children, and siblings—were in an immigration processing backlog that could take decades to clear.[33] (Contrary to the "chain migration" narrative, these immediate family members are the only ones eligible to migrate via the family-based system.)

Other avenues for legal immigration have traditionally had bipartisan consensus, such as the belief that we have moral and legal obligations (under U.S. and international law) to take in asylum seekers and refugees from around the world. These people are often fleeing the very forces of oppression, war, and dictatorship that threaten the world's safety, including America's. Going back to the resettlement of Vietnamese refugees in the wake of the Vietnam War to the lessons learned from our country's initial rejection of Jews during World War II, Republicans and Democrats have previously given real weight to the belief that consigning millions of people to refugee camps with little freedom, dire living conditions, and no hope of determining their own futures is a moral question for any nation that seeks to lead the world. Still, even as leaders from all faiths (including evangelicals) emphasize the need to strengthen not cut our refugee resettlement program, the United States still only ranks fiftieth in the world for welcoming refugees.[34]

Most Americans have no idea of this history, or that there is currently is no orderly, functioning process for people to come to America. Under Presidents Reagan and Bush, there were superficial, temporary fixes, such as legalizations or "amnesties" for those who were undocumented at the time. But without underlying reform to make the system function, we were bound to end up in the same place again. Most Republicans—and too many Democrats—have given in to the simplistic narratives supplied by anti-immigrant forces, throwing billions of taxpayer dollars into mass deportations, a vast labyrinth of expensive private prisons, and a border that is already one of the most secure and militarized in the world.

The problems caused by indiscriminate enforcement and the lack of comprehensive reforms certainly did not start with Donald Trump, but he has taken an approach dramatically different from that of every Republican and Democratic president of the past several decades. Instead of embracing the fact that immigration has been the unique genius of America's history and is necessary to the economic vitality of our nation, Trump has welcomed the rigidly restrictionist agenda of anti-immigrant zealots. He has instituted inhumane policies such as ripping children from their parents and imprisoning them indefinitely, shackling pregnant women, cutting refugee admissions to their lowest level in decades, curbing all forms of legal migration, and vilifying immigrants at every opportunity. This is not an administration or a Republican Party that has displayed any interest in principled compromises to fix the underlying broken and outdated immigration system or allow it to be fixed. If they did so, they would lose what they see as a potent tool to rile up their base.

That means it is up to us, us in the broadest sense of the word. I don't just mean Democrats, though Democrats should—in my view—be leading this charge. I mean an *us* that includes those who remember and care about their own immigration histories, those who recognize that without this, America loses the very soul of who we are. We need to recapture the moral imagination of immigration, the idea of an America that was rooted in the idea of a land of freedom, refuge, and acceptance to those turned away by other places; a land that took the tired and poor, those yearning to breathe free.

And while America has the right to control her borders, the real challenge in front of us must be to emerge with a new definition of borders in our global context and show that America can display real leadership again in a world reeling from so many conditions that cause people to seek a new life.

When my parents used all their savings to send me across the oceans from India at the age of sixteen, they made the ultimate sacrifice of separating from their child without knowing if we would ever live on the same continent again. They did so because they believed America was where I would get the best education and have the most opportunity. Seventeen years later, when I finally got my citizenship, I was surrounded by people from all over the world. Hands over our hearts, we pledged allegiance to our new country. We knew we were the lucky ones and we were grateful, even as we felt our loss in saying goodbye to the families and countries we had left behind. Through my work, I have met many new Americans and am constantly amazed at the sheer diversity of how they came here and what they end up doing—as farmworkers, doctors, caregivers, entrepreneurs, or researchers. Their stories add to the long tapestry of this uniquely American experience, one that is central to our national identity.

Today's immigration stories are stitched to the stories and experiences of each successive wave of new arrivals: the Irish, Polish, Germans, Chinese, Mexicans, Jews, Greeks, Nigerians, Somalis, and many others. More than most others, America is a nation of the imagination: its imagined horizons promised our forebears the freedoms of a nobler, more resilient, more just society, one that did not exist anywhere else and would be created from whole cloth by daring trailblazers and idealists who celebrated the land of plenty. It was this imagined America that spurred people to come. In their coming, and their working here, they built America and their successors continue to do so.

It was Dr. Martin Luther King who said in his letters from the Birmingham jail that "an unjust law is no law at all." As we fix our laws, we can create a new moral imagination on immigration.

Imagine how, with an underlying system of laws that actually works and meets the needs of our economy, we would dramatically reduce the need for the kind of costly and cruel enforcement we have today, saving American taxpayers billions of dollars. We would be able to target only those who are serious threats. Our immigration judges could be empowered to use their extensive knowledge of the immigration system to make humane and smart decisions that are consistent with our values, including embracing second chances for those who make mistakes as we have done in the criminal justice system.

Imagine becoming, again, a country of family values by emphasizing the bedrock principle of family immigration and allowing the families who have been separated for decades to be able to reunite again. Family immigration has and will continue to bring us strivers of all kinds to fill jobs at every skill level, while at the same time allowing families to get essential support at home that immigrants need in order to integrate and become self-sufficient more quickly: think of grandparents taking care of grandchildren while parents work or of children taking care of aging parents. Those who enter through the family immigration system have identities far beyond family members: they go on to contribute their skills to our economy as service workers, doctors, lawyers, and small business entrepreneurs. It is their family that keeps them whole and their work—in and out of the home—that keeps America prosperous.

Imagine if our government was not stuck in political gridlock but instead doing the job we should be doing: updating our immigration system regularly to prioritize certain industries that are seeing rapid growth and need workers, such as domestic workers and home health-care workers. Our country needs the labor of immigrants, and we have a responsibility to do provide it in a way that addresses the problems of declining economic conditions for both American-born and immigrant workers.

Imagine getting rid of the divisive conversation that pits U.S.-born workers against immigrants, and instead simultaneously investing in measures like retraining initiatives and new investment programs that would help displaced workers in industries that are undergoing structural change or decline to find reliable new jobs quickly. At the same time, we can put resources into helping immigrants integrate rapidly in their new home, learning English and obtaining the skills that will help our nation see the full economic and civic benefits of their presence.

Finally, imagine recognizing our strong national interest in development, diplomacy, and the protection of human rights around the world. Rather than using the blunt tool of a militaristic foreign policy, American investments in countries that uphold the rule of law pays off by encouraging people to make their own opportunities where they live, rather than feeling forced to make perilous migrations.

We cannot lose hope, no matter how complex the issues and how difficult the path ahead seems. Failing to address immigration and leaving it as a pawn for those who seek to divide us will undo every other piece of progress we hope to achieve as a nation. I have been working for twenty years to reform our broken immigration system, from those early days after 9/11 when I helped lead a bus load of immigrants across the country on the Immigrant Workers Freedom Ride, to the long and sometimes painful journey to build a truly broad and diverse coalition of likely and unlikely allies. I know it is not easy, that it sometimes feels like two steps back for every step forward. But in the long run, perhaps it is better for this racism to be exposed for what it is, better for xenophobia to come into the open so that we can see it more clearly and fight it more strategically.

In the end, perhaps our biggest hope comes in the goodness of the American people and the nation's deep connection to immigration. Somewhere in the recesses of the American psyche, I believe Americans understand that it is only the indigenous peoples of this land that have any claim to it. The rest of us have come from somewhere else, helping America to remake itself through each of our new arrivals and the underlying hope that we could all make something different of our lives here.

Our moral imagination is the only thing that will take us forward. Morality and imagination together will help us find our way back to our hearts again.

9

Moral Vision—Medicare for All

ON THE MORNING OF APRIL 30, 2019, I GATHERED IN THE THIRD FLOOR OF the Capitol Building, in the Democratic anteroom for the Rules Committee, with a small group of healthcare advocates including Bonnie Castillo from National Nurses United, Jennifer Epps-Addison and Ana Maria Archila from Center for Popular Democracy, and Alex Lawson from Social Security Works. We were about to hold the first hearing on Medicare for All—a bill that I had introduced in March and spent over six months crafting with health advocates, Senator Bernie Sanders, and other House colleagues. This was a historic hearing: it would be the first time in decades that Congress would hold a hearing on a single-payer bill.

It was a hard-won, hard-fought-for moment for all of us, but it was an activist named Ady Barkan whose struggle and journey here most embodied all of the sickness of a for-profit healthcare system and also the tremendous courage and resilience of the movement for Medicare for All.

Ady is a thirty-five-year-old husband, father, lawyer, and lifelong activist. In 2016, Ady was diagnosed with ALS, or Lou Gehrig's disease. The degenerative, neurological disease is devastating; its sufferers are typically given three to five years to live, as their motor functions slowly disappear over time.[1] Ady's work was legendary in the activist community: he helped to establish the powerful, progressive organization called Local Progress that organized progressive city councilmembers across the country, founded the Fed Up campaign to show the impact of the Federal Reserve's monetary policy on low-income communities, and then carried out courageous civil disobedience actions, including getting handcuffed in his wheelchair protesting the 2017 GOP tax bill that would have cut Medicare and Medicaid.[2] Most recently, as a member of the Center for Popular Democracy and the founder of his own Be A Hero project, Ady had become a leading voice in the fight for Medicare for All.

Getting Ady on the witness list to testify had been complicated, and almost did not happen. The Rules Committee chairman, Jim McGovern, is a dedicated progressive and a champion of single-payer healthcare; I had worked closely with him to pull off the hearing. Still, working with staff in leadership and on the committee, it was difficult to ensure that we got the voices we needed to testify. Our witness list had to be small, and there was argument around what kind of testimonies to include. I had been advocating hard for a patient voice—and we wanted it to be Ady. Others on the various staffs felt that we should stick with the "experts"—people who could answer the detailed questions they felt sure would be asked. When it became clear that the patient testimony was not going to happen, Ady decided to utilize his own relationship with Speaker Pelosi. He told her it would be his dream to testify at the hearing and she did not let him down. She immediately weighed in and we managed to get Ady on the testimony list. It was a huge victory that was celebrated across the movement, because we knew that Ady was powerful—in his knowledge, in his story, and in his fearlessness. I knew immediately that the hearing would be defined by Ady's testimony, and that would be a good thing for Medicare for All.

By April of 2019, Ady's condition had worsened. It was not certain that he would have the energy to make the trip. He could not walk, talk or even type, but he came to the hearing and spoke to us through a sophisticated machine that tracked his eye movements onto a computer, which then typed the words and delivered them electronically.

I had worked closely with Jennifer and Ana Maria of CPD for years, and certainly knew of Ady through that. But the first time we really met was in that anteroom. I leaned over Ady's wheelchair to hug him gently so as not to hurt his frail body, and I saw that he was typing out a message to me on his screen:

"Thank you. I cannot imagine the politics you have had to negotiate to get this hearing."

It was certainly true that I had to negotiate a lot of politics to get the hearing. But that day belonged to Ady, and to the grassroots movement for Medicare for All that got us to this point.

That first historic Rules Committee hearing almost didn't happen at all.

We had to clear a number of hurdles on the road to April 30, and the first one came about in the first days of our new Democratically controlled House. It involved a wonky, procedural rule in Congress known as PAYGO. PAYGO required Congress to offset any new mandatory spending—whether that spending was for a program like Medicare or tax cuts—with a cut from someplace else in the federal budget, or with tax increases. This had been around in Congress for about two decades, passed into rules packages and then waived whenever leadership saw fit so that bills could be brought to the floor without a corresponding "pay for" method. These typically got worked out during the appropriations process anyway, so the whole idea of PAYGO seemed more of a symbolic, messaging rule than a practical one, designed to appeal to fiscal conservatives. PAYGO was also, at its core, bad policy. The question should have been about which investments would generate balanced economic growth in the future, not about how to pay for it in the moment—especially when it seemed the only things that people demanded payment for were things that benefited Main Street not Wall Street or the Pentagon. Democrats had gone along with decades of austerity spending, cutting domestic discretionary spending for things like education, housing, and transportation, even as wasteful military spending continued to skyrocket. It seemed like a final indignity that we Democrats would have to jump through hoops to pay for an agenda that benefited working families when the folks on the other side of the aisle didn't have to pay for tax cuts for the wealthiest.

In 2010, in the eternally misguided Democratic quest to be seen as fiscally conservative, President Obama signed a PAYGO provision into statute so that it was no longer just in the rules of the House, it was now locked completely in law. And yet, during my first term in Congress, in a sign of the absurdity of the statute, my Democratic colleagues and I watched as then-House speaker Paul Ryan and his ilk waived PAYGO to enact draconian tax cuts and other measures that ran up the federal deficit by $800 billion in the first fiscal year of President Trump's administration.[3]

Now, in 2019, Democrats had taken back power in the House of Representatives. In our first week in Congress, we would pick our new leaders and decide the rules by which we'd operate. Still hewing to the idea that voters wanted us to be fiscally responsible even though it was Republicans that had just run up the deficit, Speaker Pelosi asked us to vote on a rules package that still included PAYGO as it had before.

In the Congressional Progressive Caucus, where I had just been elected as a co-chair along with Congressman Mark Pocan, we didn't want PAYGO. In addition to the fact that it meant nothing when it was constantly waived as had been the case, it also acted as an excuse for why we couldn't bring forward progressive policies.

Mark and I had raised getting rid of PAYGO to Pelosi back in November but she was noncommittal on the point. Later, when we negotiated a number of wins as part of our agreement to support Pelosi as Speaker, PAYGO was the one provision we were not able to win. Still, Rules Committee Chairman Jim McGovern had promised us that we would simply waive PAYGO as needed for our progressive priorities, and it wouldn't be a problem. Most of the CPC members were supporting the overall rules package—even though it included PAYGO—because there were so many other good things in it. But days before the vote, Warren Gunnels (Bernie Sanders's policy director) began tweeting about bringing down the rules package over PAYGO. Ro Khanna picked up the mantle and then newly elected progressive star Alexandria Ocasio-Cortez announced she would vote against the package and encouraged others to do so, calling the rule "a dark political maneuver designed to hamstring progress on healthcare and other legislation."[4]

I agreed with Alex and Ro—PAYGO was bad policy—but I also knew that PAYGO was enshrined in statute whether we put it into that rules package or not. Representative Ilhan Omar, also a newly elected CPC whip, agreed that while we would prefer to eliminate PAYGO, it wasn't worth bringing the rules package down for it. She had obtained some great wins in the rules package as well—including changing House rules so she could wear her head covering (*hijab*) on the House floor—and she too had something at stake in not bringing down the package.

Still, as pressure rose from progressives on the outside, framing this as one of the first tests of progressive power, CPC members began to get worried. What was our plan? Most were not planning to vote against the package, but they also didn't want to get caught in an early progressive firestorm. Nor were any of us sure we had enough votes to win the fight of bringing down the rules package as one of our very first moves. Rules Chairman Jim McGovern—whom I have always liked and respected—was now calling me in a panic, asking for my help in getting enough votes from progressive members to pass the package. I realized this could be an opportunity to get something more negotiated—and I had a hunch of what that could be.

"Look," I told him, "I will try to help, but we need something in exchange for this."

The insistence by some House Democrats that we include PAYGO in the rules package had caused real concern that we would not be able to bring our bold ideas to the floor, even though Jim had assured us we could waive PAYGO for bills like Medicare for All, if we could show we had enough votes to pass them. We needed to have a win that would really matter and would show some commitment to moving some of these progressive priorities forward. I had an idea. "Help me get the Speaker to commit that I will be able to have hearings on my Medicare for All bill," I said to Jim.

"I can do a hearing in rules," he said immediately. "It's not typical but I'll do it."

I saw immediately the real benefits of having Jim chair the first-ever hearing: he was a good friend, he believed whole-heartedly in Medicare for All, and he was one of my favorite people in Congress—remember, he had been one of the only two white guys who had stood up with all of us people of color when we protested the electoral college count during my first week of Congress. Doing the first hearing with Jim as chairman meant that we would have much more control over the hearing and that was very, very good. It would be a great trial run for us.

But it wasn't enough. I wanted hearings in the committees of jurisdiction—Budget, Ways and Means, and Energy and Commerce, as well. And I wanted Pelosi's blessing that these hearings would happen, because I knew nothing would happen without that.

I spent the better part of twenty-four hours on the phone negotiating with Jim, going back and forth with him as he went back and forth with Pelosi and her staff. Finally, late in the night, he called me back and said, "She'll do it," with tremendous relief in his voice. Pelosi herself called me, too, to say that she was supportive of doing hearings, that it was important to discuss all these ideas, and that we should start with the Rules and Budget Committee and then she would help me to move to hearings in Ways and Means and Energy and Commerce. That was good enough for me—this was an enormous win.

It was the first of many moments when I would have to assess the landscape, determine what power we might have, and decide when to fight and when to negotiate and get something in return for a vote.

In the end, all but a handful of my congressional progressive caucus members fell in line with the CPC position and voted for the rules package, accepting a wonky budgetary technicality for a bigger promise. In the months to come, leadership would also do exactly what Jim promised and waive PAYGO a number of times to bring progressive priority bills to the floor, from the American Dream and Promise Act to the Cadillac Tax Repeal.

For now, what was most important was that we had negotiated something truly historic: for the first time, we would hold a full committee hearing on Medicare for All, a healthcare proposal that would guarantee coverage to all Americans. In doing so, we would get that much closer to making healthcare a right for all, not a privilege for some, a new bedrock principle of the Democratic Party.

When the founding framers outlined those "unalienable rights" in the Declaration of Independence—"Life, Liberty and the Pursuit of Happiness"—I don't think they would have ever imagined a time when half a million Americans would file for bankruptcy every year due to medical costs. I don't think they could have imagined that life would end every day for countless Americans who could not afford cancer or insulin treatments. And how could you possibly have liberty or pursue happiness if you were sick, so sick that you would have to choose between paying your mortgage or paying your hospital bills?

The question of healthcare has been one that we have struggled with in America through the ages. In 1916, the economist Irving Fisher reminded the country that the United States at that time had "the unenviable distinction of being the only great industrial nation without compulsory health insurance."

In 1945, just seven months into his presidency, Harry Truman put forward the idea of a universal national health insurance program, saying: "Millions of our citizens do not now have a full measure of opportunity to achieve and enjoy good health. Millions do not now have protection or security against the economic effects of sickness. The time has arrived for action to help them attain that opportunity and that protection."[5]

Truman knew that fixing the broken healthcare system required the federal government to even out the playing field for Americans, regardless of income or whether they lived in urban or rural areas. He also believed strongly that any good health-care system had to address the spread of infectious diseases—which affected the whole public—and the health of children, in particular, "like their education, should be recognized as a definite public responsibility." Truman emphasized that not being able to pay for healthcare when you needed it was a major source of concern, not just for low-income Americans, but for many others.

Truman faced attacks very similar to those we see now. The fear of "socialized medicine" figures prominently in the speech he gave then: "[Americans] will not be frightened off from health insurance because some people have misnamed it 'socialized medicine.' I repeat—what I am recommending is not socialized medicine. Socialized medicine means that all doctors work as employees of government. The American people want no such system. No such system is here proposed."[6]

Truman's fight was not successful, as we now know. His opponents were many of the same ones we face today. Leading the charge was the American Medical Association, which has had a longstanding opposition to single-payer healthcare and has poured money into propping up support for private insurance. And yet, Truman's fight almost certainly paved the way for one of the largest expansions of healthcare in history. In 1965, President Lyndon Johnson signed into law Medicare and Medicaid, providing healthcare for nearly 20 million seniors as well as the poorest Americans.

Today, as we take up the fight for universal healthcare based on a guaranteed insurance program provided by the government, I hear the echoes of Dr. Martin Luther King's words in 1966: "Of all the forms of inequality, injustice in health is the most inhuman."

Since becoming the lead sponsor of Medicare for All in the House, I have heard thousands of stories of Americans who labor under truly inhuman conditions.

A man with a disability who is insured through his work but still pays $40,000 a year in medical costs. He is not physically strong enough to work, but he also cannot afford to quit because he needs the insurance.

A gay man with HIV/AIDS whose medical bills are so high, he says he works in a company that provides healthcare even though he disagrees with the mission of the company.

The many people who took out second mortgages or raided their kids' college funds to pay for life-saving cancer treatments.

The small businesses who want to be good employers, who provide healthcare to their employees at enormous cost that makes it impossible for them to be competitive.

The tens of thousands of Go Fund Me campaigns, appealing to the generosity of friends, families, and strangers to cover medical costs that are simply too high to afford alone.

The doctors and nurses who have to confront the injustice of a healthcare system where they are literally not allowed to give patients the care they need and have to watch patients walk out to die because they cannot afford the necessary treatments.

One evening, I ended up in the emergency room for a hand injury. In the curtained stall next to me, I could hear the doctor talking to a young-ish sounding man.

"You cannot leave here," the doctor was saying in an almost panicked voice. "I need you to understand that you may die."

"I know," said the patient. "But I don't have insurance and I can't afford the medical bills so I'm just going to take my chances."

This went on for minutes—the doctor pleading with the man to please stay and be treated, they would apply for charity care; the young man responding back: but what if the charity care didn't come through? He refused to be saddled with bills he would never be able to pay off. In the end, the doctor emerged looking defeated and the young man left to take his chances with death. All because he didn't have insurance and he couldn't afford to take care of his health.

So, whenever people ask if we can really afford to insure and care for all Americans, I always turn that question back around: What does it cost us *not* to fix our broken system and ensure healthcare for all Americans?

You see, the stories I mention here pour in by the thousands. They aren't isolated. They aren't the exception. They are the rule. Just about every American can tell you either a story of outrageous medical costs, or they can tell you about a sister, mother, brother, father, or friend who faced insurmountable bills. Medical heartbreak is present in every single community, every family, every state.

Today, in America, 70 million people are uninsured or underinsured and tens of millions more can't afford their healthcare costs even if they have insurance, and 500,000 Americans declare bankruptcy every year due to medical costs. In one of the richest countries in the world, one in four people pass up visiting the doctor because of the cost. And even though the Affordable Care Act, passed in 2010 under President Obama, expanded healthcare coverage for tens of millions of people, the truth is that it wasn't able to cure the deep sickness of a for-profit healthcare system that put those profits over patients. Average families that purchased healthcare in the marketplace under the ACA paid an average of $10,000 per year— and even higher if they met their deductible. Employer plans—which pay premiums to the same for-profit insurance companies—were getting more and more expensive while covering less and less and passing on more of the costs to employees.

Our healthcare system is the most expensive *in the world*. In 1970, the U.S. devoted 6.9 percent of gross domestic product to total healthcare spending. By 2017, that amount had increased to almost 18 percent of GDP, about $3.5 trillion per year. In the next decade, that number is expected to increase to almost $6 trillion per year. In people terms, that means more and more people walking out of emergency rooms because they can't afford care, driving to Canada where the cost of insulin is one-tenth of the cost in America, or making untenable choices to forego rent to pay for medical care.

For low-income people, frontline communities, and communities of color, the effects are even worse. These are the communities least likely to have employer-covered health insurance and most likely to bear more of the health burdens of climate change—higher rates of asthma, heat strokes, unclean air and water—that make accessible, affordable healthcare even more essential.

The fact is that our healthcare costs in the United States are almost double those of all our peer countries—and unlike them, we still can't guarantee comprehensive healthcare to every single person. And if you think that an expensive healthcare system means we've got great outcomes, think again. When it comes to the health indicators that measure the health of a whole society, ours in the United States are some of the worst of all our peer countries: we have the highest maternal mortality rates, the highest infant mortality rates, and our life expectancy is going down instead of up.

So once again, the question is: how can we afford to stick with the system we have when people are literally dying because of healthcare costs?

That healthcare should be a basic and universal human right is not a trendy new idea to me. I've believed this for a long time—both in my work and in my blood. In the 1990s, when I was employed at PATH, I was working hard at ensuring communities around the world could have preventive care—so illnesses would be diagnosed at the beginning not at the end, when it would get much more dire, complex, and expensive. During the Obamacare fight, I was at OneAmerica, working in a coalition of groups pushing for a single-payer system that took private insurers out of the picture. When we didn't get that, our fallback position became a public option as a transition to a single-payer system. The U.S. House of Representatives, under Speaker Pelosi, actually included the public option, but it was stripped from the bill in the Senate by moderate Democrats and not included in the final Affordable Care Act legislation signed into law. Many years later, when I got to the Washington State Senate, I served on the healthcare committee, and we were still pushing to try to get to a statewide single-payer system.

So healthcare has always been front and center for me, and when I got to Congress, the first bill I signed on to was Representative John Conyers's H.R. 676. The bill had the sketches of a healthcare system the way I wanted to see it: one that covers everyone, under a single guaranteed insurance plan provided by the government. When Conyers first introduced it more than fifteen years ago, it was considered "out there" by many establishment Democrats and had just twenty-five cosponsors.[7] At just thirty pages, it was an overview of principles, not a detailed plan, and it hadn't changed much since its introduction. Each year, as healthcare costs continued to rise, more and more sponsors came onto the bill as a way to show their constituents they wanted a real solution to the healthcare crisis. By the end of my first term in Congress in mid-2018, Conyers's bill had 126 co-sponsors.[8] Still, neither that bill nor Bernie Sanders's bill in the Senate had ever been granted a hearing in either chamber.

Since the introduction of HR 676 fifteen years ago, however, the country's views on healthcare had definitely changed. The ACA had moved the needle tremendously, particularly with its elimination of rules that allowed insurers to deny coverage to people with pre-existing conditions. Suddenly, people realized what they had not had—and they liked it a whole lot. At the same time, however, the ACA had problems that Republicans refused to fix, and healthcare costs continued to soar. Some of the ACA marketplace plans had high premiums but covered very little. Pharmaceutical drug prices were still increasing because the ACA had not enabled the government to negotiate with the pharmaceutical companies to bring down drug prices, and the drug manufacturers were rolling in greed.

Fundamentally, although the ACA had tried to address some pieces of cost containment, it hadn't worked across the board because the system still relied on the services of for-profit insurance and drug companies where the majority of administrative waste and healthcare profit is contained. Healthcare costs continued to rise and, by 2016, when Bernie Sanders decided to run for president, healthcare was a fundamental pocketbook issue for Americans across the country.

Bernie's 2016 presidential run, and the movement around him was a game changer for single-payer healthcare. In a stroke of genius, he called his universal healthcare plan Medicare for All. Medicare is a tremendously popular government-provided insurance plan that covers seniors over the age of sixty-five. Bernie's proposal built on that already successful system, improving Medicare and expanding it to all Americans. At rallies with tens of thousands of people across the country, Bernie argued that our system was sick with profiteering, and that healthcare was a human right not a privilege for the wealthiest few. Americans responded. In a fundamental shift in mindset, they now believed they *deserved* healthcare.

In 2018, Democrats took the majority in the House, and much of that election was won on the issue of healthcare. In 2017 and 2018, Republicans had done all they could to gut the Affordable Care Act, including some of its most popular provisions, with nothing to replace it. Healthcare costs were out of control and scandals had erupted with pharmaceutical drug manufacturers' out-of-control greed that led to out-of-control prices. From 2007 to 2016, Mylan raised the list price of its EpiPen about 500 percent, from just under $100 to more than $600. Insulin prices had tripled and Humira, which treats rheumatoid arthritis, had climbed from $19,000 to $60,000 per year. To add insult to injury, many of the most promising drugs are funded by the National Institutes of Health using taxpayer dollars. This meant that after being an early investor in these drugs, the federal government essentially turned over proprietary control to the drug companies, who then turned around and price-gouged taxpayers to literal death. It was an absurd cruelty of epic proportions and the greed of these for-profit companies captured the attention of Americans across the country.

By now, polling was through the roof on Medicare for All with 70 percent of the American people supporting the idea in red and blue districts across the country.

The idea of a universal, single-payer healthcare system seemed finally ready for primetime.

Inside Congress, leadership of the universal healthcare bill was going through changes. When Conyers stepped down in 2018, Representative Keith Ellison took over as the lead sponsor on HR 676, but shortly after that, Keith decided to run for Minnesota Attorney General. Healthcare advocates and progressive organizations were pushing me to take over as the lead sponsor of the bill. I wanted to do it, but I also wanted to re-write it. Bernie had introduced a detailed Medicare for All proposal in the Senate, and I thought we should combine the best of Bernie's bill with the best of Conyers's bill and have a proposal in the House that was as detailed and thoughtful. I knew this was going to be a tough bill to lead, and that I was sure to get attacked by insurance companies and Big Pharma. But I was itching for this fight. I cared deeply about healthcare and I saw this as a chance for the perfect confluence of inside-outside organizing.

While Keith was still in the House, I started by establishing a Medicare for All Caucus with Keith and Representative Debbie Dingell as my co-chairs. Debbie's husband, John Dingell, Sr. (who passed away in 2019), had been the powerful chairman of the Ways and Means Committee and also a real champion for a single-payer healthcare system. Debbie herself had spent time as a healthcare executive and was deeply committed to this too. My idea for the Caucus was to build buy-in within Congress: this would be a place where we could share information about Medicare for All, work to craft a new bill, and organize on the inside.

Next, I set about pulling together a new bill, building a small table of groups like Center for Popular Democracy, Physicians for a National Health Program, National Nurses United, Public Citizen, and Social Security Works—all of whom had been in the fight for single-payer healthcare for decades and were eager to use my transition to lead sponsor as an opportunity to breathe new life into the bill and the movement. I knew that anything I did on the inside had to be bolstered by a movement—Bernie had helped build that but we needed to keep it going. We needed people on the ground to speak up, organize, and fight; to tell their stories about the hours of their lives they'd lost to fighting with an insurance company and the debt they'd racked up just to get their family members the proper care.

In organizing, when you build a coalition, you often think in terms of concentric circles. The small group with NNU, Public Citizen, and Social Security Works, among others, needed to be smart on policy and get into the weeds of what the legislation could look like. Some of those groups, like Physicians for a National Health Program, were invested deeply in Conyers's bill and didn't trust that anything else would be as good. Some, like the disability rights coalition, were worried about specific pieces of the bill and ensuring they would be covered, no matter what. Some groups were downright resistant to change, which created a great deal of tension as we worked to update and redo the bill. Others saw this as an opportunity to make some important changes to Bernie's Senate bill, such as the inclusion of long-term care supports and services, which they knew I was in favor of adding. All of these policy fights had to be carefully worked through before we would settle on the final language.

The second concentric circle was made up of organizations that represented the breadth and depth of the movement. These were groups that had a national presence, represented diverse communities, and whose support would be influential. These included National People's Action, the Leadership Conference on Civil Rights, and others.

The third circle was everyone else that could be helpful and whose buy-in we would need. Because we didn't want to let information out too quickly and begin mobilizing the insurance companies and Big Pharma against our effort, we kept information close to our chests initially and this, too, created suspicion and resistance even among the left.

I also knew that many of my colleagues had signed on to Conyers's original bill because it was clearly aspirational: it was essentially a set of principles, relatively vague on the details. That made it much easier to support than a bill that would be over 125 pages long with technical details and clear policy positions that co-sponsors would have to explain. Further, as President Trump and Senate Republicans were trying to strip away healthcare from millions of Americans, there was a concern in the Democratic caucus that pushing for Medicare for All would undermine the work we needed to do immediately to shore up the ACA and blame the Republicans for tearing it down. I began reaching out to all the co-sponsors of HR 676, inviting feedback and sharing what we were doing.

It took us more than seven months to craft a new bill. I would never have been able to do it without my new legislative director, Lindsay Owens, who came to our office via Senator Elizabeth Warren and then Representative Keith Ellison in the final months of the drafting process. She was absolutely brilliant, knew enough about the policy to know what she didn't know and get input, and was masterful at managing complex relationships. At that point, we had no health staffer in the office, so she became the de facto health policy person. Later, we added a brilliant health policy aide named Stephanie Kang who was getting her PhD in global health from Harvard.

In the end, our House Medicare for All bill included several critical changes from Bernie's Senate bill. These changes, in the minds of most advocates, ended up making my House Medicare for All bill the "gold standard" bill. First, I included in my bill a cost-containment measure called global budgeting that added details to the question of how providers would get paid in an efficient and effective way. Under global budgeting, the Secretary of Health and Human Services would appoint regional directors based on geographic area who would negotiate with healthcare providers—from hospitals to family practices to nursing homes and dialysis facilities—for a lump sum payment from the government that would cover their operating expenses. Those estimates could be adjusted as needed to account for medical emergencies such as pandemics or other factors.

I also included my colleague Representative Lloyd Doggett's bill to control skyrocketing pharmaceutical drug prices. Lloyd's bill introduced competition into the marketplace as a stick: if name-brand pharmaceutical drug manufacturers did not want to negotiate the cost of those drugs, then the government could implement compulsory licensing of generics into the marketplace. We figured that only would need to happen once before it would never happen again. It was a heavy stick that would keep Big Pharma in line.

Our bill also cut the transition time to a Medicare for All system from the four years in the Senate bill to two years. For a long time, research and conventional wisdom said a gradual transition from our current healthcare system to a single-payer system made more sense. In reality, a gradual drawdown would mean your premium payment would likely spike as insurance companies scrambled to make profits during that bridge period, knowing they would soon be out. It would also give insurance companies more time to kill the bill before it could be implemented.

Two years was not unreasonably fast in my mind: every single day, ten thousand people were being added to Medicare—and the vast majority of names were now in Medicare, Medicaid, or employer databases. My plan proposed that the first year would be used to make sure we had the proper administrative and data systems aligned and in place. In the second year, we'd test the new system out with a smaller population. By the third year, everyone would be covered. Every time I got a little nervous about this time-line, I would remind myself that Medicare was fully implemented in a year![9]

The final change was a big one, and it really set our bill apart from the Senate version. It also required enormous discussion in our coalition as we put it forward. For the first time in history, our House Medicare for All bill would provide universal coverage for long-term care supports and services for individuals with disabilities and older Americans without requiring cost-sharing. I believe strongly that this is a civil rights issue and a moral issue. We needed to look after our elderly and our most vulnerable and allow them to live out their last days with their loved ones in their own homes. So, our bill made sure that community-based care—not institutional care—would be the default coverage. To me, covering long-term supports and services was also a women's issue—it was finally time to ensure that the millions of Americans, who were largely women, who had left their jobs and risked their own financial stability to take care of their parents and relatives would have the help they needed. Adding this piece also ended up bringing us partners in unions who represent home health-care workers, one of the fastest areas of job growth in our economy.[10]

During his poignant testimony, Ady had brought attention to this pro-vision, explaining to the crowded Rules Committee hearing room that he and his family pay $9,000 a month so he can receive proper care in the comfort of his own home, surrounded by his wife and young son. Ady was lucky to have good medical insurance, but that simply wasn't available for the vast majority of people. As he told us, "Go Fund Me is a terrible substitute for smart congressional action."

Deciding on the policy we wanted to include took enormous negoti-ating, discussion, and time. Given that, we now risked losing the bill's historical number. In the past, Conyers's bill had always had the same number: H.R. 676. A small set of advocates had grown very attached to the number. However, in order to get the same number, we needed to be ready to officially introduce the bill in the House by mid-January 2019 so it would be assigned that number in the queue. By mid-December, it became clear that was not going to be possible. I didn't want to introduce the bill without being completely battle ready. I wanted a momentous launch with lots of press and at least a hundred co-sponsors in the House so that we could show that there was significant momentum behind Medicare for All. I also thought that, when all was said and done, it might actually be better for us to have a different bill number than Conyers's, given that it was a completely different bill. I knew our decision to give up the bill number was causing some advocates tremendous angst, but I made the decision that we needed to push the launch to late February 2019 to be completely ready with a strong bill and a strong rollout.

The pressure was now massive: some groups in our coalition were growing impatient. Without the full text of the bill out in the open, there were rumors starting that I was killing the old Conyers bill and watering down the new one. The truth was that the Conyers bill had been a good start, but it was not a roadmap to a real transition. Our bill would not just be principles, it would be a drop-dead serious legislative pathway to universal, single-payer healthcare.

This entire process was both an old challenge and a new one for me. I'd built coalitions and brought advocates and lawmakers together in the Washington State Legislature to pass bills that funded job-training programs in the transportation sector for women and people of color and made sure low-income women on Medicaid had access to the same contraceptive rates as all women—just to name a few examples. But this was the first time in my career as a lawmaker where my party would be in the majority, which meant the stakes were higher and the political risks were greater, but the possibility of real, transformative change was closer too.

So, what is Medicare for All? The bill we debuted in March 2019, with a massive coalition of groups and with dozens of my colleagues in attendance, was all about making sure that everybody was in and nobody was out. If healthcare was truly a right, then everyone needed to have access to the same kind of care: rich or poor, young or old, no matter your color or religion or gender, you would have the same guaranteed healthcare.

The Expanded and Improved Medicare for All Act of 2019 was similar to Bernie's Medicare for All bill in that both bills replaced multiple private insurance provider plans with a guaranteed government insurance plan that would provide comprehensive coverage for everyone. The coverage would include primary care, vision, hearing, dental, prescription drugs, mental health and substance abuse care, maternal health, and more. It would be based on medical necessity rather than what insurance companies are willing to pay for.

No longer would people be tied to soulless jobs just to get health insurance, nor would they have to constantly worry about giving up insurance when changing jobs. No longer would creative entrepreneurs have to give up their dreams of going out on their own and starting a business because they couldn't afford healthcare. Everyone would be covered, all the time with the same coverage. As is true with Medicare, private insurance providers would no longer be able to offer plans that covered the same duplicative coverage—and because our bills provided such comprehensive coverage, this left only a little room for private insurance to operate. We want people to never have to worry about spending hours fighting with insurance companies to justify the services that their own doctors had prescribed. We also wanted to end the business model of private insurance companies, which is to rake in as many dollars as possible in premiums, and pay out as few dollars as possible in actual healthcare coverage. We want people to get the treatment they need when they need it—not when insurers were willing to pay for it.

Medicare for All also eliminates the thousands of dollars Americans spend on co-pays, private insurance premiums, and deductibles. We *want* people to go see the doctor if they are sick, not to delay treatment until it's too late or too expensive. And it also eliminates the administrative waste and profit of the private, for-profit insurance companies that are greedily milking illness for profit. A 2017 study estimated that over 30 percent of total health expenditures are administrative costs. Because of the complex requirements of our for-profit insurance system, private insurance spends, on average, 12 percent of revenue on maintaining claims and billing processes. Hospitals spend even more: 25 percent on overhead costs. CEO salaries for the major pharmaceutical companies range from $40 million to $80 million annually, even as people are dying for lack of care. Medicare's administrative costs are only 1.1 percent, or 6–7 percent if you include the administration of its private plans. Taking the private companies, and their loyalty to shareholders rather than patients, out of the equation would result in enormous savings for the American people.[11]

And contrary to the myths of socialized medicine, Medicare for All does not take over the hospital or provider system—just like Truman's plan decades before it. That system would continue as it is, so everyone would keep the same doctors or hospitals they have if they wanted. We believe that Medicare for All would actually give you more choice because you would no longer be tied to the same rapidly narrowing set of "in-network" doctors and hospitals. As I would explain countless times on national television over the months to come, this was not a socialist takeover of the provider system; it is not that there is no role for the private sector in anything. I'm not looking to buy my coffee or my computer from the government. But I am looking to have the government do what it does in every other peer industrialized country: provide guaranteed health insurance so when you get sick, you can get care. That should just not be about profits, it should be about patients.

I knew that this was a bold, ambitious plan. I knew it had to be. If we could end legalized slavery, give women the right to vote, and send a man to the moon, then I knew we could absolutely provide healthcare to everyone in America.

The scale of our healthcare crisis is enormous and if we truly want to tackle it, our solution needs to match the scale of the crisis. Our plan has to tackle the deep sickness within our for-profit healthcare system. Other countries have done this, and I just know we can too. It is just a question of political will. And that political will has to be pushed and prodded into being by an active and vast movement for healthcare justice on the outside and the inside.

Once we had the commitment from Speaker Pelosi to hold hearings, including the first Rules Committee hearing, I felt a whole new level of pressure. The next hurdle was getting at least a hundred co-sponsors on the bill and having a successful rollout. Everything had been delayed because we were still finalizing the content. Every day, reporters would ask me when we were introducing the bill. We had to manage the varying expectations of the coalition of groups and I needed to get as many of my colleagues on board as quickly as possible.

Remaining optimistic and strategic while staying true to my bold principles and policies was key for me. In a number of instances that winter, someone—usually a reporter—would try to coax cynicism: "But you only got a commitment for the Rules Committee and it's not even a committee of record," they would say. They didn't trust that Pelosi would actually allow the hearings to proceed, and the chairs of the other committees of record were being coy, refusing to commit to holding hearings.

There were many things to worry about, but how to get the future hearings was not one of them. I was focused on Rules. I am probably odd in that I have big, bold visions but I am also a disciplined step-by-step person. I work hard at being successful at whatever the step is in front of me, and I am always convinced that will give us the momentum for the next step. My experience as an organizer told me that if we could pull off a hugely successful Rules Committee hearing, we would put others at ease that we could do this, ramp up pressure, and get the next hearing in one of the major committees of record. I also had faith that Jim McGovern was precisely the right shepherd for that first hearing.

I had colleagues in the House who were more nervous, even members who seemed like obvious, progressive champions of Medicare for All. It was my job to get them on board and this was no easy task. As elected officials, it's much easier to attach your name to something when it's just an idea or framework, when you're in the minority, and when the bill is not yet ready for primetime. It takes a lot more courage to step up and back something that is specific about how to get where you want to go, not to mention a bill that would occupy a big part of the national conversation in an important election year.

By late February, I was still racking up co-sponsors, preparing to release the bill's text. Many in the DC press corps, looking for sexy, horserace-style coverage, seemed to question why I didn't have as many as we'd had by the end of the last session.[12]

My conversations, though, gave me hope. I was genuinely impressed with the courage of many of my colleagues when I went to speak with them about my bill. There were many new members, some of whom had won election in previously Trump-held districts. I wanted them on board too, because I wanted to show that Medicare for All could be supported even in those swing districts.

Jahana Hayes was an example of a courageous new member. Elected in 2018 as the first African American woman from her home state of Connecticut to serve, Jahana represented some of the biggest insurance companies, making her support of a bill that put people's health over the profits of these companies a political risk. In fact, no representative from Connecticut had *ever* been on the bill, reminding me of how badly we needed to get money out of politics.

I'll never forget what Jahana said to me when she signed on to Medicare for All: "I am here to do the right thing. If I lose reelection because I'm doing the right thing for people in my district, then so be it."

Four of the five new representatives from Orange County—Katie Porter, Katie Hill, Mike Levin, and Josh Harder—who had flipped Republican-held districts for the first time had also courageously come on board. All of them had run their campaigns on Medicare for All, and I had supported all of them during the campaign. They were the epitome of bold members who ran on their principles and on the critical idea that Americans supported—that healthcare should be a right and not a privilege—and they had been elected in spite of enormous negative advertising. However, some of them had questions that needed to be answered before they came on board, and even some language changes that we negotiated through.

I also wanted to have someone on board who would highlight the long-term services aspect of the bill. Jim Langevin from Rhode Island was my choice. Jim had been on the Conyers bill but had not been particularly vocal about it. Jim is a quadriplegic and serves as co-chair of the Bipartisan Disabilities Caucus and, for all these reasons, Jim's vocal support would be a big plus for the bill. When I spoke to him about the bill and the addition of long-term care, and asked if he would speak at the launch, Jim was visibly moved and agreed almost immediately.

And then there was Joe Kennedy III. When I looked at my colleagues who'd backed the original Conyers bill, I noticed Joe wasn't one of them. This surprised me and I doubted that it was a mistake or oversight. Joe is incredibly thoughtful on policy, and he represents a very progressive district in the Boston area. I wanted to know why he had not signed on so I set up meetings between our two staffs and got right to the point.

"I'm working on this new bill, and I want to know why you weren't on the old Medicare for All bill," I told him. "What can I do to get you on mine?"

As I had guessed, it wasn't a mistake. Joe and his staff did have a few concerns. For one thing, the Conyers bill did not get rid of a relic of federal healthcare policy known as the Hyde Amendment, which stipulated that no federal funds could be used to pay for abortion except in cases of rape, incest, or the life of the mother. Reproductive justice champions have admirably railed against the Hyde Amendment for years, and Joe and others wanted to see healthcare legislation that put this antiquated, fear-based stipulation in the past once and for all. Fortunately, my bill had eliminated the Hyde Amendment, so that concern was addressed already.

Joe's second concern was around the several safety-net hospitals in his district. He did not know about some of the provisions in our bill that increased rates for these safety-net hospitals and made them more financially viable. He seemed impressed with our conversation and the many ways in which we had addressed some big issues. He told me he would continue to think about it, and we kept in touch. In late February, Joe signed on to the bill, praising the thoughtfulness of the bill and commending me for engaging in discussion with members of our caucus around the bill text. Given that he had never signed on to HR 676, Joe's support made news with the congressional press: "Medicare for All is no longer purely theoretical," one headline crowed.[13] Shortly after he joined, several other congressmembers from Massachusetts signed on to the bill as well.

Getting my colleagues on board required a tremendous amount of my time and energy as well as my staff's. One colleague had concerns about the language that gave Medicare for All to all residents, including undocumented immigrants. Immigrant rights groups suddenly became worried, even though the language I had included was far better than the language in Bernie's bill. Other colleagues wanted more information on the cost of the proposal and how we would pay for it. We worked it hard, on the floor, in staff conversations, and with groups pushing on the outside as well. The groups organized lobby days in districts across the country and in DC. Our Revolution organized an ambulance tour to target districts. We worked with Local Progress, a group of progressive city councilmembers from across the country, to begin passing local resolutions endorsing the bill—Seattle, of course, was first!

All of us fighting for real change must find our own styles and theories of persuasion. For me, I have found success leading with a spirit of generosity and abundance instead of scarcity and fear. I am less interested in shaming and blaming; I approach every difficult conversation believing in the better angels of everyone involved. Once people had the facts on my bill—beyond the headlines that suggested we were proposing something that was too unrealistic, too bold, too socialist, too *much*—of course they'd come on board. And they did. I finally reached the one hundred-sponsors mark, and we rolled out the bill to a cheering, nationally live-streamed coalition of folks right in front of the steps of the Capitol.

Now there was one last hurdle to clear: the first-ever hearing.

This hearing was going to be historic: no one had managed to get a full committee hearing on a single-payer healthcare bill before. We needed powerful testimony that would meet the moment. Politics at its best has human stories at its heart, and logic and methodology in its bones.

When the House of Representatives convenes a hearing, the minority party is entitled to call witnesses that represent its views.[14] Since the Republicans would inevitably choose witnesses that would undermine our bill, I knew it was important we heard stories from the patients and families buried under medical bills, and it was important that we have true Medicare for All advocates who also respected the incremental progress we had made with the passage of the Affordable Care Act.

While we worked hard to find the right balance, rumors flew that there would not be any "true" single-payer advocates at our hearing to help us make our case. One particularly damaging story began by conceding the unprecedented nature of our hearing, then went on to declare that "Medicare for All advocates may actually be getting screwed."[15]

The hearing had been scheduled for two days after Congress returned from Easter recess. Ironically, Steve and I had—months before—scheduled a trip to Italy, a twelve-year-delayed honeymoon that we had never taken because my parents had come from India for the wedding and we went off with them afterwards instead. Each year, we talked about going and we had finally decided this was the year to do it. At the time, we had no idea that we might have a major hearing on the books. Talking with my staff, I decided to go anyway. Most of the details seemed squared away and I felt like we could make it work and avoid suffering huge cancellation fees for the long-planned trip. It wasn't a great time, for sure, but I have found that in the fight for justice, there really is never a right time for the things that are important to you and the people you love unless you make a commitment to them.

A few days before we were due to return, I was awakened by my cell phone. It was Gautam, my chief of staff, and his voice was urgent. "Jim McGovern wants to talk to you," he said. The stories about our hearing had become more damaging; Jim was facing a lot of heat, particularly from progressives who had supported my legislation. I understood their point. It was true that the folks most associated with Medicare for All, from the nurses union, National Nurses United, to the Physicians for National Healthcare Program—were not on our witness panel.

If I had been in the states, I would have happily taken a call from Jim in the middle of the night—it's part of the job description as a member of Congress. But away from the bubble of Washington, DC, and the constant hum of news—often bad—I had some added calm and perspective. I chose to call him back the next day instead.

Jim was taking a big risk for me, and I appreciated it. Other co-chairs weren't happy with him, my colleagues who had also championed Medicare for All weren't happy, the leftist press was clearly critical. He was ready to scratch the hearing. But to his credit, he left its fate in my hands: "Pramila," he said, "are you happy with this hearing, are *you* satisfied?" In his mind, if the co-author of the bill was okay, he could take the heat from all corners: "If you're satisfied, I will put up with all the other crap."

I was satisfied. It was true that our biggest, rowdiest champions were absent. But for as hard as we'd worked to get those signatures, many House Democrats had not signed onto our bill. We needed empirical witnesses who'd have some credibility with those members. We needed economists, think-tank experts, emergency room physicians.

We needed Ady.

I knew that if we could get him in, the hearing would be about Ady, which is what I wanted. It wasn't clear he would join what was now apparently a controversial roster of witnesses in some quarters until just a few days before the hearing, when Ady texted Speaker Pelosi and told her he was up for the cross-country trip from his home in California.

His testimony that day was emotional (even some Republicans on the committee were moved). Since I was not a member of the Rules Committee, I sat in the front row next to Ady's father and just a foot or so away from Ady and his caregivers. I watched as he painstakingly used his eyes to select letters and words. He would begin to type a word, the computer would add it, then he'd need to backspace. But his mind was clearly strong: he was typing up questions and comments during the entire hearing, challenging congressmembers on the committee, and refusing to let untruths sit unchallenged.

He testified first. Through his machine, he told America his story. He'd had everything: a fulfilling, stable career; a loving marriage; a brand-new beautiful baby boy. As he put it, "The sun was shining and there was not a cloud in sight. And then, out of the clear blue sky, we were struck by lightning."

He explained ALS and its many mysteries and devastations. Perhaps most devastating of all was that Ady had been a fierce advocate for many causes and given many presentations throughout his legal and advocacy career. He was a high school debater. Now, all of his passion and persuasion had to be distilled through the voice of the robot.

But Ady was no less convincing in this way. He spoke of his insurance company's denials of their claims, on top of never-ending and unsustainable bills for his care.

"Too many corporations make too much money off of our illnesses," he said. "It is very important to emphasize the following point: these cost savings are only possible through a Medicare for All System. It will save us all tremendous time. It will mean more time to give high-quality care. For patients and our families, it will mean less time dealing with a broken healthcare system and more time doing the things we love, together."

Each of our witnesses was excellent, but Ady was most poignant, reminding us that his time was running out.

"Some people argue that although Medicare for All is a great idea, we need to move slowly to get there. But I needed Medicare for All yesterday. Millions of people need it today. The time to pass this law is now."

There was not a dry eye in the House. It quickly became clear that something magical happened that day. Now, nobody could say that Medicare for All advocates lacked a real plan. America could see how extensive and serious our bill was, they could see how many supporters we had, and they could feel the urgency of the issue.

In the middle of the hearing, I had to hurry out of the committee room for a regularly scheduled Progressive Caucus meeting. Two congressmen, Frank Pallone and Richie Neal, who were working on a separate bill on pharmaceutical drug pricing would be in attendance, and I wanted to relay that day's successes to them. They chaired the two committees that were the primary committees of jurisdiction for healthcare policy: Ways and Means, and Energy and Commerce. Those were the committees that we needed to hold similar Medicare for All hearings, and I intended to ask for those hearings at this meeting.

When I relayed the tremendous success of the Rules Committee hearing and the moving testimony we were hearing, I put the question to Richie first: could we have a similar hearing for our bill in his committee?

To my tremendous surprise, he said yes!

Frank was noncommittal but this was huge—our next hearing would be in the prestigious Ways and Means Committee.

I ran back to the Rules Committee hearing to spread the good news. This historic day in April would not be our bill's last. I ran into some reporters on my way back and told them we'd secured a second hearing. The headline came out quickly: "Ways and Means Committee to Hold Hearing on Medicare For All."[16]

When I got back to the committee room, I showed him my phone with the headline. "Ady, look what you've done!" I said. "Because of you, we got ourselves another hearing. You're going to have to come back for it."

He looked at me, then he typed on his screen: "It would be my honor to do that. I will come back. For me, this is life giving and energizing."

It is for me too.

I expected to be hit hard by the for-profit insurance companies and pharmaceutical companies that stood to lose enormous profits and huge salaries for their top executives if Medicare for All ever became a reality. I was ready for that. What I was not quite ready for was the onslaught from Democrats running for president who began to attack Medicare for All using corporate and Republican talking points to try and quell the rising support for Medicare for All across the country.

From Joe Biden to Pete Buttigieg to Amy Klobuchar, the attacks started coming fast and furious, aided and abetted by television pundits, including some Obama administration senior officials who were now part and parcel of a new so-called "healthcare coalition," funded by drug and insurance companies and formed specifically to preserve the status quo and kill any progress on Medicare for All. Hundreds of millions of dollars were now being poured into confusing the public, generating polls designed to undermine Medicare for All, spreading lies about what Medicare for All is and isn't, and driving up fear in the public—all to preserve corporate profits. As the presidential primary debates got underway, moderators asked loaded and biased questions of Bernie Sanders and Elizabeth Warren, the only two remaining candidates who had not backed away from Medicare for All. Often, those questions focused on the cost of a new Medicare for All system without even addressing the fact that the cost of our current system was even more expensive than Medicare for All, even in the estimates of the conservative Koch Brothers. No one questioned other candidates on a real plan to bring down these costs that would only continue to rise, or why they were protecting the administrative waste generated by big for-profit corporations in our healthcare system.

Biden, Buttigieg, and Klobuchar went hard against Medicare for All, claiming: 1) that labor unions were against Medicare for All (not true: thirty-two unions had signed on in support of my bill, including some of the largest like American Federation of Teachers, National Education Association, United Auto Workers, and Service Employees International Union, among others); 2) that people currently covered by employer insurance loved their private insurance and wanted the "choice" that private insurance offered; 3) that the only way to pay for Medicare for All was through raising taxes on middle-class families; and 4) that there were plenty of other ways to address the healthcare crisis we faced, such as (surprise!) the public option, a Medicare "buy-in" that lowered the eligibility age of Medicare, or even "Medicare for All Who Want It."

By late summer, I was furious at these candidates and I was starting to fight back on Twitter. On August 1, 2019, following the second

Democratic presidential debate, I published an op-ed in the *Washington Post* titled "It's Time for Democrats to Get Their Facts Right About Medicare for All" taking on many of these points.

> First, it is a myth that Americans love private insurance. The vast majority of Americans are deeply frustrated with the health-care system—even if they have private insurance. Opponents and pundits often quote polling that suggests support for Medicare-for-all drops when you tell people that their private insurance plan would go away. But when polls accurately describe Medicare-for-all, and explain that you can keep your doctor or hospital, the majority support increases. People are happy to get rid of private insurance; they just want to know they can keep their doctors and hospitals, even if they switch or lose their jobs. Medicare-for-all would let them do so.
>
> Second, it's wrong to assert that taxes will rise without talking about what health care *currently* costs Americans in premiums, co-pays and deductibles. The average American family with employer-sponsored insurance incurs more than $28,000 dollars in health-care costs per year, of which about $15,800, or 56 percent, is paid by employers. And many argue that they still can't get the care they need. Americans are smart enough to be asked questions like: Would you be willing to pay more in taxes each month if you saved more money by not paying private insurance premiums, deductibles and co-pays and were guaranteed high-quality health care?
>
> Third, it is simply false that labor unions don't want Medicare-for-all. Sure, they fought hard for employer-sponsored health insurance plans for their workers. But they, above all others, recognize that the rising costs of insurance premiums are directly related to stagnating wages and, more and more, the pressure of those costs hurts worker power at the bargaining table. Take a look at the unprecedented number of unions

that have endorsed our bill, all of which know Medicare-for-all is necessary.

Fourth, comparisons of Medicare-for-all to the GOP's push to "repeal and replace" the Affordable Care Act are simply unfounded. Republicans are the only ones trying to take away health care. There is absolutely no daylight between leading on Medicare-for-all and fighting to shore up the ACA right now, or stopping the GOP from stripping care away. The Affordable Care Act made profound improvements to our health-care system. But it was never meant to be the end goal, because it does not address the real disease in our system: a profit motive that leaves millions either without access to care, bankrupt or unable to afford medication in the world's richest country. We can strengthen the ACA and work towards Medicare-for-all at the same time. Even former president Barack Obama agrees.[17]

Fifth, we simply cannot expect to bring down the costs of health care in the United States without taking on the for-profit insurance and pharmaceutical corporations, which are raking in billions of dollars at the cost of American lives. Incremental steps such as a public option might sound appealing but would still leave more than 10 million people without coverage while keeping in place a costly private-insurance middleman that eats up 25 to 30 percent in administrative waste and profits. If we want to achieve true universal health care while containing costs, Medicare-for-all is the only answer.

Finally, Democratic candidates should stop using one-liners from industry front groups and Republican playbooks—such as "Medicare-for-all would shutter hospitals," or telling seniors that "Medicare goes away as you know it. All the Medicare you have is gone." These claims—amplified by contributions from the private health-care industry—are designed to incite fear and sow confusion. I've spoken with several hospital CEOs who see Medicare-for-all as a lifeline for their hospitals—particularly safety-net and rural hospitals that are barely surviving under the current system. And my Medicare-for-all bill *improves* Medicare for seniors by adding additional benefits such as dental, vision, hearing and long-term care.

I also had to take on mainstream TV hosts. I kept trying to get dedicated time with hosts like Chris Cuomo and others, but they rarely wanted to give it to me. They seemed completely taken with the arguments of the opposition, and they brought on people like former White House Chief of Staff Rahm Emanuel to spread the talking points of industry. When I saw even my friend, progressive TV commentator Van Jones, talking about "choice" and pushing Buttigieg's approach of something much less than Medicare for All on CNN, I called him up to question what he was doing. It was an extremely tense conversation, but at the end of it, Van agreed to have me on his show to talk about why Medicare for All was the best solution and to give me a full ten minutes to do it. He was true to his word, and he gave me a chance to highlight two of my arguments that he felt really had not been made and needed to be put out there.

The first was about choice. I saw this as a huge red herring argument. The truth is that even those people who are covered by employer health insurance don't have any "choice." They don't choose which plan they will enroll in: their employers make that choice. They don't choose what benefits those plans will cover or what doctors and hospitals are "in-network": the for-profit insurance companies make that choice and those companies had been increasingly excluding more and more doctors and hospitals from coverage, cutting the kinds of benefits and treatments that were covered and leaving more and more uncovered. Many insurance plans now even require that people's claims have to be reviewed by doctors paid for by the insurance companies who had never even seen the patient but could simply decide to deny a claim even if person's private doctor had recommended the treatment. And if, by some chance, a person was too sick to go to work and lost their job, their insurance was terminated and now they had no choice at all. For people who did not have insurance to start with, there also was no choice. You could simply think about dying, or foreclosing on your home to pay for your treatments, or drawing on a kid's college fund if you were lucky enough to have one. This was simply not choice, period, I said on Van's show.

The second thing that Van wanted me to talk about was why a public option—which had been the backup position for progressives during the Affordable Care Act fight—or a Medicare buy-in would not get us where we needed to go. We had learned a lot from enacting the Affordable Care Act, including that unless you take on the private system, you also can't bring down the overall costs for both the private and public systems in order to cover everyone with the same comprehensive coverage. All of the plans—other than Medicare for All—lacked a way to cover everybody with comprehensive care and to bring down the overall costs of health-care. Without doing those two things, Americans would continue to face a healthcare crisis. *These half-measures would not solve the problem and we would be right back where we started.*

Sure, you could cover some more people by dropping the eligibility age of Medicare, but you still wouldn't cover everybody. If you did not cut out the administrative waste of the current for-profit system, you could not bring down the costs. None of the other plans did this. And as long as you had a for-profit insurance system competing with a government insurance system, you would allow for-profit companies to game the system and cherry pick the healthiest people onto their plan while funneling the sickest people onto the public option, driving costs up for everyone while garnering none of the savings of a single-payer system.

Finally, none of the other plans expanded the overall set of benefits to include the kinds of comprehensive care that people needed. They didn't propose expanding Medicare to cover dental, hearing or vision; they didn't repeal the Hyde Amendment to allow for reproductive care to be covered; and they certainly weren't thinking about expansions such as long-term care. Without this, people would still be paying enormous out-of-pocket costs for care they desperately needed to stay alive.

At the time of this writing, the debate is still raging on television and in the press. But across the country, a funny thing has happened: Medicare for All appears to be one of the most resilient policy proposals out there. In a recent poll conducted by advocates for Medicare for All and designed to test out the attacks from the opposition in a real way, the results showed that as long as a counter-argument was given to the worst attacks from drug and insurance companies, support for Medicare for All stayed strong even after those attacks: 66 percent of registered voters nationally and 63 percent of swing-state voters supported Medicare for All, including huge majorities of Democratic voters and even substantial numbers of independent voters, by narrower margins. A poll conducted for the *New York Times* in November 2019, at the height of attacks from industry, Biden, and Buttigieg, showed that "Medicare for all doesn't divide Democrats the way a wealth tax does. Democrats of all ages, races and education and levels support the policy by similar margins."[18] Among Democrats, whose turnout will be essential for the 2020 election, support for Medicare for All is well over 70 percent in every single poll and the intensity is high.

Earlier, I alluded to the challenge of taking on your own party. It's not what you go looking for, but sometimes there is no getting around the bear. You've got to go straight through.

Democrats lost in 2016 for many reasons, and it's all been explored and discussed. But one of the underlying reasons was voters' belief that Democrats got it wrong—all wrong—on trade. And voters were right. Democrats abandoned working people in favor of corporations and the wealthy.

Today, Democrats have been able to fashion themselves as fighting for healthcare through the Affordable Care Act; and the fact that support for the ACA grew even as it was attacked is proof that Democrats were right in fighting for the people while Republicans showed their true colors as defenders of corporations and the elites.

But don't be fooled into thinking that healthcare is settled ground; it isn't. Working families are increasingly frustrated, and they no longer believe that there can't or shouldn't be a better way. Working people across this country are seething, and their anger is genuine. If the crises that working families face today, including on healthcare, are not solved, they absolutely will visit a price on one party or the other.

This unsettled turf is exactly the scenario that Trump seeks out like a heat-seeking missile. Even a Trump-led salvo that truly and honestly lowered prescription drug costs for families would be a game-changer, and Republicans will own healthcare, just like with trade.

I've laid out all my policy reasons, my health data and health expert reasons, and the real-person reasons—like the life-and-death situation that people like Ady Barkan face—for Medicare for All. Now I am sounding a warning as loudly as I can: Democrats better put working families ahead of corporations on healthcare or it WILL cost us politically in a big way, not just in this election but in elections to come and in the belief that a democracy is the right form of government to respond to the needs of people across this country.

At the time I write this, there are two presidential candidates willing to fight for Medicare for All: Bernie Sanders and Elizabeth Warren. There is no guarantee that either of them makes it through as the Democratic nominee for president. But whoever does make it through, I hope the points I make sound an alarm bell. Presidential elections often define an issue or two and readjust the trajectory of the nation. Healthcare is just such an issue, if ever there was one. The reality is that working people trying to keep themselves and their families going through the healthcare crises they face can easily sniff out tepid, fearful, leadership that parrots industry talking points. Just as in trade, average Americans are wary about who will fight for *them*. At the end of the day, I believe Medicare for All is the biggest political opportunity Democrats have to show the American people that we care about them and we will fight for them. We will be defined by how we advance the healthcare debate to solve problems for the American people in meaningful ways.

Imagine what would happen if, instead of attacking Medicare for All, the Democratic nominee for president lifted it up as the real solution for solving our healthcare crisis. What we learned from the impeachment debate over the summer of 2019 was that once Democrats united on the message of the importance of an impeachment inquiry to our constitutional responsibilities, public polling moved dramatically by over ten points. Polling, as I say over and over again, is not static; people are looking for us to lead and to make the arguments for why we should move in a particular direction.

In the scenario where Democrats refuse to stand up to a system that puts profits over patients, we will face a dire situation. Imagine Democrats who run on a half-measure like a Medicare buy-in, promising Americans that it will solve their healthcare crisis. It won't. Americans, disillusioned once again with a system that caters only to the wealthiest corporations with literally hundreds of lobbyists pushing ideas that hurt Americans and put money in the pockets of the greediest, could very well throw up their hands in despair and vote for Trump again or a Trump-like figure who promises to "drain the swamp" all over again. Remember, Trump is a symptom of a system that is rigged against regular working folks and the despair of everyday families. If that were to happen, Democrats would have only themselves to blame.

Imagine a different scenario now, where a Democratic president uses his or her entire might and platform to call out the special interests that control our country, works to capitalize on the two-thirds of the country that already supports Medicare for All and to bring along those who can be brought along. This would require going up against the powerful insurance companies and drug companies. It would require building on the movement for Medicare for All both on the outside and on the inside. It would require thoughtful strategy, yes, but it would be a real solution that fights for regular people and restores the faith of people in the power of government to be the great equalizer of opportunity.

That's a fight worth having and I intend to help lead it.

10

Moral Vision—The Fight for $15 and the Three Supremacies

WHEN IT COMES TO THE MORALITY OF INEQUALITY, THE FIRST THING we should stipulate to is that there is enough wealth to go around. It's just about who has it and the trajectory of how it is distributed. Take any metric: wealth, income, ability to address an emergency, bankruptcies, debt, tax burden, market investments, or any other. Then, disaggregate that metric across race, gender, or age in many cases, and it gets uglier and even more immoral. The moral north star is that the masses of millions are generating wealth only for the relatively few and this inequality has been getting dramatically more unfair each year.

Tremendous wealth exists in America today. Livable incomes for all could be a reality as they are in other nations. Working people would not have to go into medical or education debt that weighs on them for decades, and tax policies do not have to favor those who already have the most wealth or income for the world to turn on its axis. As a nation, we do not have a wealth problem; we have a greed problem.

Today, we face the worst inequality since the 1920s. Almost all of the income inequality we've experienced since 1980 comes from the fact that top incomes have taken off, pulling away from the bottom incomes which have stagnated. The three richest people in the country—two of whom live in my state—have more wealth than the bottom half of Americans combined. In other words, three people have more wealth than 160 million people combined.

And although pundits like to tout increasing gross domestic product (GDP) as a sign of economic growth, GDP growth doesn't mean a damn thing when 90 percent of that growth goes to the top 1 percent, as is true today. Part of our job as activists on the outside or legislators inside is to not let others get away with touting GDP or other benchmarks without qualification. The facts matter, but only if we assert them in their totality.

There is a very real story that needs to be told more broadly about how that top-income takeoff happened: a result of decreasing top marginal tax rates, rocketing CEO pay relative to worker pay made possible in part by declining union density, corporate consolidation, shareholder capitalism, and deregulation. Here, too, the disparities in effects by race and gender are stunning.

All of the trends, the daily realities for everyone, and the tax implications come down simply to choices we have been making—and choices we can unmake. Inequality of the sheer scale that we have today is a moral issue that we can and must take on. And we begin by talking about it just that way.

Consider a for moment, that today in America, 60 percent of Americans do not even have $1,000 in their savings accounts and 40 percent cannot afford a $400 emergency expenditure. Every night, families across American toss and turn, worrying about how they will fix a car that has broken down, a roof that is leaking or a parent who has fallen ill.

If we are going to be real about the situation we are in, we have to recognize that Trumpism did not emerge out of the ether. Deepening economic divides, austerity measures that cut social safety nets and punished the most vulnerable, and the increasing criminalization of poverty and of black and brown communities under both Democratic and Republican administrations have all contributed to creating deep and widespread economic insecurity for decades.

Wages have stagnated even as the costs of basic food, housing, and transportation have climbed rapidly. People are working two or three jobs instead of one, a paycheck buys you less and less, and too many Americans are one crisis away from bankruptcy.

Healthcare is unaffordable so people are needlessly sick—literally—and sometimes even dying because of the unaffordable costs. The United States remains the only industrialized country in the world that does not mandate paid maternity leave, and moms and dads wonder how they will take days off from work to look after their sick children when they have no paid sick leave.

Black and brown kids predict their futures based on their zip code, and too many young people decide not to go to get higher education or trade skills because they can't afford to come out loaded with debt. Over 44 million Americans—including older Americans and grandparents—are working to pay off $1.5 trillion in student debt that they literally will never be rid of.

Our immigration system is broken, and although we know what the solutions are, we refuse to fix the system, instead exploiting the labor of immigrants and then criminalizing them, putting 56,000 immigrants every day into for-profit prisons, when the vast majority have never been charged with a crime, much less convicted of one.

As the Amazon burns, water shortages plague our poorest communities, and 100 million more people could be driven into poverty by 2030 due to climate change, Republicans—funded by fossil fuel companies—want to tell you that climate change is not real.

Is it any wonder, with all this, that Americans feel disillusioned and left behind by their own government and wanting anyone who they think will fight *for them* and *against* those entrenched interests?

The gaping hole of economic insecurity is a wound that is being poked, prodded, and inflamed by white supremacists, racists, and corrupt people who, far from draining the swamp, are only making it swampier. They exploit the understandable anger of that economic insecurity and misdirect it from the real causes of a system rigged against them toward blaming black and brown folks, poor people, immigrants, and those who need a hand up.

Trumpism, Exhibit A today, is a symptom and a cause. But it is our failure that helped create this situation; it was our refusal to take on bold structural changes that were needed to fix the growing power imbalance between workers and corporations, to address institutionalized racism, and to restrain greed. Nibbling around the edges simply won't do it.

To rebuild our country properly, we must be willing to take on three deeply intertwined supremacies that are tearing us apart: white supremacy and anti-blackness, corporate supremacy, and individual supremacy. I understand this is a tall order and I am not naïve to the challenges of what I propose. However, if we don't face the need for structural change and the interconnectedness of our structural systems of oppression, we will continue our downward slide. I have found the three supremacies as one good way to convey what is really an Age of Separateness. Each supremacy capitalizes on disconnection: the ultimate Big Lie, because at the root of everything, we are deeply interconnected. Any separation is, by design, an attempt to profit from the lie that we are separate.

White supremacy has a long and tragic history in America, going back to the genocide of Indigenous Peoples and the enslavement of Africans, Chinese exclusion, and Japanese internment. It persists in our education and housing systems, and is felt deeply in the brutal use of force against black and brown people by law enforcement, rising hate crimes against Muslims, Latinos, Jews, and so many more—and in the barbaric treatment of immigrants, refugees, and asylum seekers. Worst of all, it is lodged, often without awareness, in too many of our brains and exploited in too many stereotypes, rising rapidly with seemingly no checks.

The concept of anti-blackness, which is appropriately emerging in some of the most important thought spaces of taking on racism, is the corollary to white supremacy. In 2012, Pacific Northwest activist Scot Nakagawa wrote that "anti-black racism is the fulcrum of white supremacy."[1] Without understanding the core tenets of anti-blackness to the development of the United States and its economy, tenets that made not just possible but necessary the enslavement of millions of African people, you cannot truly understand white supremacy, the development of the manufactured concepts of race that put black people at the bottom of a hierarchy of races. Nor can you, without these core understandings, begin to heal or transform the past trauma or our future.

The alarm bells for the rising tide of white supremacy should not have taken so long. In August 2017, white supremacists held a Unite the Right white supremacist rally in Charlottesville, where marchers chanted anti-Semitic slogans, carried semi-automatic rifles, swastikas, and Confederate flags. Following clashes between protestors and counterprotesters, a self-identified white supremacist deliberately rammed his car into a group of counterprotesters, killing Heather Heyer and injuring nineteen other people. Instead of condemning the display of white supremacy, President Donald Trump refused to denounce the white supremacist marchers explicitly and instead referring to "very fine people on both sides." In spite of criticism from both Republicans and Democrats, Trump did not back down, only fueling further hate and white supremacist movements around the world. It wasn't until the horrific shooting in Christchurch, New Zealand, and the accompanying white supremacist manifesto that the broader public attention became more focused on the issue. In September 2019, the Department of Homeland Security seemed to finally spring into action, issuing a new framework for countering domestic terrorism and associated targeted violence.

Just the month before, in August, a man with an assault rifle drove six hundred miles across Texas to find enough brown people to kill. Stopping at a Walmart in El Paso because he was hungry, he walked in to get a bite to eat and saw, all around him, a heavily Latinx crowd. This would be the place, he decided. He went back to his car, got his weapon of war, and massacred twenty-two people, injuring twenty-four more. Shortly before his shooting spree, he posted a white nationalist, anti-immigrant manifesto online that used many of the same words and phrases used by President Donald Trump and other Republicans, describing "Hispanic invasions" and "cultural and ethnic replacement."

In September, I went to El Paso for a House Judiciary Committee field hearing on white nationalist terrorism and Trump's border policies. The evening before the hearing, I went to visit the heartbreaking, and yet gorgeous, memorial to the twenty-two victims who had been massacred. I walked through the row of twenty-two three-foot-high crosses, decorated with rosaries, flowers, pictures, and signs—signs like "How many more?" "Give me love not guns," or one sign with just the word, "Believe." The El Paso community had been tending those memorials every day, through rain and shine. One man, whose wife was killed, sat and slept there, handing out flowers to every person who visited. It was a community reeling from pain but refusing to bend to hate.

Our solutions to this kind of white nationalist terrorism are not easy, because they are not only institutional, they are cultural. The causes are being fueled by economic instability and the political divisiveness of some of our highest political leaders. But at the core, this is also about organizing, about building a movement and bringing those voices to the forefront. Just as we did after 9/11, we must again organize ourselves into hate-free zones; speak out against the hate, racism, and xenophobia; and demand that the social media companies who are complicit in encouraging clickbait and inflammatory content, stop making profits off of death and destruction. We need fundamental reforms in our laws around hate crimes, voting rights, immigration reform, and criminal justice reform. But we also need to take on the culture of violence that is in us and around us. Some of that is institutional and legislative, but some is also individual: refusing to allow hate to drive out love and remembering that we human beings have goodness in us that can triumph over evil, as we insist on maintaining the connection of community.

Corporate supremacy has elevated the corporation *over* the community, shareholders *over* stakeholders, and too often sanctioned greed and the consolidation of power. This wasn't always so. For many decades, corporations were well-regulated, profits were distributed to everyone in the company and not just to a tiny group of already wealthy shareholders and corporate executives. In 1965, the average CEO-to-typical-worker compensation ratio was 20:1. By 2018, it had risen to 221:1. The average pay of CEOs at the top 350 firms in the country in 2018 was at least $14 million. It is a destructive myth that CEOs deserve such a high ratio: this undervalues the important work of the employees, without whom there would be no corporation. CEOs get more simply by virtue of their power to set pay—and this is directly related to their ability to squelch the wages of those underneath them.[2]

Today, corporations seem to believe—with some good reason—that they make the rules and they can rig the system to benefit only them. At the time of this writing, angered by the headtax on Amazon that the Seattle City Council had passed (and the mayor had vetoed) to pay for more affordable housing, Amazon responded by pouring $1.1 million into local Seattle City Council elections in just the last three weeks of the election to try to elect a pro-Amazon slate that they could more easily control. Their bid backfired terribly, assisted by my own statement opposing this kind of money in politics and my reaching out to Elizabeth Warren and Bernie Sanders to weigh in and draw attention to this local election that epitomized the arrogance of corporations. In the end, Seattle elected the most progressive city council yet, with only one of Amazon's candidates winning—and he would have won without their money.

When we look at the mega-corporations that exist today and their control over all aspects of our life, including our health and location data, our shopping preferences, and so much more, we begin to understand that today's monopolies are more powerful than we can even begin to imagine. Today's mega-corporations need regulation on every front. In addition to investigating monopolistic practices and anti-trust violations, we also need to go back to regulating corporations much more substantially to prove their benefit to the community.

Remember, for example, that corporate charters used to not be handed out for an unlimited time; to renew your charter, you actually had to show that the corporation was benefiting the community. The amount of land that a corporation owned was limited, which prevented behemoths like Amazon from owning substantial amounts of a city's land—as they do in Seattle—and using that as a threat to stop government from regulating them.

Anti-trust laws and government regulations fostered the idea that power consolidated in the hands of a few hurt innovation and entrepreneurship. Breaking up monopoly power was something that people saw as helping small businesses to thrive and survive, preserving consumer choice, and regulating price and profit.

Corporations beat down labor unions while politicians from both parties did little to stop them. This decimated worker power. While more reliable than Republicans who have seen labor unions as a threat to the corporate power that keeps them wealthy and in office, Democrats have too often been unreliable labor allies. In the 1970s, Democratic mayors even participated in many strikebreaking activities in their own cities. Democrats have not just allowed, but bought into, the privatization of entire industries under the theory that they will be more "efficient" than government. In so doing, they have helped contribute to the argument that government wastes money and is inefficient, even though most research shows example after example of the wasteful administration and high profits and salaries of the private sector when it comes to functions that serve the public good. Democrats just haven't fought hard enough for stronger labor laws and increased rights of workers to organize and collectively bargain. It used to be a given understanding that worker organizing was a good thing for the community, but in the last forty years, too many elected officials have hidden behind a *faux* neutrality while corporations beat down workers attempting to organize unions.

Labor unions, too, must think through new ways to organize workers. Some of that is happening now, with a robust conversation beginning around ideas like sectoral bargaining, where instead of bargaining with each individual employer, bargaining occurs by sector. Think of the enormously successful teacher strikes in states like West Virginia, California, Illinois, and Arizona that inspired the country, as teachers across school districts banded together demanding not only higher wages and benefits for themselves but resources for their students, forcing the question at state legislatures with their bigger and more organized power.

My National Domestic Workers Bill of Rights, introduced in 2019, also takes a new approach to organizing a sector of workers that is overwhelmingly female, made up of low-income, mostly women of color who care for our children, people with disabilities, and seniors. These types of jobs are in the fields with the largest projected growth over the next decade. Like my Dignity for Detained Immigrants Bill, the legislation was drafted in coalition with domestic workers from around the country along with a broad and diverse set of groups. The bill aims not only to include domestic workers in current federal civil rights protections from which they had been excluded, but also to extend new benefits such as guaranteed paid time off, privacy protections, and written employment contracts.

To counter corporate supremacy, we need to reverse the backward motion of laws and policies that focus on short-term profit for a few at the expense of the common good. The policies we propose now—from new labor laws to canceling student debt to sectoral organizing to breaking up monopolies to limiting corporate power—must take on these deep structural problems and replace greed with true commitment to the simple idea that Senator Paul Wellstone used to speak about: we all do better when we all do better.

Finally, we must take on *individual supremacy*. At the national level, this is the "America first policy," using military might and dismissing coalition allies. At the individual level, it is NIMBYism that rejects compassion in favor of fear of others, blame in favor of collective action, individual needs versus what is best for whole communities. We appear to have forgotten what Dr. King said, that "Whatever affects one directly, affects us all indirectly."

This is exactly the case when we look at climate change and the need for climate justice, or even at the conversation ensuing now around gun reform. We have seen, over and over again, the ways in which our communities are deeply interconnected; how changes in ocean temperature affect the ability of salmon to survive and tribal communities to eat; or how the pollution of automobiles used to transport so many people across the country have the biggest effect on those communities that are forced to live near those highways; or how the burning of the Amazon for corporate profit and the warming of the earth helps lead to forest fires that cause people to lose homes and firefighters to lose lives.

And yet, corporate and individual supremacy have combined to stop us from thinking about the ways in which we are linked and the responsibility we have to urgently address climate change. Even more disturbing are the ways in which the burden of climate change affects those who are most vulnerable—often people of color and low-income people, as well as the workers who have been doing their work in environments that are toxic to their health. Some of our solutions may require that we reprioritize our own individual comforts relative to the benefits for the common good, but this is increasingly difficult to achieve in a capitalist society designed for immediate ease and short-term gain.

In the gun debate, I have been most struck by the students who have led the movement for reform, many of them personally affected by the wave mass shootings. The Second Amendment right to bear arms was never intended to override the right to live, nor does it need to with sensible reforms. But once again, the destructive selfishness of a corporate gun lobby that promotes the idea that individual rights override community good are the simplified expressions of the debate.

At the core of dismantling the idea of individual supremacy is reinstating the idea of a social contract, where government is the great equalizer of opportunity and the members of our society have an implicit agreement to all be a part of obtaining greater benefits for the whole, even sacrificing some individual freedom for state protection.

These supremacies are powerful and powerfully intertwined; changing them will require the courage to push for big structural change that doesn't just nibble at the edges but goes deep to root causes. It will require leaders who are willing to lead conversations on tough issues, not just follow the polls, people who will act for what is right, not what is easy. And if we are going to rebuild the trust of people to see government as something that truly does act for them, then we will need to show that quickly and boldly. We're going to have to rewrite the script that most Americans see into one where elected officials are fighting for them and not for the corporations who fill the halls of Congress and state legislatures with armies of lobbyists while the ordinary man or woman tries desperately to call their elected official to tell them their tale of woe.

Tying all these supremacies together will require, of course, getting money out of politics. We need sweeping campaign finance reform that focuses not only on democratizing our voting through public funding of campaigns and stopping the flow of "dark money" into our elections, but also closes the revolving door of politicians and senior staff, who go on to lobby for the biggest companies at double and triple the salary they earned in Congress. We'll have to stop the voter suppression and gerrymandering from happening across the country and give people a chance to believe for good reason that their vote actually matters.

Fixing deep wealth and income inequality and taking on the supremacies that are tearing apart our nation will require boldness and courage. It will require solutions that match the scale of our crisis, not ones that nibble around the edges but do not take on the structural problems we have. I know we can do it, but it will require organizing, collective action, and all the tools we have in our toolbox. It will require us to be strategic and to take risks; to do things that might feel bigger than we can pull off, perhaps even utilizing the tools of mass civil disobedience, which we can learn from mass nonviolent movements for change around the world as well as our own struggles for civil rights and women's suffrage in this country.

To do that, we have to claim our power, we have to have faith, and we have to build discipline.

Even now, in this divided political era, I've seen what can happen when we claim power and act with discipline. On July 18, 2019, the U.S. House of Representatives passed the Raise the Wage Act with 231 Democrats and 3 Republicans voting for it. The bill would gradually increase the federal minimum wage to $15 by 2025 and give 33 million workers across the country a raise.[3] It would also phase out the subminimum wage for tipped workers and index future wage increases to wage growth so the minimum wage keeps its value over time.

This was a truly historic day and it was a moment of tremendous pride for me to literally be a part of the fight for $15—from almost its beginning in the streets as an activist to the moment of passing legislation on the floor of the House. In 2012, a hundred courageous fast-food workers walked off their jobs in New York City, demanding higher wages and the right to be represented by a union. Now, in 2019, the United States House of Representatives was passing a bill to raise the current federal minimum wage of $7.25 for the first time since 2009.[4] The grassroots was claiming its power.

Take a moment to think about what $7.25 an hour means to a worker who works a full-time job for 40 hours a week and 2,080 hours a year. If they are earning the federal minimum wage, that worker will earn a total of $15,000 per year.[5] Imagine trying to feed a family and pay rent on $15,000 per year, not to mention healthcare, childcare, and transportation costs. Forget about saving for college, forget about emergency expenses, and absolutely throw out of the window the idea of accumulating wealth for future generations.

Now, compare the minimum wage worker's situation to that of the richest 5 percent of Americans, who in 2017 earned $15,000 in just six and a half weeks compared to a year for a minimum wage worker.[6] This sad comparison says everything about how we have disrespected the principle of hard work and undermined the value and the futures of millions of workers.

It was President Roosevelt who first passed minimum wage laws as part of the Fair Labor Standards Act in 1938, setting the wage at 25¢ per hour. He wanted the wage to ensure that people could earn a decent living, yes, but he was even more fiery about a business's obligation to its workers, saying that "no business which depends for existence on paying less than living wages to its workers has any right to continue in this country." If our system regulated wages by that very simple standard today, we would have a very different model than the one we have today, where entire industries—discount stores to name but one—are premised on paying wages way below the poverty line, often with few if any legitimate health, vacation, or other benefits.

I like to note here that women and girls played a big part in the push for a minimum wage, even back then. When Roosevelt asked Frances Perkins to be his labor secretary in 1933, according to Department of Labor historical records, she told him that she would accept only if she could advocate a law to put a floor under wages and a ceiling over hours of work and to abolish abuses of child labor.[7] It was also a young girl who passed Roosevelt a note when he was campaigning in Bedford, Massachusetts, that read

> I wish you could do something to help us girls. . . . We have been working in a sewing factory . . . and up to a few months ago we were getting our minimum pay of $11 a week . . . Today the 200 of us girls have been cut down to $4 and $5 and $6 a week.

To a reporter's question right after that, Roosevelt said "Something has to be done about the elimination of child labor and long hours and starvation wages."[8]

Roosevelt's idea was that if you worked forty hours a week—one full-time job—it should be enough to take care of your family and put away a little for savings for your kids. That is exactly what we have been striving for but failing at for decades. Adjusted for inflation, the federal minimum wage peaked in 1968. At that time, someone working a full-time minimum wage job would be right about at the poverty level.[9] Since 1989, that has dropped considerably so that workers working full-time at the federal minimum wage would be earning about 40 percent *less* than the poverty level.[10] Here's the kicker: if that minimum wage in 1968 had kept up with labor's productivity growth, the minimum wage in 2017 would be at $19.33.[11]

So here we were, in 2019, fighting for a $15 minimum wage . . . by 2025. It shouldn't have been considered radical to start with, and by 2025, workers will have fallen behind again, but it was still the biggest and most radical proposal in a decade. The fight for $15 had come to symbolize the depth of income inequality in America and the callous disregard for workers at the bottom of the wage scale—from corporations and from both Republicans and Democrats in Congress. It also had come to symbolize the power of a movement in the streets that bubbled up, creating change as it went, transforming a policy proposal from being a "radical left" idea into the mainstream.

When I talk about building intersectional movements, it sounds like jargon or some too vague notion. But there's probably no better illustration of this than how my early work with Somali Muslims post-9/11 intersected with the very first successful fight for a $15 minimum wage almost a decade later in the city of SeaTac, just south of Seattle, where the airport is the main employer. Many of the airport workers are immigrants, and the airport had long been a place of union organizing around baggage handlers, retail, aircraft service workers, and food service workers. By 2011, a quarter of SeaTac's residents were Somali Muslim immigrants.[12]

My work at the airport went back to just a few years after I started Hate Free Zone in 2001. I had participated in some protests organized by the union SEIU 6, which represented many of the immigrant baggage handlers. Later, because of the work we were doing with Muslims around Somali deportations and the raids on grocery stores, we were beginning to receive a tremendous number of requests around intervening for workers concerning the discrimination they were facing. We celebrated the successful resolution of a case where we worked to engage an attorney on behalf of six Muslim women workers at Oberto Sausage Factory who were not being allowed religious accommodation for their prayers. Working with the Equal Opportunity Employment Commission, we were able to get Oberto to pay $362,000 to the workers and agree to change their practices around religious accommodation.

At the airport, similar issues were happening. In 2003, a group of fifteen Somali workers had been suspended for taking a break to pray during Ramadan. They went to their religious leader, who called the Teamsters representative. After four or five meetings with the union rep, the workers were frustrated at the inaction and perceived disrespect by the union officials for these new immigrant workers. Because I knew the religious leader well and had worked closely with the community around the deportations and the grocery store raids, the Somali leaders then reached out to me. I was stunned at the stories I heard: these workers were being asked to take the stairs instead of the elevators. They were being shunned when they went into the bathrooms and told they could not take breaks to pray. I was furious that this was happening in 2003, no less. It was clear that the workers at that time had little to no relationship with the Teamsters union that represented them, and it also seemed clear that the union was not willing to negotiate on their behalf.

I decided I needed to speak with the union directly. I reached out to Steve Williamson, the head of the King County Labor Council at the time (the same person who is now my husband), and asked if he would help mediate. A tense set of conversations between the union rep, Steve, and I followed, but I was not satisfied with the pace of progress. I decided that to help the workers, we should work with an attorney again to file an EEOC lawsuit, which successfully led to the ability for workers to pray on the job without clocking out.

But I had seen the problem was far deeper. If we were going to see real progress, we needed to combine our movements for racial justice with economic justice. Minimum wage workers were largely people of color, and certainly that was the case at the airport. Union leaders were mostly white and too often had little understanding of these new immigrants who now were making up the workforce. I decided we needed to establish a new understanding between the immigrant workers of the union and the union leadership.

Our greatest ally was the legal counsel for the union, a woman named Tracey Thompson who had shown great sensitivity to the plight of the workers and had helped us as much as she could. She understood the issue and worked with us from the inside to help us organize, for the first time ever, a day of education and relationship building with these newer immigrant workers. Much later, that would be the groundwork for new worker organizing around a $15 minimum wage, supported by a number of different unions, including SEIU and the Teamsters. Still, trust is not built easily, and those stories of the union's lack of responsiveness embedded a sense in the community that it would be community allies and religious leaders who would be the real champions for these immigrant workers.

When the historic SeaTac Airport Workers Coalition formed to make SeaTac a test case for passing a $15 minimum wage, the campaign director, Jonathan Rosenblum, reached out to us for help in connecting with Somali workers. They had hired a dynamic organizer to organize inside the Somali community, but he was new to the community and needed help building that trust. The Somali leaders with whom I had become close—Abdullahi Jama, who worked for me for over seven years as an organizer and later senior advisor at OneAmerica, and Mohamed Sheikh Hassan, who was always at the forefront of every struggle in the community—were constant advisors and bridge builders. I asked them to help with the SeaTac campaign and they did, helping to organize forums in the mosques on how to take on religious discrimination and the need to raise wages. But the campaign needed a pivot point, an organizing moment that would help put everything on the line and show what collective action and power could do.

It came in the form of yet more religious discrimination—at the rental car company, Hertz. On September 30, 2011, a Hertz manager told the Muslim workers that they now had to clock out if they were going to pray—and if they didn't, they could forget about their jobs and go home. It was a Friday, the most important prayer day for Muslims. After our first fights in 2003, the workers had been allowed to pray without clocking out. Now, they were being told all over again that they would not be able to pray. The workers knew what they had to do: faith was important to them; the practice of praying five times a day is absolutely essential in

Islam. They went to pray. Three days later, thirty-four workers had been suspended.

Leadership, organizing, and relationships make all the difference. The new head of the Teamsters union was Tracey Thompson, the woman who had been legal counsel in 2003 and had seen the suffering of these immigrant workers back then. When she heard about what was happening, she responded immediately, saying, "This is bullshit. We're not going to stand for this. We're going to take them on."

The organizing efforts got a high-octane boost. Workers felt empowered and they had support—from the union and the community. Ties were being made between the largely white-led Occupy movement in Seattle and the immigrant organizing at the airport. Everything was about worker power, but now—as had happened after 9/11—we were also starting to see immigrant workers at the forefront. Still at OneAmerica at the time, I spoke in front of almost one thousand people at a big rally in April 2012 with the theme "Make Every Airport Job a Good Job." It was as if I was looking at the first Justice for All hearing again! There were Sikh cab drivers, Somali car-rental shuttle drivers, Latino baggage handlers, and black skycaps. We had helped organize immigrant rights organizations to attend and support, and multiple unions and faith leaders were also represented. Congressman Adam Smith, who represented the SeaTac area, was on hand as well and gave a fiery speech in support of the workers and in support of a $15 minimum wage. This time, though, the campaign included racial justice issues, such as the discrimination workers were facing. This was a game changer.

Fast forward to November 2013, when a coalition of unions, community-based organizations and faith organizations put together a SeaTac Good Jobs Initiative that would appear as a citizen initiative on the ballot.[13] The initiative included not only a $15 minimum wage, but also paid sick leave and several other pieces designed to support good wages and benefits and rights on the job. At OneAmerica, we went to community centers to register voters and then launching a huge Get Out the Vote effort. With tremendous organizing around voter turnout and a new impetus to get immigrant voters to cast ballots this time around, the initiative ultimately passed by just seventy-seven votes—making SeaTac the first city in the country to pass a $15 minimum wage. For the immigrant leaders who had put everything on the line to turn out their community, register new voters, and help lead the campaign, it was a sweet victory and it showed that every single vote really does count.

SeaTac showed what was possible in Seattle, and it showed, of course, that it took everyone to make it happen. I played my part, but the real work was done by workers with their worker peers, who took on a corrupt system. In 2011 and 2012, OneAmerica had been part of the coalition—initiated and led by the Equal Opportunity Institute and joined by many community organizations and unions including the United Food and Commercial Workers Union Local 21—that had advocated for a successful paid sick days legislation at the City of Seattle. The labor-community organizing model had been tested and we wanted to do the same thing again around the fight for $15. SEIU, UFCW, and several other unions, along with community organizations, had begun organizing.

In May 2013, at Seattle University, I kicked off a panel where low-wage workers told their stories of living on poverty wages. They were joined by a fast-food worker who had been part of the very first walkout in New York City. Their stories were powerful. They spoke of the choices they had to make between rent and food; about the dreams they let go of; and about the daily struggle to work in environments where they were often treated as dispensable, as garbage.

The previous month, two hundred fast food workers in New York City had gone on strike, and that strike was replicated in Chicago, Detroit, St. Louis, and Seattle. Our strike in Seattle was on May 30. I remember the surge of energy as hundreds of fast-food workers walked out on their jobs and joined thousands more in the streets of Seattle, demanding a $15 minimum wage. I went to speak to some fast-food workers who were leaving their workplace at one of the restaurants in Seattle's Capitol Hill neighborhood, showing solidarity as they walked out, and then I joined the throngs in the street who were chanting powerfully for $15. Workers were using their collective power, and our movement felt strong and full of anger channeled into action.

At the same time, we had an election for mayor happening in Seattle. I had endorsed Ed Murray, a former state senator who had worked with me on some immigrant rights issues and was challenging the incumbent. It was a contentious race. The incumbent—with whom I had clashed previously—was also a progressive. In the summer of 2013, Murray called together a small table of people including me and David Rolf, a good friend of mine and the influential head of the largest SEIU union in the region, who is one of the most creative minds on economic policy and worker organizing. Murray wanted to put together an Economic Opportunity Agenda and wanted our thoughts on it. I still have the draft document from September 2013, with my marked-up changes, which calls clearly for a $15 minimum wage, but also for other pieces of legislation like a Domestic Workers Bill of Rights, pay equity for women, and specific policies to address economic opportunity for workers of color.

The Fight for $15 organizing, the election of Socialist Alternative Councilmember Kshama Sawant, whom I had strongly supported, the passage of SeaTac's $15 minimum wage initiative in November 2013, and the mayoral election set the stage for our success. It was a perfect storm of coinciding things that supported each other and built the momentum for the campaign, the kind of tipping point we often look for in organizing but can't always predict. In organizing, you simply have to keep your eyes open for those opportunities and be closely attuned to when the ground shifts and the time seems right. Then you have to be ready to strike. And we were.

Murray ran hard on a $15 minimum-wage platform, and when he won, he kept his promise. Shortly after he took office in January 2014, he formed an Income Inequality Committee with twenty-four members from labor, business, and community organizations to hash out the details of a $15 minimum-wage proposal. The committee was co-chaired by SEIU's Rolf and a prominent businessman who owned the Seattle Space Needle,

Howard Wright. Wright and Rolf had strangely forged a strong connection and seemed excited to try to work together to come to some agreement on a $15 proposal by May 2013. By this time, I had left OneAmerica and was a senior fellow at the national Center for Community Change. Because I had been a key supporter of Murray's during the campaign, he appointed me to be a member of the committee as well as the co-chair of his police chief search committee.

I knew my role on the Income Inequality Committee would be important on multiple levels, including representing people of color: out of the twenty-four, six of us were people of color and I felt strongly that to be successful, we needed to frame minimum wage as what it was: an issue that disproportionately affects women and people of color, a frame that hearkened back to the one put forth by Roosevelt's secretary of labor, Frances Perkins.

The Committee's meetings were contentious, to say the least. There was no consensus around a $15 minimum wage yet. Businesses were fighting back hard, particularly the restaurant owners and hotel owners who hoped that this might be an opportunity to institute a "tipped minimum wage." This meant that an employer of an employee who receives tips is required only to pay $2.13 an hour in direct wages, as long as that amount plus the tips the employee receives from customers equals at least the federal minimum wage. Employers called this a "tip credit" but those of us who were opposed called it a "tip penalty," robbing an employee of the tips they earned and subjecting the wages of workers to the whims and pocketbooks of customers. I was particularly opposed to a tipped minimum wage because the large majority of restaurant workers were women and low-income people of color, whose reliance on tips for income also forced them to tolerate sexual harassment and other inappropriate behavior from customers, co-workers, and management.[14]

In Washington State, we were one of the few states that had resisted—thanks to labor and community—moving to a lower minimum wage for tipped workers. That meant that the minimum wage was the same for everyone, and if workers in restaurants earned tips, they could keep them on top of the minimum wage. Restaurants admittedly have tight profit margins, and they had been lobbying hard to allow for a tipped minimum wage so that they could pay less and have customers make up the wage with tips. But we were clear that was not going to happen. It was one of the many fights we had on the committee that erupted in some yelling and even stomping out and banging doors.

Even among those of us who were advocating for a $15 minimum wage there were disagreements about strategy and the importance of different bargaining items. During this time, I forged a friendship with Nick Hanauer, the wealthy and also brilliant entrepreneur who has bankrolled and masterminded some of the most important advances in policies to address inequality. At that time, we disagreed vehemently about the tipped wage, and it wasn't until a year later, during a public panel, that Nick turned to me and said, "You were right and I was wrong about that tipped wage."

Our own organizing included pulling together meetings outside of the meetings with our own sub-caucus. I often commiserated with Nicole Vallestero Keenan, another woman of color who led research for the labor-community organization Puget Sound Sage, about the challenges of lifting up those most affected during these meetings. Together, we worked hard to center women and folks of color in our messages.

At the time, the biggest arguments against a $15 minimum wage were that it would kill businesses and hurt the economy. Opponents of $15 argued, also, that if minimum wage was to be raised at all, it should be done regionally because one wage is too high for smaller communities, and it hurts teenagers who want to work part-time and get experience and wouldn't otherwise be able to do so. These arguments stayed the same when I introduced my minimum wage bill in the state senate, and they would be the exact same arguments we would face when debating the Raise the Wage Act in Congress many years later.

Small business owners who had been organized by the larger Restaurant Association testified that they would be put out of business if we moved to $15. The Chamber of Commerce and others were fighting hard, citing this as job-killing government regulation. Meanwhile, nasty and often personal fights between City Councilmember Sawant and Mayor Murray were intensifying.

To counter the argument that raising the minimum wage was bad for business, we relied heavily on some wonderful high-road employers who wanted to do right for their employees and pay good wages and benefits. Washington Community Action Network built a small business coalition called Main Street Alliance to lift up the voices of small business. These owners were crucial in our fight for $15, because they allowed us to pierce the narrative of opposition from business. Small business owners were closely connected to their communities and felt the responsibilities of that connection: they articulated very well the argument of the virtuous cycle we were aiming to strengthen: when workers have more money in their pockets, they spend more as customers. When they do so, their earnings go directly back into the economy, boosting the sales of businesses and helping them to do better. When businesses do better, the economy does better, and the virtuous cycle continues. On top of that, the research all showed that turnover decreased dramatically when workers were paid better.

Ironically, many of the small businesses who came and complained to us that they would go under ended up expanding after we passed the $15 minimum wage law, adding one or more restaurants after the minimum-wage law went into effect. We were able to document that raising the wage does not hurt the economy, even as business funded studies to try and generate conflicting data.

In the end, after many fractious debates, we knew we would have to compromise to cobble together something that could win the majority of votes on the committee. The biggest concession ended up being the length of the transition—five years for big businesses with more than five hundred employees and seven for smaller businesses to get to $15. That meant that workers at behemoths like McDonald's, Boeing, and Amazon would be at $15 by 2017 while smaller businesses would reach that wage by 2021. In practice, we knew that once large businesses went to $15, it was likely the market would drive small businesses to pay the same as well in order to compete for workers.

The other major concession was one that looked worse than it was, but it created enormous dissonance and divides in the broader community of movement allies and within our own coalition. The final agreement was to include a nominal and temporary tip penalty in the sense that tipped workers in businesses with under five hundred workers would make less than their nontipped counterparts until 2025, when the tip penalty would sunset. I say nominal, because even though there was a tip penalty included, the deal also negotiated a much higher starting wage for workers that essentially compensated for the tip penalty. But it was complicated enough to explain that it allowed the chamber to say they had won on a tip penalty. That was a big public relations loss and it undermined the unity of the movement on the final deal. It also, in many people's minds, squandered an opportunity to do better.

Around the same time, San Francisco had gone down a different route. Not trusting the mayor to get the job done, activists and organizers had put a $15 minimum-wage initiative on the ballot with just a two-year timeline—and it passed with a resounding 77 percent of the vote. That meant that San Francisco would reach $15 an hour for all workers even before Seattle, and that stuck in the throats of many. I hated to leave anything on the table, but I also felt we were at an impasse and going down the initiative route was simply not possible at this point.

It was messy and difficult—which is the often-repeated lesson on how social change on big policies happens. Negotiating with power IS messy, and the concept of success is sometimes ephemeral, depending on how success is measured, by whom, and at what time. We learn as we go. The places that go first are crucial in defining the debate and creating the momentum, but those that come later can craft even better policy that learns from what came before.

On May 1, 2014, Mayor Murray announced the terms of a deal, a watershed moment in the national Fight for $15. We became the first major city to pass a $15 minimum-wage policy. What fast-food workers in New York

City started led to a chain of events across the country, and our Seattle victory gave hope to other cities and states that they, too, could move forward without waiting for a lackadaisical, special interest–controlled Congress to act.

By the time Democrats took the majority in the House of Representatives in January 2019, twenty-nine states and the District of Columbia had enacted minimum-wage laws above the federal minimum wage. With Trump's election in 2016, Democrats had begun to understand how badly we had failed workers and the party was beginning to prioritize solutions to the extreme inequality in our country. Minimum-wage increases had passed at the ballot in multiple red states like Arkansas and Arizona, defying Republican-controlled legislatures that refused to raise the wages.[15] Workers were organizing and the movement had swept the country.

Democrats now had power in the House and we had to show we could get the job done. Our For the People agenda that Democrats had run on in 2018 included raising the minimum wage to $15, despite the grumblings of conservative Democrats who still did not seem to get the message. To be fair, some were running in difficult districts and states, and business interests continued to pour money into opposing minimum-wage increases. Chairman of the Education and Labor Committee, Bobby Scott, had staked his ground on passing a $15 bill. So had Speaker of the House Nancy Pelosi. If we wanted to show we cared about workers, we had to throw down on this bill. It wasn't the be-all-and-end-all answer to income inequality, but it was a strong policy solution whose time had come.

In spite of our commitment to get it done, it took months to garner enough votes to get it through committee. Behind the scenes, fights broke out between conservative Democrats who were still pushing for a regional minimum wage or tax credits for small businesses and the rest of the Democrats who believed we should just get it done simply and quickly. We were less than a dozen votes short of the 218 we needed to get the bill across the finish line in the House. Mark Pocan, my co-chair of the Progressive Caucus, and I together mobilized our progressive allies on the outside to stick together and to push hard to get the remaining sponsors.

One of the Republicans' top talking points, ironically, was what a failure the $15 minimum wage in Seattle had been. That was a joke, of course!

For all the doom and gloom of the business interests that fought us, the Seattle experiment was proving them wrong. We have one of the lowest unemployment rates in the country and jobs have continued to grow steadily. In 2018, *Forbes* magazine named Seattle the number one place for businesses and careers.[16] Even the *Seattle Times*, which had been staunchly anti-$15 minimum wage, continued to cover what it calls our city's "crazy restaurant boom," where many new jobs are being created each year.[17]

Most credible research showed that wages for our workers went up without any negative impact on employment.[18] Local food prices remain constant; you can still afford to feed your family plenty of healthy food and know that it was prepared by workers making a decent living. The truth was what I had said all along: when we increase the minimum wage, we get strong businesses, healthy families, and flourishing communities.

Still, Republicans didn't care about the truth and would fling lies about Seattle around without care. I printed out fact sheets about the truth of what we accomplished in Seattle and handed them to every Democrat to try to stop bad amendments on the floor. We had already fought back and stopped a number of amendments from being added by Democrats that would have weakened the bill, but we had made one major concession in increasing the transition time to 2025 instead of the original 2024. That had to be the only concession and we needed to organize to make that so.

The Progressive Caucus organized on the inside as well as the outside. The bill was less than a dozen co-sponsors short of the 218 we needed for ultimate passage on the House floor, but Mark and I were convinced that if we simply brought the bill to the floor, we would have the votes we needed to pass it. Some of our colleagues had told us that they would not co-sponsor the legislation but if it came to the floor, they would vote for it. However, we needed to convince leadership to bring the bill to the floor. In a bold move, Mark and I used our regular press conference for the Progressive Caucus to announce that the minimum-wage legislation had the votes to pass and called for the legislation to come to the floor. That call forced leadership's hand. About an hour after the press conference, in response to reporters' questions, Majority Leader Hoyer put out a press release saying they would put the bill on the floor before the August recess.

We immediately got to work mobilizing our progressive allies on the outside to stick together and to push hard to get the remaining sponsors. I spoke to nervous colleagues and made sure they were armed with statistics that made them more comfortable. We asked our labor allies to make it clear that they would "score" any attempts to weaken the bill on the floor as if those were the final vote. "Scoring" meant that those unions would look at these votes as part of their assessment of whether or not someone was a labor champion. Typically, scoring happened on a final vote, not on the amendment votes that can often weaken a bill. Scoring these types of votes as essentially a "NO" vote on the final legislation was a tough, audacious, and new strategy and it upset many of the Democrats who wanted a weaker bill. Mark and I also conveyed to Democratic leadership that if any additional changes were made to weaken the bill, we would be forced to rally progressive votes to oppose the bill, even if it meant the bill would fail.

These were high-stakes negotiations. But the time was right and the powerful, broad, and deep organizing coalition on the outside—which I had been privileged to be a part since the early 2000s, before I even knew what it would create—had created the conditions to make organizing on the inside possible.

This *was* my theory of change. My old mantra—if politics is the art of the possible, then it is our job to change the limits of what is possible—still held true, and now I was doing it not only on the outside but here in Congress too.

What a joy it was to be on the floor as the bill passed. In a time of rising inequality and desperation for so many millions of workers, and led by a movement of grassroots workers whose courage mobilized all of us to action, the passage of the Raise the Wage Act gave hope to tens of millions of workers across the country that government CAN work for them. Truth be told, it also gave me much-needed hope that my theory of change of inside-outside organizing—the whole reason I had run for office—was working.

Brittany Howard, the former lead singer of Alabama Shakes, refers to all the hate and racism that has been unleashed as a "necessary evil to get to the next place where we can fix the ruptures in our own society."

There are ruptures for sure, tearing apart the fabric of America all around us. But this book is for those who are ready to step into the void and fix the ruptures. This book is for the organizers and the activists; the knitters, sewers, and darners who are working to stitch our country back together and create an even better tapestry than what we had before, people who are authentically ready to use power for good. And when you are depressed about our country seemingly taking steps backward, remember that ruptures allow for that which is hidden or kept underground to emerge into the daylight, giving us the opportunity to see and diagnose our problems clearly, to strategize better, and then to take bold action together.

America is a country that makes and remakes itself over and over again, every single generation. Our work now is to restore America to a country where the American Dream is truly available to every one of us, rich or poor; white, black, or brown; gay, trans, or straight; immigrant or U.S. born. Our work must be disciplined, loving, fierce, and intersectional. We have to learn to always be part of the solution.

What I have found through my organizing is that we organizers are optimists. We don't just believe that something else is possible, we *know* it. We believe not that we are the ones we have been waiting for, but rather we ask *why wait?* Our movement of *we* believes that our strength comes in joining our voices and rolling up our sleeves, not just walking the walk but running the run to create a real community of opportunity, a society grounded in equality, a country not just of open doors but of open hearts, an America more just, more compassionate, more loving than the one we were handed.

It is our time to claim our power and use it. Our future depends on it.

Afterword

You may be reading this book in the waning days of the first Trump administration, the early dark days of his second term, or the much brighter time of a new, progressive Democratic presidency. But in a sense, the political lessons of this time in history are still the same: we must not only envision a new and better world, but we have to find, build, and nurture the pathway to making it a reality. Sometimes, this work feels far more urgent than it does at any other time. I would contend that this is exactly one of those significant moments when so much is on the line. But even in those moments where it may seem like we can sit back and relax, the truth of democracy is that it takes work *all the time*. Creating that more perfect union was the charge given to us so long ago by our founding framers, and that work is hard. My abiding belief is that progress comes only in the form of individual efforts and collective movements for change, through struggle and resilience, and through the deep conviction that something else is possible.

I wrote this book because I saw this myself. I wanted to share the belief that democracy requires something of us, and that our efforts—no matter how small we might feel they are—matter. I certainly would never have guessed that my life would take the path it did, or that the outrage

I felt after 9/11 in the wake of discrimination against so many would lead to the formation of the state's largest immigrant advocacy organization, much less to my becoming a member of Congress. Along the way, I met countless people who themselves were agents of change, people who saw an injustice and responded, and through their own individual efforts helped build collective and intersecting movements that sought a whole greater than its parts.

As a country, we have great divides to heal, great wrongs to right, and great achievements to learn from. We cannot be stuck in either our challenges or our advances, but we also cannot paper over the foundational inequities and injustices that landed us where we are. We have made immense headway into electoral politics, but so much more remains to be done. Women, immigrants, people of color, and allies of all stripes are beginning to understand how to bend the power structures to their needs—but our existing structures and ways have long histories and they are not easy to break down.

Trump has shown us in the starkest terms what is at stake when we allow government to be taken for granted by some, and when we allow it to be appropriated by others for personal gain at the expense of public good. I became an activist in the wake of September 11, 2001, and I remember the feeling of despair that led me to act for change. I did not think it would get worse, but it certainly has. It sometimes feels like our Constitution and our democracy are being shredded piece by piece, with only the wealthiest left standing. That cannot be our America—we cannot let it be our America.

Many young women, particularly women of color, ask me for advice on their lives or their careers. When I tell them that I used to be terrified of public speaking or that I wandered a lot before I found a path that was more straight than circuitous, they are amazed or disbelieving. I hope this book helps to show that our achievements are not preordained, they are obtained through believing in ourselves, paying attention to our own intuitions that the mainstream world tries to beat out of us, learning from those who came before, and plain and simple hard work.

Here are the top lessons learned in this brown woman's rise to political power. While focused on my own experiences of politics, I also believe they can apply to anyone in any field. This isn't an all-inclusive list, and perhaps you've taken other lessons from the pages of this book that resonate even more. If so, please share them and let's keep building this list to benefit everyone.

Own yourself. Stay open.

Don't try to be who you are not. Politics is filled with people who are inauthentic or trying to *be* someone instead of *do* something. Owning yourself and your story is your key to success. Make sure you think about your story in the larger context; it's not really about you, it's about all the others who have similar stories. Your ability to connect with yourself actually enables your ability to connect with others. Don't ever let people talk you out of sharing who you really are at the core. Authenticity shines through with the words you choose, the people you seek out, and the way you listen. Keep it real. Voters, like kids and animals, have a nose for evasions and anything fake. You are your own storyteller, and your story is important.

Don't let anyone buy you, with their money or their promises of power. Money in politics is corrosive—that's why I don't take corporate PAC money because I want there to be no illusions, not even a hint of anything that undermines people's confidence that I work *for the people* and not for corporate lobbyists. So, too, is power if it is used for self-promotion and not for the collective good. Don't let power tilt your head away from what it is you are really fighting for.

The imperative to stay open is as true in organizing as it is in your career. As organizers, you work hard building coalitions, gathering signatures, and knocking on doors for the causes you fiercely believe in, not always knowing whether your efforts will bear fruit and make change. But you have to keep your eyes open and look for that moment when your stomach turns over an injustice that makes you unable to sit still. That's how I started Hate Free Zone/OneAmerica, based on a gut feeling that I had to do something; I could not stay silent any longer. I didn't have a grand plan, but I knew that I had to act and I figured everything out step by step, thanks to the skills I had gained along the way.

You also have to stay attuned to subtle shifts, anticipating a tipping point when your moment has come. I saw us seize the moment when we were able to win a $15 minimum wage for all workers in Seattle, and I saw it again when I organized with my movement allies a massive protest in Washington, DC, against Trump's immigration policies—in just a few short days.

I respect people who map out their futures, but I personally have found much greater success staying open to new possibilities, staying attuned to my heart, rather than mapping out a plan of where I wanted to be in ten years. I followed my desire to help the most vulnerable while earning an MBA when I worked with community organizers in housing projects in Chicago on the weekends. I learned that I liked working in public health from my time selling defibrillators and working at PATH, and when it felt like that wasn't enough, I followed my inner compass back to India to engage these topics on a more global scale. When I was touched by tragedy—both my own trauma surrounding my child's birth, and the division I saw unfolding all around me in the wake of September 11, 2001—I found the tragedy made me stronger and more creative about what I wanted to do with my life and why it was so important.

Look for the better angels in everyone. Don't let the lesser angels diminish you.

The fight for equity and justice can often become rancorous and brutal: it's what turns many citizens off to engaging with politics in the first place. Even our own movements for justice are filled with competition and sharp elbows. There's nothing wrong with being ambitious; ambition helps fuel the drive and the passion for change. But ambition can go side by side with generosity if you recognize that our collective movement is more powerful than our individual movement. It's not easy to do this because we're trained to operate in environments of scarcity. But we have inordinate capacity for generosity and kindness and we have to remind ourselves that doing well for ourself at the expense of others hurts not only our long-term goals but also our souls.

I've learned, too, that you can't write anyone off. If you're willing to calmly engage with perceived "enemies" every now and then people will surprise you. When I was in the minority party in the state senate, I couldn't afford to ignore Republican colleagues. My instinct was vindicated in Olympia when a Republican senator unexpectedly voted with me against a bill that would have boosted the predatory payday lending industry in our state on the backs of struggling people who desperately needed the money to make next month's rent. I thanked him for his vote, and he became an unusual ally later down the line. Of course, many times this does not work, and it can be hard to keep the faith in others in a time when the GOP refuses to work with us and has been feckless time and again in their support of a lawless president. But going into difficult conversations and confrontations seeking the good in others—while staying true and bold in your convictions—isn't just good politics, it's simply good for the soul to let our own better angels take precedence in our work.

At the same time, don't let the lesser angels diminish us. Some people operate on the principle that they can only be big by making you small. Don't let them. Stand up tall, be fierce in fighting for what is right and for your own right to *be* right . . . and opinionated. White men weren't handed an exclusive patent to be leaders—we all have that right and deserve that chance. Remember that if someone is trying to make you feel small, it's probably because they are small themselves. Breathe in power, breathe out negativity. In your toughest moments, connect yourself back to *you* and to the earth. Dig your feet into the floor and imagine your arms reaching to the sky, growing bigger and stronger with every breathe. Keep the great poet Maya Angelou's words with you: you have every right to be just where you are, always rising.

You may shoot me with your words,
You may cut me with your eyes,
You may kill me with your hatefulness,
But still, like air, I'll rise.

Courage is a muscle. Learn to flex it in the face of urgency.

It's easier to go along to get along. It may even bring you more power more quickly. But change requires struggle, and that struggle is not only with those who are clearly on the opposite side, but also with those who say they are on your side but tell you to be patient or not to rock the boat.

I remember when I first read the full text of Dr. Martin Luther King's "I Have a Dream Speech." This was years after I had heard largely the parts of the speech that everyone always quotes. What struck me in the speech was not those often-repeated parts but the section of the speech where he says clearly, "This is no time to engage in the luxury of cooling off or to take the tranquilizing drug of gradualism. Now is the time to make real the promises of democracy."

How often we are told to be patient, to put our faith into what we perceive is achievable rather than what we make possible! Often, this "great lesson" comes from those who have the least to lose. I say this with the urgency that imbues itself into the life of every black mother who has lost a child to gun violence; every immigrant who is separated from their beloved family; every young person who watched their planet literally burn. Our job is to reassert urgency, not to be lulled into that "tranquilizing drug of gradualism." And that often means that we have to be courageous in taking on even those we love or those we see to be on "our side."

Courage takes effort and intentionality. It is a muscle that grows when flexed—not only for the people who are courageous but for those around them. Courageous acts are like snowballs rolling down a hill, gathering steam, first one, then a hundred, then a thousand acts of courage, coming together like a symphony orchestra. Here, I think of the #MeToo movement, of the #BlackLivesMatter movement, of Dreamers who came out to protest in spite of the threat of deportation, of the fast-food workers in New York City, or of the teachers in West Virginia who went on strike. I think of the first whistle-blower who came forward to call out presidential abuses of power related to Ukraine, which then emboldened another whistle-blower to come forward as well, and even more at the time of this writing.

Re-building institutions differently to deal with the challenges of ineffectiveness, institutionalized inequities, and a broken status quo often requires challenging our own leaders. I loved President Obama and I wept at the significance of the moment when he was elected to the highest office of the land, giving new hope and possibility to the paths of so many others across the country. It was not easy to take him on, then, when I felt he played in to a negative narrative about immigrants, and ended up deporting more immigrants than any president before him. I and many of our immigrant rights colleagues called him out as Deporter-in-Chief, protested him—and, yes, worked with him on new solutions. That eventually led to real progress: the creation of the DACA program that has given essential temporary relief to Dreamers across the country and a refocus on the most important priorities for deportation, called the prosecutorial discretion policy.

Later, at the Congressional Progressive Caucus, we had to do this too— often challenging our own leadership. By flexing our muscle, we won important gains for the progressive movement and for our caucus members, pushing for House passage of the $15 minimum wage, an end to the illegal war in Yemen, and essential limits on presidential power related to immigration. By holding out for a coordinated strategy on endorsing our own speaker, we were able to get members onto critical "A" committees for the first time and build out opportunities for progressives to serve in leadership. If we do this work with grace, without rancor, but with an attachment to the principle of what we seek to achieve, our courage muscle will grow stronger, win or lose.

Bring the voices of the most affected to the table.

The most affected people must be at the table when we craft solutions. Indigenous people, people of color, and low-income folks have to be a part of defining the problem correctly and then helping to develop the solutions at the tables of power where policy decisions are made. When I am in a particularly tough hearing, I bring the stories and faces of those most directly impacted with me to remind me of what is at stake and to be authentic in conveying the urgency.

I have made the drafting of our most important pieces of legislation similar to the coalition work I have done in the past: we consult with and help put in the driver's seat those most directly affected by the outcome, and connect that with existing research and lessons learned. That way everyone operates from the same shared understanding about the problem; this shared foundation includes not only quantitative research but qualitative understanding of lived experiences that reveal what is needed and what we can do to build real power for those most directly affected. This not only allows for better policy solutions ultimately, but it also opens the space for new leadership and facilitates real buy-in. Every organizing moment is stronger and more powerful when everyone works together as a team, even if it includes give and take within the team.

Pick your battles. Always think about the long vision, not just the short fight.

When I became an elected official, I did so with the understanding that—as the only woman of color and first ever South Asian American woman elected to the Washington State Legislature—I was going to push to always acknowledge racial injustice and make racial justice central. I knew I would have to be unafraid in my insistence that race touches every challenge we face in this country and this was going to mean making others uncomfortable.

In my time in Congress, I've been underestimated, talked down to, even shouted at by a recalcitrant witness—the former director of ICE—during a hearing. Throughout my twenty years of activism, I've been the target of extraordinary hate, told to "go back" to where I came from, and faced death threats. I've stood up over and over again for my fellow women of color in Congress who have faced the same challenges, because I know how important this public solidarity is to countering hate. I've sometimes had to consciously screw up my courage when standing by my principles—whether it was as the first Judiciary Committee member to call for one of my own civil rights icons, John Conyers, to step down in the face of sexual harassment claims from several women, or as one of the first members of Congress to call for an impeachment inquiry in the wake of the release of the Mueller Report and serious obstruction of justice incidents detailed in that report.

There are plenty of things that I choose not to respond to, because as a woman and especially a woman of color, you can't react to every sexist, racist thing that happens to you. You have to pick your battles and conserve your energy for the ones you decide are most important, the ones where you can best use your power to stand up for people like you and change our world for the better.

You also have to learn to call people in as well as calling people out. The future will be incredibly bleak—and limited—if we don't truly believe that people have the capacity for change. Too many people walk only with people who are just like them, and our minds get trained to be comfortable in that homogeneity laced with other -isms that have been fueled in our institutions and our media. We have to be the pioneers or the space explorers, going where no other has gone before, trying to find openings, cracks, fissures, interstices that allow for education and a new understanding of who we are as human beings and that we all want the same basic things for ourselves and our families. How beautiful it is to believe in the possibility of change—for everyone!

There's never a "right" time.
Nurture those things that matter most.

In the fight for justice, there is never going to be a right time for the things that are important to you and the people you love. We are constantly on high alert for the next insidious tweet from the president, or the next threat to justice from all corners. As activists and change makers, we are driven. The goal is not to become less driven, it is to preserve enough time for ourselves and our loved ones, the capacity to think, a slate clean enough to allow our creativity to come through when it is needed the most. We have to work just as hard at keeping our humanity and our capacity to love, as well as to love and nurture those connections to those who keep us grounded.

When my husband Steve and I finally decided to take a ten-year delayed honeymoon, it was most certainly not a great time to do so: we were in the midst of finalizing the plans for the first Medicare for All hearing I'd worked so hard to secure. The Mueller report even came out while I was on the airplane! But I emerged, both during and after this trip, with a clearer and calmer head. Visiting my parents in India, even now when I am busier than ever, remains so important and dear to me and I never, ever regret taking that time to be with them in their older years of life. I have immovable dates on my calendar: Janak's performances; family birthdays, weddings, and funerals; walks with my dearest girlfriends and my dog, Otis; and quiet time at our rustic cabin, chopping wood with Steve. All this roots me, but it also allows me to give back to those who give me so much. As I get more power, there are more people who want more from me. It only makes me appreciate that much more those who replenish me every single day, week, month, and year.

Build your own theory of change. Then build the
infrastructure that your theory demands.

Everyone—from political insiders to activist fighters to concerned community members and everyday voters—has a role to play in the fight for bold, progressive change. During much of my twenty years as an activist and organizer, my activist friends and I turned up our pure noses at elected officials as we demanded change—government was far too unrepresentative, too cautious, and most lawmakers looked nothing like me. But suddenly, I realized that I could be the one to change this problem. I could, as Gandhi teaches us, be the change I wished to see.

If we wanted bold, progressive change, we needed to train and elect more "movement electeds"—a term I coined to describe people who come from an outside movement and have a strong allegiance to it. Our political system and its traditions and hierarchies are entrenched and tough to topple, and we need to keep up the pressure on political parties to let them know they are not simply beholden to their donor bases and their party leadership. Just electing a person of color or a candidate who is good on an equity issue won't be enough if they do not have a coalition of movement support behind them.

All this required me to test that theory of change—by running myself. That also gave me a front-row seat to what actually happens in campaigns and in elected office. That front-row seat then allowed me to see clearly what infrastructure was missing and to focus on building it, leading to the creation of the newly refurbished Congressional Progressive Caucus Center and building on the lessons of the past Democratic Study Group, updated for our current moment. It also led to strengthening the internal structures of the Congressional Progressive Caucus. I have learned that as strong and powerful as we might be as individuals, we really do need an infrastructure that supports our movements for change. Without that, we simply don't have the support or the resources to make real the change we seek.

Practice makes perfect.
And fear can be conquered.

I want to be the one who is always prepared—and you will often find this to be the case with women and with people of color. Some say it's a shame that we have to do this; I say it's a shame other people don't. Imagine how much better the world would be if people actually prepared for their jobs with the same diligence that we put into ours!

Here's the other thing I've learned. Our deepest fears can be conquered, with time, effort, and the right conditions. Lore (and some research) shows that people's fear of public speaking is greater even than the fear of death and snakes. I am always met with complete disbelief when I tell my staff or people I mentor that I, too, used to be terrified of public speaking. So much so that, in my early years of work, I would sometimes call in sick right before a major presentation to a group of twenty or twenty-five because I was too terrified to speak publicly, even to that small of a group. Sometimes in meetings, I would spend so long formulating thoughts in my mind that by the time I raised my hand to speak, the topic was long gone and my thought was irrelevant. I certainly never, ever, in a million years would have imagined speaking in front of crowds of thousands, much less the 250,000 people who attended the final Immigrant Workers Freedom Ride rally!

How did I do it? The change began when my first book came out and I was doing book readings of my own words, which were near and dear to my heart because I had spent years putting them down on the page. That gave me the comfort to forget all the people who were in the room for the readings. By the end, when people would ask me questions, I realized that I enjoyed answering them, even though there were so many people listening. Then, when September 11, 2001, happened and I suddenly was in the forefront of convening rallies for those who were about to be deported or put in detention, it seemed ludicrous to be afraid of speaking out when the stakes were so high for them and I was so passionate about what I was doing. Suddenly, I found my fear wiped away by the strength of my convictions and the need to speak out about injustice around me.

I still practice—a lot. I read my speeches out loud, I make sure the rhythm is right, and I write and rewrite until I feel it says what I want it to say. With the conviction of the words and the poetry of the rhythm and thoughts, any slight fear I may have gets wiped away when I start speaking. I also think that a little nervousness is good—it keeps you on your toes and makes sure that you treat every event like the new opportunity it is: a new stage to bring more people on board to the justice train you are driving.

As my own faith in myself has grown, my fears have reduced. Sure, we all have insecurities, but we build our confidence through experience and practice. Everyone has this capacity, I promise.

Leave space for new leadership to emerge, always. Don't hang on to power.

When I was at OneAmerica, I loved working with young people. Some of our funders asked me how we built such incredible leadership among these young people. "We don't build leadership," I said. "We just provide the space for leadership to emerge."

Emerge it has. I am completely inspired by the leadership of our young people on climate change, on gun reform, and on addressing our student debt crisis. They are not just our future, they are leading some of the most important present moments. Our job is to step out of the way, to learn from them, to contribute the wisdom we have built, and to collectively find the resources to support these emerging prescient voices. Theirs are voices unfiltered by reasonableness, and most responsive to the urgency of now.

We may want to think that we are the leaders forever, but to me, the sign of a good leader is one who can step down when her work is at its peak and who can put as much time into mentoring and building the power of others as part of the vision of her own success. I have tried to do both these things. I stepped down from OneAmerica after founding, leading, and growing the organization into tremendous success. Founder transitions are notoriously difficult and often fail, but I was determined that my success should be measured by how well I managed the transition to a new leader, not just by what I had done while at the helm of the organization. I felt strongly that a successful transition would only happen with serious planning, which I invested in for several years, and also stepping aside when the organization was working well. People around me were stunned that I would give up that platform of power when things were going so well, but I knew that was the only way it would continue to be successful. So, I resigned and I am proud that the organization is still doing incredible work and has moved on to play a leadership role on even more frontiers.

My mentoring role also gives me enormous joy and pride. I enjoy looking around at some of our new leaders in government and social justice and seeing women like Yasmin Christopher, Hamdi Mohamed, Jennifer Chan, and others who started as interns and volunteers thrive and develop into the capable leaders they are today. They got the space to lead and the gift of someone's deep belief in them and what they could achieve. I was blessed to have incredible women do this for me as well: Mary Houghton, Gloria Steinem, Eve Ensler, Barbara Lee, and many others. I also had the perpetual courage and wisdom of those I worked side-by-side with: the undocumented women who got arrested with me and had so much to lose, the domestic workers who spoke out for rights on the job, and the Dreamers who painted a different vision of what was possible. The stories of Shirley Chisholm, Sojourner Truth, and Frances Perkins all created a deep foundation of possibility and hope that were essential too.

We pay it forward—that is our legacy, as much a part of the work as anything else we must do to build a more powerful union and a more powerful movement. And here's the secret truth: this building of others replenishes me too, reminding me always of the power of WE.

We are in a time when we must help America lead from her heart again. That is actually why I ran for office after decades as a civil and human rights activist and advocate, and it is what I, now as a congresswoman, wake up thinking about every day.

The Oath of Office I took declares that I will support and defend the Constitution of the United States. The First Amendment reads as follows:

Congress shall make no law respecting an establishment of religion, or prohibiting the free exercise thereof; or abridging the freedom of speech, or of the press; or the right of the people peaceably to assemble, and to petition the Government for a redress of grievances.

This constitutional recitation of rights is *one* version of America, the individual liberties America. In this America, naming our rights is how we insist that others tolerate us.

But before our Constitution, the Declaration of Independence put forth a deeper, more loving, and aspirational America. This America proclaims that the *purpose* of liberty or independence is the pursuit of Truths—truths that were instilled in me through my early readings of Mahatma Gandhi and that bring us all back to the region of our hearts. Our Declaration of Independence is a grand proposition that begins with these words (with a slight change of the word "men" to the word "people"):

We hold these truths to be self-evident, that all people are created equal, that they are endowed by their Creator with certain unalienable Rights, that among these are Life, Liberty and the pursuit of Happiness.

This is the promise of America, however dissonant it appears in the moment. Despite lurches this way and that, America has never been a country defined by people who say "Love it or leave it." Rather, it has been a country where people make it better through service, critique, and yes, dissent.

In 1990, Václav Havel urged the U.S. Congress to remember that a legacy of human suffering doesn't only create destruction and poverty. It also gives, said Havel, those who have suffered "a special capacity to look, from time to time, somewhat further than those who have not undergone this bitter experience. We too can offer something to you: our experience and the knowledge that has come from it. The specific experience I am talking about has given me one certainty: Consciousness precedes being, and not the other way around. For this reason, the salvation of the human world lies nowhere else than in the human heart, in the human power to reflect, in human modesty, in human responsibility. Without a global revolution in the sphere of human consciousness, nothing will change for the better."

This understanding has revealed itself more and more to me through the years. There is an underlying paradigm shift required to get to the basic understanding that we are all better off when we are all better off. We need to understand the inherent connections that exist: between a farmer and the earth she ploughs; between the effects of climate change and migration; between growing inequality and concentration of power among the fewest in a long time in our history.

There is a story I love about how on a particular night, some people came upon the Sufi mystic, Nasruddin, crawling around on his hands and knees under a lamppost. "What are you looking for?" the people asked him. "I've lost the key to my house," he said. They all started to help him look, but to no avail. "Are you sure you lost it here?" one person finally asked. "No," he said. "I lost it in the house, but there's more light under the lamppost."

I suggest to you now that it is time to start looking for our answers in different places, even if the spaces they reside in are not as well lit. In the end, it is these very places that may well hold the most light.

In the work we do, creating a different kind of world may seem sometimes too difficult. Our efforts may seem too small given the scope of the problem. But in those times, I ask you to remember a time when you have created something new. Remember a time when you have created a change for someone that they never thought was possible. Remember a time when you have dreamed and the dream has come true. Remember a time and place when you felt completely whole and alive, when you were surrounded by people you loved and who loved you.

Do you remember? Do you remember those sounds, those smells, those thoughts? Do you remember the look on the face of the person for whom you created that change? Hold those feelings with you now. That is your possibility. That is the world that we fight for and believe in. That is the experience upon which our imagination can build.

I believe that change is not just coming, she is breathing down our neck. We are a proud nation, filled with the promise of a different tomorrow, predicated on the idea that struggle is essential to progress.

Here is my prayer for all of us as we walk the paths that unfold in front of us.

I wish for rebellion and laughter, the grace of fate, and the dreams of the day as well as the night.

I wish for a respect of ourselves and our intuition, and a respect of that which we cannot know.

I wish that we remember those who came before, and those who have yet to come; that we do not forget where we have come from, or what has been taken that must have time to replenish.

I wish for the fertility of imagination and the conviction of possibility. If politics is the art of the possible, then never forget: it is our job to push the boundaries of what is seen as possible.

It is our job to bring the movement of WE to life.

Acknowledgments

To my agent, Jill Marr from Dykstra Literary Agency, who believed in me and this book and kept that belief going for years, my deepest gratitude.

Marc Favreau at The New Press wanted this book way back in 2013 when it was originally to be a book on immigration. Each year, something new came up, the book was not written, and the topic changed. Through my campaigns for state senate and for Congress, Marc still believed there was a book that needed to come out and he continued to encourage me to write it, helped me collate and cull my many articles and speeches, helped me shape the overall structure of the book, and found me support to help me get it to its finished shape. I'm ever grateful to Marc, Emily, Sarah, zakia, Brian, and the many hands I don't even know about at The New Press that helped this book come into being and out in the world. The work of nonprofit presses like The New Press is so critical to the work of bringing important voices for justice to the world.

At a time when I doubted I would ever finish this book, Amanda Palleschi entered with force and made the impossible seem possible. She held me to account for finishing chapters, helped to research material and pull together a storytelling arc, and read everything I had written as well as interviewing me to create strong working drafts of different sections of the manuscript. This book would not have been finished without her hard work, creativity, and perseverance.

I tried to name people throughout the book who stood out to me as partners, co-conspirators, teachers, mentors, allies in the struggle, and inspirations—from Dreamers to fast-food workers; from civil rights leaders to suffragettes; from movement leaders of #BlackLivesMatter to #MeToo; from my friends at MoveOn and Indivisible, to my many partners in the movement and in elected office, including the co-chair of the Congressional Progressive Caucus, Mark Pocan; and to my incredible staff at every stage of my work, without whom we simply could not have achieved what we have together. I know I have fallen short in not being able to name everyone here; there are simply too many leaders who have been part of building these movements with me. But if you see yourself in this book in some form or another, if you know you have a place in these movements for change, if you have been a part at some point of these struggles, pains, and joys: please accept my thanks for what you do and the leadership you have shown.

I am grateful to the many people who reviewed different parts of the book and offered their edits, thoughts, and reflections to ensure accuracy and the right telling of our collective work for justice: Gautam Raghavan, my chief of staff, who has literally and figuratively had my back on everything, and also reviewed the entire book and offered critical edits; Yasmin Christopher, who agreed to embark on that first journey into the state senate as my legislative aide; Jennifer Chan, now with me in different ways for more than a decade; and Lindsay Owens and Mike Darner, who were part and parcel of building a stronger Progressive Caucus inside Congress.

A special recognition to Hedgebrook and its founder, Nancy Nordhoff, for nurturing and feeding my love of writing and bringing powerful women's voices to the world that need to be heard.

To my small, loving circle of friends and family, the people I call on when I need replenishment and a reminder of joy in a difficult world—including the next generation: Michael, Tara, Josh, Kian, Raisah—you all know who you are. Thank you for always being there, making me laugh, helping me to be present, and teaching and sustaining me through good and bad times. A particular thank you to my sister, Susheela, who showed me the way by coming to America by herself first and laying the path for me; and to my dearest friend, Aaliyah Gupta, for always being willing to jump into the journey for justice and for being the truest and most generous friend I have ever had.

To Janak, my incredible miracle child: you have turned into a trusted partner and advisor, in life and in politics. You teach me every single day and give me new ways to think about analyzing our history and our future. Thank you for reviewing drafts of almost every chapter of the book, and offering incisive comments and excellent editing. Most of all, know that who you are in this world and how you continue to grow every day gives me the deepest pride and joy as a mother.

To my love, Steve, thank you for reading this manuscript and giving edits that cut to the core of what I was trying to convey. Far beyond any manuscript, there are no words sufficient to describe what we have together. Thank you for all you have done for justice and building movements in your own life; for teaching me and learning from our different perspectives; and for showing me the beauty of true partnership and deep connection. If everyone in the world could experience this kind of love, the world would be a much different place.

Finally, to my parents: I am so very grateful for your sacrifices and for imbuing me with the core values that have made me who I am. For all our physical separation, you have been with me every step of the way.

None of us uses the power we have without the contributions of everyone in our lives, for truly, "our power," as we call it, isn't ours at all. My love force arises from connections with others, as does yours. My inspiration, my essential taking in of each breath, flows most from my brown and black sisters who risk it all for the rest of us. To them and to you, I am ever indebted.

Notes

1: My Immigrant Story

1. United Nations Department of Economic and Social Affairs, *International Migration Report 2017: Highlights* (New York: United Nations, 2017). www.un.org/en /development/desa/population/migration/publications/migrationreport/docs/Migra-tionReport2017_Highlights.pdf.

2. Department of Economics and Social Affairs, *International Migration Report 2017*.

3. "Kerala Population 2011–2019 Census," www.census2011.co.in/census/state /kerala.html.

4. *Encyclopedia Britannica Online*, "Saul Alinsky," www.britannica.com/biography /Saul-Alinsky.

2: Becoming an American, Becoming an Activist

1. Valerie Kaur, "His Brother Was Murdered for Wearing a Turban After 9/11. 15 Years Later, He Spoke to the Killer," *PRI's The World*, September 23, 2016, www.pri .org/stories/2016-09-23/his-brother-was-murdered-wearing-turban-after-911-last-week -he-spoke-killer.

2. Niraj Warikoo, "Vincent Chin Murder 35 Years Later: History Repeating Itself?" *Detroit Free Press*, June 23, 2017, www.freep.com/story/news/2017/06/24/murder -vincent-chin-35-years-ago-remembered-asian-americans/420354001.

3. "Bush: 'You Are Either with Us, Or with the Terrorists'–2001-09-21," *VOA News*, October 27, 2009, www.voanews.com/archive/bush-you-are-either-us-or-terrorists-2001 -09-21.

4. Alexandra Werner-Winslow, et al., "Ten Days After: Harassment and Intimidation

in the Aftermath of the Election," *Southern Poverty Law Center Publication*, November 29, 2016, www.splcenter.org/20161129/ten-days-after-harassment-and-intimidation -aftermath-election.

5. Ana Sofia Knauf, "While WA Politicians Declare State a 'Hate-Free Zone,' Protesters Make a Call for Action," *The Stranger*, December 19, 2016, www .thestranger.com/slog/2016/12/19/24754963/while-wa-politicians-declare-sta te-a-hate-free-zone-protesters-make-a-call-for-action.

6. "A Nation Challenged: Money; 5 Months After Sanctions Against Somalia, Scant Proof of Al Qaeda Tie," *New York Times*, April 13, 2002, www.nytimes.com/2002/04 /13/world/nation-challenged-money-5-months-after-sanctions-against-somali-company -scant.html.

7. Steven Greenhouse, "Immigrants Rally in City, Seeking Rights," *New York Times*, October 5, 2003, www.nytimes.com/2003/10/05/nyregion/immigrants-rally-in -city-seeking-rights.html.

8. Walt Crowley, "Tens of Thousands March in Seattle and Other Cities to Protest War Against Iraq on February 15, 2003," *HistoryLink*, March 6, 2003, www.historylink .org/File/5389.

9. "The Feministing Five: Pramila Jayapal," feministing.com/2013/09/14 /the-feministing-five-pramila-jayapal.

4: State Senate: A Proving Ground

1. Christine Clarridge, "Putting a Face on Human Trafficking," *Seattle Times*, February 16, 2013, www.seattletimes.com/seattle-news/putting-a-face-on-human-trafficking.

2. Sarah Hagi (@geekylonglegs), "Daily Prayer to Combat Imposter Syndrome: God give me the confidence of a mediocre white dude," Twitter, January 21, 2015, 1:22 p.m., twitter.com/geekylonglegs/status/557966555313868800.

3. Pramila Jayapal and Tina Podlodowski, "It's Time for Republicans to Get Voting Rights Right: A Democratic Response to an Undemocratic Voting System," *Seattle Met*, April 8, 2014, www.seattlemet.com/articles/2016/4/8/it-s-time-for-republicans-to -get-voting-rights-right.

4. Phil Ferolito, "Filipino Community Celebrates Its History in the Yakima Valley," *Yakima Herald*, March 27, 2019, www.yakimaherald.com/news/filipino-community -celebrates-its-history-in-the-yakima-valley/article_d019b9be-50e9-11e9-9866 -0f67be0a623a.html.

5. Mike Faulk, "Sen. Honeyford Apologizes for Comments on Race, Crime," *Seattle Times*, March 5, 2015, www.seattletimes.com/seattle-news/politics/sen-honeyford -apologizes-for-comments-on-race-crime.

6. Consumer Federation of America, "Payday Loan Consumer Information," paydayloaninfo.org/facts.

7. Jim Brunner, "Moneytree Leads Push to Loosen State's Payday-Lending Law," *Seattle Times*, March 3, 2015, www.seattletimes.com/seattle-news/moneytree-leads-push -to-loosen-states-payday-lending-law.

8. Jim Brunner, "Bill to Change Payday Lending Rules Wins Approval, 30–18, in the State," *Seattle Times*, March 10, 2015, www.seattletimes.com/seattle-news/politics/bill -to-change-payday-lending-rules-wins-approval-30-18-in-the-state-senate.

9. *The Colbert Report*, "The Word—Have Your Cake and Eat It, Too," Comedy Central video, www.cc.com/video-clips/5rzknc/the-colbert-report-the-word---have-your-cake-and-eat-it--too.

10. Brunner, "Bill to Change Payday Lending Rules."

11. "Distance from Seattle, WA to Monroe, WA," Distance Between Cities, www.distance-cities.com/distance-seattle-wa-to-monroe-wa.

12. Second Engrossed House Bill 1115, 64th Legislature, 2015, 3rd Special Session, leap.leg.wa.gov/leap/budget/lbns/1517Cap1115-PL.pdf.

13. "Crews Break Ground on Project to Bring Jobs to South Seattle Neighborhood," Q13 Fox News, q13fox.com/2019/06/10/crews-break-ground-on-project-to-bring-jobs-affordable-housing-to-south-seattle-neighborhood.

14. Erika Schultz, "Free College in Seattle and Beyond Is an Idea Worth Pursuing," *Seattle Times*, December 14, 2017, www.seattletimes.com/opinion/editorials/free-college-in-seattle-and-beyond-is-an-idea-worth-pursuing.

5: Congress: Testing My Theory at the Highest Level

1. Simone Pathé, "Jim McDermott Announces Retirement," *Roll Call*, January 4, 2016, www.rollcall.com/news/jim-mcdermott-announce-retirement-14-terms.

2. Associated Press, "Big Names Enlist Campaign Against Wal-Mart," NBC News, www.nbcnews.com/id/12452314/ns/business-us_business/t/big-names-enlist-campaign-against-wal-mart/#.XTG62pNKgdU.

3. Heidi Groover, "Pledging to Work on Income Inequality and Reproductive Rights, Pramila Jayapal Launches Her Congressional Campaign," *The Stranger*, January 21, 2016, www.thestranger.com/blogs/slog/2016/01/21/23457466/pledging-to-work-on-income-inequality-and-reproductive-rights-pramila-jayapal-launches-her-congressional-campaign.

4. Josh Feit, "Jayapal and Walkinshaw in Fundraising Dead Heat in Race for Congress," *Seattle Met*, April 18, 2016, www.seattlemet.com/articles/2016/4/18/jayapal-and-walkinshaw-in-fundraising-dead-heat-in-race-for-congress.

5. Feit, "Jayapal and Walkinshaw in Fundraising Dead Heat."

6. Li Zhou, "Washington Has a Top-Two Primary: Here's How It Works," *Vox*, August 7, 2018, www.vox.com/2018/8/7/17649564/washington-primary-results.

7. Pramila Jayapal, "Guest Editorial: Why Saturday's Bernie Sanders Rally Left Me Feeling Heartbroken," *The Stranger*, August 9, 2015, www.thestranger.com/blogs/slog/2015/08/09/22671957/guest-editorial-why-saturdays-bernie-sanders-rally-left-me-feeling-heartbroken.

8. Gabrielle Debenedetti, "Bernie Begins Raising Cash for Down-Ballot Progressives," *Politico*, April 13, 2016, www.politico.com/story/2016/04/bernie-sanders-progressives-fundraising-221887.

9. Daniel Beekman, "Boost from Bernie Sanders Playing into Seattle Race for Congress," *Seattle Times*, July 6, 2016, www.seattletimes.com/seattle-news/politics/boost-from-bernie-sanders-playing-into-seattle-race-for-congress.

10. Casey Jaywork, "In Effort to Push Dems to the Left, Sanders Is Sending Donors to Jayapal," *Seattle Weekly*, May 4, 2016, www.seattleweekly.com/news/in-effort-to-push-dems-to-the-left-sanders-is-sending-donors-to-jayapal.

11. Cambria Roth, "Why Pramila Jayapal Is Winning," *Crosscut*, August 22, 2016, crosscut.com/2016/08/pramila-jayapal-7th-congressional-district-race-immigration -activist.

12. Roth, "Why Pramila Jayapal Is Winning."

13. "Washington's 7th Congressional District Election 2018," Ballotopedia, ballotpedia .org/Washington%27s_7th_Congressional_District_election,_2018.

14. "PVI Measures How Much More Democratic or Republican a District Performs Compared to the National Average," *Cook Political Report*, cookpolitical.com/pvi-map -and-district-list.

15. KeyWiki, "Pramila Jayapal," keywiki.org/Pramila_Jayapal#Congressional_run.

16. Nicole Vallestero Keenan-Lai, "Four Ways to Determine If Your Elected Offi- cials Are Effective," *Medium*, October 28, 2016, medium.com/@nicole.m.keenan/who -decides-what-is-effective-596d86eef6c0.

17. Daniel Beekman, "PAC Money Flowing into 7th District Race," *Seattle Times*, November 2, 2016, www.seattletimes.com/seattle-news/politics/pac-money-flowing-into -7th-district-race.

6: The Movement Goes to Washington

1. Ross Buetner and Susanne Craig, "As the Trumps Dodged Taxes, Their Tenants Paid a Price," *New York Times*, December 15, 2018, www.nytimes.com/2018/12/15/us /politics/trump-tenants-taxes.html.

2. Jim Newell, "Democrats' Last Chance to Block Trump's Presidency Is Over (Until the Next Chance)," *Slate*, January 6, 2017, slate.com/news-and-politics/2017/01 /democrats-disrupt-trumps-electoral-college-certification.html.

3. Alison Mitchell, "Over Some Objections, Congress Certifies Electoral Vote," *New York Times*, January 7, 2017, www.nytimes.com/2001/01/07/us/over-some-objections -congress-certifies-electoral-vote.html.

4. Jim Brunner, "It Is Over: Vice President Joe Biden Shuts Down Seattle Congress- woman Pramila Jayapal's Last-Ditch Effort to Halt Trump," *Seattle Times*, January 6, 2017, www.seattletimes.com/seattle-news/politics/it-is-over-vice-president-joe-biden-shuts -down-seattle-congresswoman-pramila-jayapals-last-ditch-effort-to-halt-trump.

5. David Gutman, "'We Didn't Sleep, We Didn't Eat': Families Separated by Trump's Immigration Ban Wait and Hope at SeaTac Airport," *Seattle Times*, January 30, 2017, www.seattletimes.com/seattle-news/politics/families-wait-and-hope-at-sea-tac.

6. Jim Brunner and *Seattle Times*, "Letter to Secretary Kelly," DocumentCloud, www .documentcloud.org/documents/3440711-Letter-to-Secretary-Kelly.html.

7. Rob Hotakainen and Lindsay Wise, "Dear Women, You Can't Read, Your Hair Looks Bad, and Don't Shake Your Head," *McClatchy DC Bureau*, March 31, 2017, www .mcclatchydc.com/news/politics-government/article141996689.html.

8. U.S. House Committee on the Judiciary, "Wednesday: House Judiciary to Markup Contempt Report for AG Barr," May 6, 2019, judiciary.house.gov/news/press-releases /wednesday-house-judiciary-markup-contempt-report-ag-barr.

9. Tina Vasquez, "Immigrant Minor Held 'Hostage' in Texas Because She Wants Abortion Care," *Rewire News*, October 11, 2017, rewire.news/article/2017/10/11

/immigrant-minor-held-hostage-texas-wants-abortion-care; Rep. Pramila Jayapal (@ RepJayapal), "Throwback to the last time I spoke to Scott Lloyd—he was trying to block women from exercising their reproductive rights," video, Twitter, November 19, 2018, 7:06 p.m., twitter.com/repjayapal/status/1064671274029539333.

10. Joseph O'Sullivan, "Alaska Congressman Calls Rep. Pramila Jayapal 'Young Lady,' Lectures Her on House Floor," *Seattle Times*, September 8, 2017, www.seattletimes .com/seattle-news/politics/alaska-congressman-calls-rep-pramila-japyapal-young-lady -lectures-her-on-house-floor.

11. Miranda Green, "Congressman: 'Young Lady' Colleague 'Doesn't Know a Damn Thing,'" CNN Politics, September 8, 2017, www.cnn.com/2017/09/08/politics /congressman-don-young-pramila-jayapal/index.html.

12. Steve Benen, "Don Young's Anger Management," *The MaddowBlog*, July 31, 2014, www.msnbc.com/rachel-maddow-show/don-youngs-anger-management.

13. Nation Now, "Rep. Don Young Apologizes for Irate Retort to Female Colleague," 10 News, September 8, 2017, www.wbir.com/article/news/nation-now/rep-don -young-apologizes-for-irate-retort-to-female-colleague/465-0ef84522-256a-43cd-8404 -51f8d33a2519.

14. Meghan Keneally, "List of Trump's Accusers and Their Allegations of Sexual Misconduct," ABC News, June 25, 2019, abcnews.go.com/Politics/list-trumps-accusers -allegations-sexual-misconduct/story?id=51956410.

15. Jim Brunner, "'I Believe These Women': Seattle's U.S. Rep. Pramila Jayapal Calls for John Conyers' Resignation," *Seattle Times*, November 28, 2017, www.seattletimes .com/seattle-news/politics/i-believe-these-women-seattles-u-s-rep-pramila-jayapal-calls -for-john-conyers-resignation.

7: Building, Pushing, Surging: The Squad, Pelosi, and Me

1. Julian E. Jelizer, "When Liberals Were Organized," *American Prospect*, January 22, 2015, prospect.org/article/when-liberals-were-organized.

2. Tara Golshan, "The PAYGO Fight Roiling House Democrats, Explained," *Vox*, January 3, 2019, www.vox.com/policy-and-politics/2019/1/3/18165261/paygo-house -democrats-progressives-medicare.

8: Moral Vision—Immigration

1. Bob Young, "An Immigrant Herself, Seattle's Pramila Jayapal Leads the Push for Reform," *Seattle Times*, August 7, 2010, www.seattletimes.com/pacific-nw-magazine/an -immigrant-herself-seattles-pramila-jayapal-leads-the-push-for-reform.

2. Heather Sells, "'It's Disgraceful': Franklin Graham Rebukes Immigration Policy on CBN Drawing National Attention," CBN News, June 14, 2018, www1.cbn .com/cbnnews/us/2018/june/its-disgraceful-franklin-graham-rebukes-immigration -policy-on-drawing-national-attention.

3. "Laura Bush: Separating Children from Their Parents at the Border 'Breaks My Heart,'" *Washington Post*, June 17, 2018, www.washingtonpost.com/opinions/laura-bush -separating-children-from-their-parents-at-the-border-breaks-my-heart/2018/06/17

/f2df517a-7287-11e8-9780-b1dd6a09b549_story.html.

4. United Nations Human Rights Council, Global Trends: Forced Displacement in 2017 (Geneva: United Nations Human Rights Council, 2018), www.unhcr.org /5b27be547.pdf.

5. IOM UN Migration, "Global Migration Trends," International Organization for Migration, www.iom.int/global-migration-trends.

6. Megan Brenan, "Record-High 75% of Americans Say Immigration Is Good Thing," Gallup News, June 2, 2018, news.gallup.com/poll/235793/record-high-americans-say -immigration-good-thing.aspx.

7. Brenan, "Record-High 75% of Americans Say Immigration Is Good Thing."

8. Pew Research Center, "Shifting Public Views on Legal Immigration Into the U.S.," U.S. Politics and Policy, June 28, 2018, www.people-press.org/2018/06/28/shifting -public-views-on-legal-immigration-into-the-u-s.

9. "In-Depth Topics A–Z: Immigration," Gallup, news.gallup.com/poll/1660 /immigration.aspx.

10. Julia Ainsley, "Stephen Miller Wants Border Patrol, Not Asylum Officers, to Determine Migrant Asylum Claims," NBC News, July 29, 2019, www.nbcnews.com /politics/immigration/stephen-miller-wants-use-border-agents-screen-migrants-cut -number-n1035831.

11. Office of Inspector General, "Special Review—Initial Observations Regarding Family Separation Issues Under the Zero Tolerance Policy," Department of Homeland Security, OIG-18-84, September 27, 2018, www.oig.dhs.gov/sites/default/files/assets /2018-10/OIG-18-84-Sep18.pdf.

12. Megan Specia and Rick Gladstone, "Border Agents Shot Tear Gas into Mexico. Was It Legal?" New York Times, November 28, 2018, www.nytimes.com/2018/11/28 /world/americas/tear-gas-border.html.

13. Throughout this chapter, I use pseudonyms instead of real names for all the individuals in detention to protect their identities.

14. "Rep. Jayapal Helps 5 Asylum Seekers Get Across U.S-Mexico Border," MyNorth-west, December 4, 2018, mynorthwest.com/1204759/rep-jayapal-helps-5-asylum -seekers-get-across-us-mexico-border.

15. Office of Inspector General, "Management Alert on Issues Requiring Immediate Action at the Theo Lacy Facility in Orange, California," Department of Homeland Security, OIG-17-43-MA, March 6, 2017, www.oversight.gov/sites/default/files/oig-reports /OIG-mga-030617.pdf.

16. Specia and Gladstone, "Border Agents Shot Tear Gas."

17. Matt Gaetz (@mattgaetz), ".@PramilaJayapal is a very well-studied person; pleasant to be around. But her joining the caravan as some sort of 'congressional coyote' is nuts!" link, Twitter, December 2, 2018, 12:08 p.m., twitter.com/mattgaetz/status /1069277071724171265.

18. "Members of Congress Return from Visit to Detention Center, Border Patrol Processing Center & Port of Entry in Texas," Congresswoman Lucille Roybal-Allard, July 23, 2018, roybal-allard.house.gov/news/documentsingle.aspx?DocumentID=398477.

19. Michael D. Sheer and Julie Hirschfeld Davis, "Shoot Migrants' Legs, Build Alligator Moat: Behind Trump's Ideas for the Border," New York Times, October 1, 2019, www

.nytimes.com/2019/10/01/us/politics/trump-border-wars.html.

20. A.C. Thompson,"Inside the Secret Border Patrol Facebook Group Where   Agents Joke About Migrant Deaths and Post Sexist Memes," ProPublica, July 1, 2019, www .propublica.org/article/secret-border-patrol-facebook-group-agents-joke-about -migrant-deaths-post-sexist-memes.

21. Aria Bendix, "Ice Shuts Down Program for Asylum-Seekers," *The Atlantic*, June 9, 2017, www.theatlantic.com/news/archive/2017/06/ice-shuts-down-program-for-asylum -seekers/529887.

22. Camilo Montoya-Galvez, "U.S. Cuts Millions in Aid to Central America Fulfilling Trump's Vow," CBS News, June 18, 2019, www.cbsnews.com/news/us-cuts-millions-in -aid-to-central-america-fulfilling-trumps-vow.

23. Douglas S. Massey, Jorge Durand, and Karen A. Pren, "Why Border Enforcement Backfired," *American Journal of Sociology* 121, no. 5 (March 2016): 1,557–1,600, www .ncbi.nlm.nih.gov/pmc/articles/PMC5049707.

24. House Document No. 1: Economic Report of the President, February 2005, United States Congressional Serial Set 14949 (Washington, DC: United States Government Printing Office, 20006), books.google.com/books?id=LkC9hXu8qUwC&pg.

25. House Document No. 1.

26. Kirk Johnson and Tim Kane, "The Real Problem with Immigration . . . and the Real Solution," Heritage Foundation, March 1, 2006, www.heritage.org/immigration /report/the-real-problem-immigration-and-the-real-solution.

27. The Economic Benefits of Fixing Our Broken Immigration System (Washington, DC: Executive Office of the President, 2013), obamawhitehouse.archives.gov/sites /default/files/docs/ report.pdf.

28. Emily Kassie, "Detained: How the U.S. Built the World's Largest Immigrant Detention System," *The Guardian*, September 24, 2019, www.theguardian.com/us-news /2019/sep/24/detained-us-largest-immigrant-detention-trump.

29. "New Poll Shows Voters Support Access to Asylum for Refugees," Women's Refugee Commission, October 24, 2018, www.womensrefugeecommission.org/news/press -releases-and-statements/3309-new-poll-shows-voters-support-access-to-asylum-for -refugees.

30. "Did My Family Really Come 'Legally'? Today's Immigration Laws Created a New Reality," American Immigration Council, August 10, 2016, www .americanimmigrationcouncil.org/research/did-my-family-really-come-legally-todays -immigration-laws-created-a-new-reality.

31. U.S. Department of Labor, Bureau of Labor Statistics, "Home Health Aides and Personal Care Aides," Occupational Outlook Handbook, www.bls.gov/ooh/healthcare /mobile/home-health-aides-and-personal-care-aides.htm.

32. Andorra Bruno, Congressional Research Service, "The H-2B Visa and the Statutory Cap: In Brief," April 17, 2018, fas.org/sgp/crs/homesec/R44306.pdf.

33. "Annual Report of Immigrant Visa Applicants in the Family-Sponsored and Employment-Based Preferences Registered at the National Visa Center as of November 1, 2017," U.S. Department of State, Bureau of Consular Affairs, travel.state.gov/content /dam/visas/Statistics/ Immigrant-Statistics/WaitingList/WaitingListItem_2017.pdf.

34. David Bier, "49 Nations Accept Asylees and Refugees at Higher Rates Than

America," CATO at Liberty, July 20, 2018, www.cato.org/blog/49-nations-accept-asylees -refugees-higher-rates-america.

9: Moral Vision—Medicare for All

1. National Institute of Neural Disorders and Stroke, "Amyotrophic Lateral Sclerosis (ALS) Fact Sheet," National Institutes of Health, www.ninds.nih.gov/Disorders/Patient -Caregiver-Education/Fact-Sheets/Amyotrophic-Lateral-Sclerosis-ALS-Fact-Sheet.

2. Benyamin Appelbaum, "Dying Is No Reason to Stop Fighting," *New York Times*, May 3, 2019, www.nytimes.com/2019/05/03/opinion/ady-barkan-als-health-care.html.

3. Dylan Scott, "The Deficit Is Rising, so Republicans Want to Cut Social Security and Medicare," *Vox*, October 17, 2018, www.vox.com/policy-and-politics/2018/10/17 /17989354/federal-deficit-social-security-medicare-2018-midterms.

4. Alexandria Ocasio-Cortez (@AOC), "Tomorrow I will also vote No on the rules package, which is trying to slip in #PAYGO. PAYGO isn't only bad economics, as @ RoKhanna explains; it's also a dark political maneuver designed to hamstring progress on healthcare+other leg. We shouldn't hinder ourselves from the start," link, Twitter, January 2, 2019, 10:52 a.m., twitter.com/aoc/status/1080492088356159489.

5. "Special Message to the Congress Recommending Comprehensive Health Program," https://www.healthcare-now.org/legislation/president-trumans-special-message-to -the-congress-recommending-a-comprehensive-health-program.

6. Howard Markel, "69 Years Ago, a President Pitches His Idea for National Health Care," *PBS News Hour*, November 19, 2014, www.pbs.org/newshour/health/november -19-1945-harry-truman-calls-national-health-insurance-program.

7. "History of Single-Payer Legislation," Healthcare-Now!, www.healthcare-now.org /legislation/national-timeline.

8. Sarah Kliff, "Pramila Jayapal Thinks We Can Get to Medicare-for-All Fast," *Vox*, February 28, 2019, www.vox.com/2019/2/28/18244547/jayapal-medicare-for-all-ezra -klein-show.

9. "Medicare and Medicaid Milestones: 1937–2015," Centers for Medicare and Medicaid Services, www.cms.gov/About-CMS/Agency-Information/History/Downloads /Medicare-and-Medicaid-Milestones-1937-2015.pdf.

10. U.S. Department of Labor, Bureau of Labor Statistics, "Home Health Aides and Personal Care Aides."

11. Emily Gee and Topher Spiro, "Excess Administrative Costs Burden the U.S. Health Care System," Center for American Progress, www.americanprogress.org/issues /healthcare/reports/2019/04/08/468302/excess-administrative-costs-burden-u-s -health-care-system.

12. Mary Ellen McIntire, "'Medicare-for-All' Is No Longer Purely Theoretical. Democrats Are Coming to Terms with That," *Roll Call*, February 23, 2019, www.rollcall.com /news/ congress/medicare-for-all-political-calculations.

13. McIntire, "'Medicare-for-All' Is No Longer Purely Theoretical."

14. Christopher M. Davis, Congressional Research Service, "House Committee Hearings: Arranging Witnesses," August 25, 2015, fas.org/sgp/crs/misc/98-304.pdf.

15. Matt Fuller, "Single-Payer Advocates Worry 'Medicare for All' Hearing Could Be

a 'Farce,'" *HuffPost*, April 25, 2019, www.huffpost.com/entry/medicare-for-all-hearing-farce_n_5cc1dfbee4b0ad77ff8164fe.

16. Nathaniel Weixel, "Ways and Means Committee to Hold Hearing on 'Medicare for All,'" *The Hill*, April 30, 2019, thehill.com/policy/healthcare/441406-ways-and-means-committee-to-hold-hearing-on-medicare-for-all.

17. Jessie Hellmann, "Obama Calls 'Medicare for All' a 'Good' Idea," *The Hill*, September 7, 2018, https://thehill.com/policy/healthcare/405597-obama-calls-medicare-for-all-a-good-idea.

18. Ben Casselman and Jim Tankersley, "Warren Wealth Tax Has Wide Support, Except Among One Group," *New York Times*, November 29, 2019, www.nytimes.com/2019/11/29/business/economy/economy-politics-survey.html.

10: Moral Vision—The Fight for $15 and the Three Supremacies

1. Scot Nakagawa, "Blackness Is the Fulcrum," Race Files, May 4, 2012, www.racefiles.com/2012/05/04/blackness-is-the-fulcrum.

2. Lawrence Mishel and Julia Wolfe, "CEO Compensation Has Grown 940% Since 1978," Economic Policy Institute, August 14, 2019, www.epi.org/publication/ceo-compensation-2018.

3. Addy Baird, "Progressives Won the Minimum Wage Fight—Now They Think They Can Do It Again with Health Care and the Green New Deal," *BuzzFeed News*, July 18, 2019, www.buzzfeednews.com/article/addybaird/progressives-15-wage-medicare-all-green-new-deal.

4. "When Was the Last Time the Minimum Wage Was Raised?" Raise the Minimum Wage, August 29, 2016, raisetheminimumwage.com/question-answer/when-was-the-last-minimum-wage-increased.

5. "What Are the Annual Earnings for a Full-Time Minimum Wage Worker?" Center for Poverty Research, University of California, Davis, January 12, 2018, poverty.ucdavis.edu/faq/what-are-annual-earnings-full-time-minimum-wage-worker.

6. Emmie Martin, "Here's How Much the Top 5% of Americans Make in an Hour," CNBC Make It, August 2, 2017, www.cnbc.com/2017/08/02/how-much-the-richest-americans-earn-per-hour.html.

7. Jonathan Grossman, "Fair Labor Standards Act of 1938: Maximum Struggle for a Minimum Wage," U.S. Department of Labor, www.dol.gov/general/aboutdol/history/flsa1938.

8. *Franklin D. Roosevelt Public Papers and Addresses*, vol. 5 (New York, Random House, 1936), 624–25.

9. "Minimum Wage History," Oregon State University Instructional Sites: Anth. 484, oregonstate.edu/instruct/anth484/minwage.html.

10. Apurva Bose, "History of Minimum Wage," *BeBusinessEd*, bebusinessed.com/history/history-of-minimum-wage.

11. Matthew Michaels, "If the US Minimum Wage Had Kept Up with the Economy, Many Low-Wage Earners Could Earn Double What They're Making Now," *Business Insider*, December 22, 2017, www.businessinsider.com/how-much-higher-the-federal-minimum-wage-should-be-2017-12.

12. Jonathan Rosenblum, *Beyond $15: Immigrant Workers, Faith Activists, and the Revival of the Labor Movement* (Boston: Beacon Press, 2017), chapter 4.

13. For an excellent account of all the SeaTac organizing that preceded the Seattle $15 minimum-wage fight, see Jonathan Rosenblum's excellent account in *Beyond $15*.

14. *The Case for Eliminating the Tipped Minimum Wage in Washington, DC*, Restaurant Opportunity Centers United Publications (New York: National Employment Law Project, 2016), rocunited.org/publications/the-case-for-one-fair-wage-in-washington-d-c.

15. National Conference of State Legislatures, "State Minimum Wages: 2019 Minimum Wage by State," January 7, 2019, ncsl.org/research/labor-and-employment/state-minimum-wage-chart.aspx.

16. Kurt Badenhausen, "The Best Places for Business and Careers 2018: Seattle Leads the Way," *Forbes*, October 24, 2018, www.forbes.com/places/wa/seattle.

17. Bethany Jean Clement, "Seattle's Crazy Restaurant Boom," *Seattle Times*, November 16, 2017, www.seattletimes.com/pacific-nw-magazine/seattles-crazy-restaurant-boom.

18. Ekaterina Jardim, Mark C. Long, Robert Plotnick, Emma van Inwegen, Jacob Vigdor, and Hilary Wething, "Minimum Wage Increases and Individual Employment Trajectories," NBER Working Paper, No. 25182, National Bureau of Economic Research, October 2018, www.nber.org/papers/w25182.

Index

Statewide Poverty Action Network
(Washington), 95
Stefan, Dorothy, 43
Steinem, Gloria, 326

Teachout, Zephyr, 125
Thomas, Dorothy, 104
Thompson, Tracey, 299–300, 301
Tirpak, John, 38
Tlaib, Rashida, 172–73, 199
To, Tony, 99
Toscano, J., 118
Trans-Pacific Partnership, 140
Truman, Harry, 255–56
Trump, Donald, 34, 54, 58, 77, 102,
113, 133–35, 137–42, 152–56, 159,
169, 181, 198, 214, 217, 222–30,
235–38, 241, 245, 263, 283–84,
289–90, 313–16
Truth, Sojourner, 326

UFCW, 111, 302
UNITE HERE, 45
United Auto Workers, 277
United Food and Commercial Workers,
45, 302
United for Climate and Environmental
Justice Task Force, 164–65
United Nations Border Relief Operations
(UNBRO), 13–14
United We Dream, 214
Universal Declaration of Human Rights,
234
Uphus, Mike, 16
U.S. Customs and Border Protection
(CBP), 153–55, 161, 198, 211–13, 217,
224–25, 229–33
U.S. Customs and Immigration Services,
25, 42, 236

U.S. Department of Agriculture, 37,
39–40
U.S. Department of Justice, 29, 37, 42,
43, 47–48, 53
U.S. Treasury Department's Office of
Foreign Asset Control, 36

Voting Justice Coalition, 90

Walkinshaw, Brady, 104, 108, 109–12,
126–34
Warren, Elizabeth, 263, 277, 283, 291
Washington Association of Churches,
65–66
Washington Community Action
Network, 84, 306
Washington State Voting Rights Act,
89–90, 93–94
Waters, Maxine, 150–51, 190, 195
We Belong Together, 56, 71, 242
Weinstein, Harvey, 169
Wellstone, Paul, 2931
Williamson, Steve, 45, 65–67, 71–73,
84, 103, 105–8, 120, 130–34, 157–58,
163, 179–80, 185–86, 273, 299, 322
Women Donors Network, 102
Women's Economic, Social and Political
Action Network (WESPAN), 104
Women's March (2017), 47, 153
Working Families Party (New York),
84, 149
Working Washington, 113
World Health Organization, 6
Wright, Howard, 304

Yarmuth, John, 197
Yoshitomi, Karen, 40–41
Young, Don, 164–68, 220

About the Author

Congresswoman **Pramila Jayapal** represents Washington's Seventh District, which encompasses most of Seattle and surrounding areas. The first Indian American woman in the House of Representatives, Jayapal has spent the last thirty years working internationally and domestically as an activist and advocate for economic, gender, and racial justice. She lives in Seattle, Washington.

Publishing in the Public Interest

Thank you for reading this book published by The New Press. The New Press is a nonprofit, public interest publisher. New Press books and authors play a crucial role in sparking conversations about the key political and social issues of our day. We hope you enjoyed this book and that you will stay in touch with The New Press. Here are a few ways to stay up to date with our books, events, and the issues we cover:

- Sign up at www.thenewpress.com/subscribe to receive updates on New Press authors and issues and to be notified about local events
- Like us on Facebook: www.facebook.com/newpressbooks
- Follow us on Twitter: www.twitter.com/thenewpress

Please consider buying New Press books for yourself; for friends and family; or to donate to schools, libraries, community centers, prison libraries, and other organizations involved with the issues our authors write about.

The New Press is a 501(c)(3) nonprofit organization. You can also support our work with a tax-deductible gift by visiting www .thenewpress.com/donate.